MW00605636

Skin Saga
Copyright © 2018 by Charles W. Stiefel

All rights are reserved.

No part of this publication may be reproduced, distributed or
transmitted in any form or by any means, including photocopying,
recording or other digital or mechanical methods, without the prior
written permission of the author, except in the cases of fair use as
permitted by U.S. and international copyright laws. For permission
requests, please submit in writing to the publisher at the address below:

Published by:
Smart Business Network
835 Sharon Drive, Suite 200
Westlake, OH 44145

Printed in the United States of America
Editor: Dustin S. Klein

ISBN: 978-1-945389-72-6
Library of Congress Control Number: 2018943075

Printed in USA

SKIN SAGA

How a Tiny Family Soap Business Evolved over Six Generations
into the #1 Dermatology Company in the World

CHARLES W. STIEFEL

SMART BUSINESS® BOOKS
An Imprint of Smart Business® Network Inc.

DEDICATION

*This book is dedicated to my wife, Daneen Stiefel,
who has steadfastly supported my every endeavor.
It is further dedicated to the six generations of Stiefels who sacrificed
so much to build a great family business, and to the thousands
of amazing men and women who shared our vision and helped
transform our dreams into reality.*

TABLE OF CONTENTS

ACKNOWLEDGMENTS

I am very grateful to a number of individuals who contributed information and anecdotes that helped me write this book. Both Werner Stiefel (my father) and Herbert Stiefel (my uncle) spoke and wrote periodically about the history of Stiefel Laboratories; during their lifetimes, they were both kind enough to share their writings with me. I would like to make special mention of a 32-page paper that Herbert Stiefel wrote in 2003 entitled "The Story of Stiefel International Division." This paper contains a wealth of information, as well as many amusing anecdotes, a few of which I have shared in this book.

My older brother, John Stiefel, my two sisters, Stephanie Stiefel Williams and Joan Stiefel Rodriguez, and my son, Todd Stiefel, all sent to me the results of their genealogical research about the Stiefel family.

Todd maintains archives on the history of Stiefel Laboratories, and he granted me full access to this invaluable collection of historical material. He and my other son, Brent Stiefel, were also very helpful to me by sharing recollections from their years working at the company.

My cousin, Catherine Stiefel, provided a considerable amount of useful information to me. The same is true of my friend, Gabriel McGlynn, who previously ran all of Europe, Africa, Asia and Australia for the company.

As the writing of this book progressed, I asked several other individuals for their recollections about specific events; and all of them graciously answered my questions. These individuals include Bill Humphries, Bill Carr, my cousin Claus Stiefel, Patricia Riley, Jim Tombros, Jerry Hirschberg, Morris Goodman and Skip Huisking; and I am grateful to all of them.

I would like to thank my editor, Dustin S. Klein, and assistant editor, Abbey Jo Deckard, for all their insightful suggestions, as well as my publisher, Smart Business Network. Finally, I would like to thank the wonderful dermatologists whose quotes about the Stiefel saga appear on the back cover of this book.

INTRODUCTION

S *kin Saga* tells the story of Stiefel Laboratories, Inc., a company founded by my great-great-grandfather and run by my family for six generations. It started as a tiny European soap business in 1847; and 162 years later, it was sold to GlaxoSmithKline for $3.6 billion. During that time span, the company encountered countless challenges and made many costly mistakes. But thanks to the dedication and perseverance of several key individuals, there were also some notable successes.

Writing this book has been a labor of love for me. I feel strongly that my ancestors' efforts to build a meaningful company deserve to be memorialized; *Skin Saga* reflects my desire to pay tribute to them. Through the years, hundreds of dermatologists have questioned me about Stiefel's history; this book answers all of their questions. Finally, I want future generations of Stiefels to know about the company to which so many family members dedicated their lives.

Because much of this story is about my family, I decided to utilize the first person to speak directly to the reader.

Thank you for your interest in the history of Stiefel. I sincerely hope that you enjoy this saga. If you have any feedback that you would like to share with me, please e-mail me at cwstiefel@yahoo.com.

CHAPTER ONE

JOHANN

"Stick to the knitting—stay with the business that you know."
– TOM PETERS AND ROBERT WATERMAN

Life is all about making choices. Sometimes the optimal choice seems obvious, but frequently there are so many factors to consider that the best course of action is difficult to determine. This difficulty can be compounded by the fact that the most important decisions in life generally entail the greatest element of risk.

Have you ever noticed that whenever life requires you to make a difficult choice, there is an oft-quoted adage that suggests which direction you should take?

Unfortunately, however, most of these time-tested adages are counterbalanced by other adages suggesting exactly the opposite. We are counseled to "look before you leap," yet "he who hesitates is lost." "Many hands make light work," but "too many cooks spoil the broth." In the world of love, "absence makes the heart grow fonder" for some; but for others, it's "out of sight, out of mind."

When making decisions in the corporate world, we can seek advice not only from adages, but from thousands of scholarly books and journal articles that address a myriad of business issues. Unfortunately, similar to the adages quoted above, the advice

1

rendered by one business expert is often directly contradicted by that of another equally-respected expert. One of the most widely read business books of all time is *In Search of Excellence,* by Tom Peters and Robert Waterman. Written in 1982, this book is considered by many to be the seminal management book; and one of its key pieces of advice is quoted at the top of this chapter. Fortunately, 135 years before this book was written, my great-great-grandfather decided not to "stay with the business that you know," but rather to embark upon a new venture that would impact the lives of generations to come.

Johann David Stiefel was born in 1822 in Offenbach am Main, an ancient European city in the Germanic state of Hesse. Offenbach was relatively small, but it was strategically located on the banks of the Main River, just across the water from Frankfurt am Main. Many people believe that Stiefel Laboratories was founded in Germany, but the country of Germany was not formed until 1871; so Stiefel predated Germany by nearly a quarter of a century. Johann was the seventh born of eleven children; and since he had several older brothers and sisters, it is not surprising that he did not enter his father's business of manufacturing dyestuffs. Instead, Johann started a small candle-making business, and he sold his candles by walking door to door, pushing a cart through the cobblestone streets of Offenbach. At first blush, this might seem like a very difficult way to earn a living, but remember that Thomas Edison did not invent the incandescent light bulb until 1879. Consequently, Johann was quite successful selling his candles to the local citizens, with his best customer being the local Catholic church.

Friendships play an important role in everyone's life, and friends can profoundly influence the decisions all of us make. When Johann Stiefel was still a very young man, he formed a close friendship with Ferdinand von Hebra, a brilliant physician from Austria. Von Hebra had earned his medical degree in Vienna in 1841 and shortly thereafter developed a passionate interest in skin

Johann David Stiefel

diseases. He became famous as the founder of the New Vienna School of Dermatology, and he authored one of the most famous dermatology textbooks of all time—*Atlas der Hautkrankheiten*—an illustrated atlas of skin diseases. Von Hebra was the first to apply scientific classifications to dermatological conditions, and several skin disorders were named after him, including Hebra's prurigo and Hebra's eczema marginatum. He was also a pioneer in developing new methods of treating cutaneous disease. In Johann, he saw someone who could help him expand the therapeutic armamentarium available to dermatologists.

Ferdinand suggested to Johann that active ingredients useful in dermatology could be conveniently delivered to the surface of the skin by incorporating these ingredients into bars of soap. Johann knew nothing about manufacturing soap, but he had a lot of experience working with fats and oils—raw materials utilized to produce both candles and soaps. Consequently, he felt learning soap technology would not be an insurmountable challenge. Like most entrepreneurs throughout history, he was filled with enthusiasm and determination. Consequently, instead of trying to expand his successful candle business, he chose to focus his energy on starting a soap manufacturing business from scratch. In April of 1847, Johann David Stiefel, then 24 years old, founded a company he named simply "J.D. Stiefel." Ferdinand was excited about this new venture and, using his dermatology expertise, suggested several formulations for Johann to market.

One year after launching the J.D. Stiefel company, Johann married his childhood sweetheart, a local girl named Elisabetha Margaretha Walther, nicknamed Lisette. Lisette's parents owned a grocery store in Offenbach, but, unfortunately, they were so frequently ill that Lisette was forced to miss school to mind the store. According to Lisette and Johann's granddaughter, Elsa Stiefel, Lisette's teacher complained one day about Lisette's poor grades, to which her father replied, "Ich bin mit meiner Tochter sehr zufrieden," which translates, "I am very pleased with my daughter."

When Lisette married Johann David Stiefel, she was only 16 years old and already an orphan. Lisette and Johann had twelve children, five of whom died before reaching their second birthday. In present day society, we often hear complaints about how much money doctors and pharmaceutical companies earn; but when one considers the miraculous medical advances that have been effected by physicians and drug companies, I submit that society should be feeling gratitude rather than resentment. Can you imagine how Lisette felt, losing both parents during her adolescence, and then watching five of her children die during infancy?

As the J.D. Stiefel company grew increasingly successful, Johann became a leader in Offenbach society, serving on the governing board of the city and co-founding the first savings bank in Offenbach. The family was not rich, but Lisette and Johann were financially able to send all of their children to private school. One of these children, Carl Friedrich Stiefel, emigrated to the United States in 1876 at the age of 20. Carl was very interested in the pharmaceutical business, and he spent the next 16 years gaining valuable experience at two prominent drug wholesale companies. In 1892, he joined the prestigious chemical and drug importing firm Schering & Glatz, eventually becoming the president and sole owner. Meanwhile, two of Carl's brothers, Anton and Ferdinand, decided to remain in Germany and work with Johann in an effort to bolster the sales of the J.D. Stiefel company. Johann David Stiefel died of stomach cancer in 1880 at the age of 58. But his legacy lives on, thanks to his willingness to take a big risk and venture into unknown business territory.

CHAPTER TWO

GLOBAL EXPANSION

"You will either step forward into growth
or you will step back into safety."
– ABRAHAM MASLOW

The middle of the nineteenth century witnessed an increasing emergence of dermatology as a recognized medical specialty. In 1845, Noah Worcester published the first American dermatology textbook. Moritz Kaposi and Heinrich Auspitz, both renowned physicians and researchers, joined Ferdinand von Hebra in Austria at the Vienna School of Dermatology; and in the 1870s, they were joined by Paul Gerson Unna, one of the pioneers in dermatopathology. Unna became famous after publishing his first book, *Histopathology of Skin Diseases*, in 1884; but he conducted research in several other areas, including the development of new therapies for skin diseases.

Like von Hebra before him, Unna developed close friendships with Johann, Anton and Ferdinand Stiefel. Unna suggested several medicated soap formulations to his friends, and these suggestions prompted the J.D. Stiefel company to launch more than a dozen new products. Some of the active ingredients suggested by Unna, such as ichthyol and resorcinol, are still utilized in dermatology to this day.

Armed with a product line conceived by the greatest medical minds of the time, the J.D. Stiefel company's reputation for quality flourished—and formal recognition soon followed. The German Apothecaries Association awarded the company its highest medal of honor in 1889; and in the decade that followed, equally prestigious honors were conferred at several other pharmaceutical and industrial expositions throughout Germany.

The highlight of these formal recognitions was in 1897, when Prince Louis Ferdinand, a medical practitioner himself, personally commended Stiefel's medicinal soaps, which he had used on himself and his patients with great success. On that occasion, the Prince awarded Stiefel the gold medal at an exhibition in Munich showcasing various remedies for pediatric diseases.

Stiefel soaps garnered so much respect after the gold metal that competitors began launching copycat products. In order to differentiate J.D. Stiefel soaps from the rest, the company registered a distinctive trademark—a flowerpot inscribed with the Latin words *nunquam retrorsum* or "never backward." This trademark was reproduced on the wrapper of every single cake of Stiefel soap. Additionally, in 1884, Anton and Ferdinand Stiefel built a new manufacturing plant to insure Stiefel soaps always exceeded even the most stringent quality standards.

Anton and Ferdinand, who by then had taken over management of the company, were very pleased with all the accolades Stiefel soaps were receiving in Germany; but they wanted their products to be used and respected worldwide. During his lifetime, Johann had exported Stiefel soaps to several other countries, but Anton and Ferdinand significantly expanded this export business.

There are many ways to do business in a foreign country, but two of the most common involve establishing a subsidiary or contracting with an agent. For the J.D. Stiefel company, establishing foreign subsidiaries would have entailed incorporating separate legal entities around the world, hiring personnel to staff these

Stiefel 1910 Price List, printed in 5 languages

subsidiaries, and opening offices to house these employees. A huge financial investment would have been required, and the Stiefel family did not have access to that level of funding.

For Anton and Ferdinand, it was a relatively easy decision to negotiate agency agreements, which placed a much smaller demand on their limited resources. The foreign agents they engaged agreed to import the soaps from Germany, warehouse them, market them and collect payment on them for a portion of the profits. Typically, agents handle the product lines of several different companies in order to achieve economies of scale; but most agency agreements prohibit the agent from marketing a competing product line.

As you might expect, one of the most significant potential markets for the J.D. Stiefel company was the United States; this made it vitally important for Anton and Ferdinand to choose the best possible U.S. agent. Fortunately, their brother Carl Friedrich Stiefel had begun working at the highly-regarded Schering & Glatz firm in 1892; and Anton and Ferdinand had enormous respect for their older brother. Within a few months, Schering & Glatz became the exclusive agent for the J.D. Stiefel company in the United States. By 1914, well over 100 different formulations of Stiefel medicinal soaps were being packaged in seven different languages and sold through agents in all major countries of the world.

CHAPTER THREE

COMING TO AMERICA

"When it comes to the American dream, no one has a corner on the market. All of us have an equal chance to share in that dream."
— J.C. WATTS

When I first began to learn about dermatology, I wondered how my ancestors' medicated soaps could possibly have been effective. Soap lather is generally washed off almost immediately, whereas an active ingredient cannot optimally fight skin disease unless it remains in contact with the epidermis for some period of time. Modern dermatological gels, creams and ointments are generally applied to the surface of the skin and left there until the next time the patient washes that area. When I eventually saw the instructions for use of my forefathers' soaps, however, I surprisingly discovered that, just like modern topical dermatology products, J.D. Stiefel medicated soaps were not intended to be rinsed off immediately.

Instead, to achieve optimal efficacy, patients were urged to follow the instructions of their physicians, but in the absence of such instructions, the company provided the following written advice to the patients: "The lather should either be permitted to dry upon the cuticle or gently massaged into the skin and, if feasible, permitted to remain so overnight." Patients were

August C. Stiefel

cautioned not to rinse off the soap immediately, because this would reduce the therapeutic benefits to a minimum. And in addition, patients were advised, "Removing the lather with a soft clean cloth is preferable to rinsing, since this permits more of the substance to penetrate the skin." We will never know for sure, but I strongly suspect that von Hebra and Unna helped the J.D. Stiefel company write these instructions.

As the company continued to expand, so did the Stiefel family. Ferdinand married and had two children, but unfortunately, both of them died at an early age. Anton also married, and he and his wife, Johanna Grünwald, had two sons and a daughter. The daughter, Lena, married her first cousin, a practice that was common in Europe at that time. (Two prominent examples of first cousins marrying in the nineteenth century are Queen Victoria and Prince Albert, and Charles Darwin and Emma Darwin.) The two sons were named August Christian Stiefel (my grandfather) and Ferdinand Stiefel (not to be confused with his Uncle Ferdinand). Ferdinand became an architect and contractor, but he also helped his father and uncle at the J.D. Stiefel company. August started his career at Merck & Co., a manufacturer of chemicals and pharmaceuticals, but in 1910, his father sent him to the United States to investigate the feasibility of opening a subsidiary there to supersede the existing agency arrangement.

August met with his uncle, Carl Friedrich Stiefel, who offered him a position at his firm, Schering & Glatz. The job would be a kind of apprenticeship—August would learn about the soap business and the complexities of the US market from a firm that had been successfully representing J.D. Stiefel for nearly two decades. The following year, at the age of 21, August C. Stiefel emigrated from Germany to the United States of America and started his new job with Schering & Glatz in New York City.

Companies, like individuals, try their utmost to control their own destinies, but sometimes outside forces intervene. On June 28, 1914, a Yugoslav nationalist named Gavrilo Princip assassinated Archduke Franz Ferdinand, heir to the throne of the Austro-Hungarian Empire; shortly thereafter, virtually all of Europe was at war. The United States did not enter World War I until 1917, but because Germany was an ally of Austria-Hungary, it became involved almost immediately in mid–1914.

That same year, a young girl from Offenbach am Main named Lili Koch decided that it was an opportune time to leave Germany and move to the United States. She did not know August Stiefel, even though they had grown up in the same small city; but they met in the United States and married in 1919. August and Lili had two sons, Werner (my father) and Herbert (my uncle), both of whom would grow up to be dynamic entrepreneurs. But their stories are for later chapters.

CHAPTER FOUR

ASHES TO ASHES

"Experience is simply the name we give our mistakes."
— OSCAR WILDE

World War I may have helped bring Lili and August Stiefel together, but it created some serious challenges for the J.D. Stiefel firm. The successful British naval blockade of Germany, coupled with German submarine attacks on foreign ships, virtually eliminated trade between the United States and Germany by 1916. J.D. Stiefel could not import all of the active ingredients it needed to manufacture its full product line, and it was almost impossible for the company to export even the limited quantities of soap it was able to produce.

Carl Friedrich Stiefel requested permission to have the Stiefel product line manufactured in America; but Anton and Ferdinand refused, voicing their concern about entrusting the family's secret formulae to any other company. Inventories of Stiefel soaps around the world were quickly exhausted; and with no source of supply other than the factory in Germany, the company struggled to stay alive.

Another problem caused by the war was the strong anti-German sentiment that developed around the world. In 1918, Schering & Glatz, obviously concerned about the German surnames of its two founders, felt compelled to issue the following notice to its customers: "Founded in New York City in 1867, the House of Schering & Glatz has been from its very inception, and throughout its existence, an American concern, entirely free and independent of foreign control, financial or otherwise." The relationship with the giant German chemical and pharmaceutical company also bearing the name "Schering" was downplayed. Customers were assured, "The German concern has never had a dollar's worth of investment in Schering & Glatz, nor have Schering & Glatz ever owned stock in the German firm, either as a firm, or as individuals." Finally, the notice guaranteed that the firm's products would in the future be manufactured in America, not Germany.

This notice posed no problem for August Stiefel because after World War I, he decided it was time to open a branch of J.D. Stiefel in the United States. International trade had resumed, so he had no problem importing Stiefel soaps from Germany. He terminated the agency agreement with Schering & Glatz and, after finding office space at 246 Pearl Street in New York City, began to apply the business lessons he had learned from his uncle. His immediate neighbor was George Merck, who had also emigrated from Germany to set up an American branch of the family business.

The J.D. Stiefel firm barely survived World War I, but in post-war America, it slowly but surely regained some of the ground it had lost during the war years. During the Roaring Twenties, August initiated a consumer marketing campaign to promote the company's Freckle Soap. Many of the "flappers" of that decade felt that it was fashionable for their skin to be alabaster in color with no freckles, so it was an opportune time to launch this product.

The exact formula had been developed personally by Ferdinand von Hebra after much experimentation, and the soap contained 5 percent borax, 2.5 percent beta naphthol and 10 percent

Freckle Soap promotional materials

sulphur. Although a product claiming to eliminate freckles in today's era might be viewed as something akin to snake oil, Stiefel stood behind the product by offering consumers a money-back guarantee. Freckle Soap actually worked by accelerating epidermal shedding; and, very importantly, patients were counseled to avoid the sun. Like most successful products, Freckle Soap attracted competitors who sought to copy it. Compared with how business is conducted today, I love the no-nonsense announcement the company issued about these copycat products: "The attention of the public is called to imitations of soap manufacturers who have no knowledge of either pharmacy or medicine, and whose bungling work is only calculated to deceive credulous people." I suspect that this announcement was not drafted by an attorney!

As the Roaring Twenties were drawing to a close, world events once again intervened to threaten the economic viability of J.D. Stiefel. On October 29, 1929, the U.S. stock market crashed, and soon the entire world was grappling with the Great Depression.

Then, in 1930, Congress passed (and President Herbert

Hoover signed) the Smoot-Hawley Tariff Act in an effort to protect American businesses from foreign competition. The act dramatically increased duties on imports from Europe and elsewhere. Other countries quickly retaliated by enacting their own protective tariffs, causing global trade to decrease by nearly 70 percent (according to the US State Department).

Almost overnight, it became prohibitively expensive for August Stiefel to import the family's medicated soaps from Germany. Once again, he begged his father and brother to allow him to have Stiefel soaps manufactured in the United States, but once again, the family refused. This turned out to be a huge mistake, but hindsight is always 20/20; I'm sure that the Stiefel family in Germany did not anticipate the Great Depression would last a decade. In any event, Stiefel soaps became exorbitantly expensive in all the company's export markets; as a result, sales plummeted precipitously.

In 1933, August Stiefel started calling his struggling business the Stiefel Medicinal Soap Company and moved his offices to 155 John Street in New York City. In an effort to make ends meet, he started working a second job as a salesman for the Air-Way Electric Appliance Corporation. Just as his Grandfather Johann had sold candles door to door, August Stiefel sold vacuum cleaners door to door.

To demonstrate his product, he offered to clean each prospective customer's house. However, in the midst of a depression, he cleaned a great number of houses while selling very few vacuum cleaners! Unable to afford Stiefel's New York location any longer, August moved his office into his family home in Montclair, New Jersey. By this time, sales were virtually non-existent, and August could no longer afford to make the mortgage payments on this home.

The bank foreclosed, and the family's only viable option was to move into what had been their summer cottage in Preston Hollow, New York. This cottage, situated in the northern part of the Catskill Mountains, was positively primitive, with no electricity, telephone, or indoor plumbing. But the family coped surprisingly well, and the location of the company office was changed yet again—the third new address within five years.

While August, Lili and their two sons were floundering in upstate New York, the J.D. Stiefel company in Offenbach am Main was faring only slightly better. Although the export market had essentially disappeared, Stiefel soaps were still being purchased within Germany, albeit in very limited quantities. When Johann's son Anton passed away in 1934, his son Ferdinand took charge of the struggling operation. But since Ferdinand's construction company was quite successful, he did not need to sell soap in order to feed his family.

Meanwhile, a few hours' drive south of Preston Hollow, August's uncle, Carl Friedrich Stiefel, was enjoying great financial success. In 1930, he sold Schering & Glatz to William R. Warner & Company, which eventually became the healthcare giant Warner-Lambert. Sadly, Carl was slowly going blind from glaucoma, a tragic development that made a profound impression on his daughter (my great-aunt), Elsa Stiefel. When Elsa passed away in 1982, she left half of her significant fortune to Lighthouse International, a charity focused exclusively on helping the blind and visually impaired. The other half went to Memorial Sloan Kettering Cancer Center (for cancer research) and the Children's Aid Society.

In the fall of 1938, August Stiefel's older son, Werner (my father), enrolled at Yale University. His family's financial plight was not an obstacle because (fortunately) he was awarded a full scholarship. He majored in chemical engineering and did well enough to land a summer job at Procter & Gamble, where he learned (what else?) the process of commercial soap-manufacturing.

Werner had always loved music, so before graduating he decided to take an elective course in harmony at the Yale School of Music. One of his classmates was a brilliant young pianist named Catherine Martyn Pierson, who later that year won the prestigious Piano Prize, awarded to the best pianist in the entire music school.

Werner and Catherine Stiefel, 1942

As fate would have it, Werner and Catherine fell in love, and they married two days after Werner graduated from Yale in 1942.

Catherine had been offered her own radio show, as well as the opportunity to embark upon a nationwide concert tour, but she happily sacrificed her own promising music career to follow Werner. Catherine was my mother, and she was the most talented musician I have ever heard. She had perfect pitch, and she could play any song in any key totally by ear. She was classically trained, so she could play Beethoven, Bach, Mozart and Chopin flawlessly. But as a kid sitting on the floor listening to my Mom play the piano, my favorite piece was George Gershwin's *Rhapsody in Blue*. To this day, I think of my mother whenever I hear that song.

The United States entered World War II in December of 1941, immediately after the Japanese bombing of Pearl Harbor. In June 1942, the government opened an explosives plant in Deer Valley, Pennsylvania and recruited talented chemists to work there. Werner was an ideal recruit because his chemical engineering background meant that he did not need any additional training. So, five days after marrying my mother, Werner joined the Ordnance Corps, a sustainment branch of the U.S. Army, and started making TNT at Deer Valley to support the war effort. In 1944, the Army transferred him to a different explosives facility, the Kankakee Ordnance Works in Joliet, Illinois, where he remained until he was released by the Army in August of 1945.

Life is filled with irony, and while Werner Stiefel was busily synthesizing TNT, the German cities of Frankfurt—and just across the Main River, Offenbach—were sustaining heavy bombing. Approximately one third of Offenbach was destroyed, and, as fate would have it, the J.D. Stiefel soap factory, now run by August's brother Ferdinand, was completely demolished. Is it possible that TNT produced by my father was used in the bomb that destroyed his family's business? As much as this question intrigues me, we will never know the answer.

Sales of Stiefel soaps outside of Germany had already been suspended, so the destruction of the factory in Offenbach killed the last remaining piece of the company. Almost 100 years after its founding in 1847, the J.D. Stiefel company essentially ceased to exist. Nothing remained except a few formulae and the good reputation of the Stiefel family. Ashes to ashes in one century.

CHAPTER FIVE

A NEW BEGINNING

"Our greatest weakness lies in giving up. The most certain way to succeed is always to try just one more time."
— THOMAS EDISON

The Stiefel soap business may have been gone, but it was hardly forgotten. On September 11, 1944, Werner Stiefel, Herbert Stiefel and August Stiefel officially incorporated the Stiefel Medicinal Soap Company, Inc. in New York State. They pooled all of their financial resources, a total of $1,200, as their initial capital investment in the new company. Their heads were filled with ambitious dreams of recapturing the prestige of the defunct J.D. Stiefel company. But these dreams had to remain on hold for a while, as Werner was still serving in the Ordnance Corps for Uncle Sam and Herb was just starting his freshman year at Yale (also on a scholarship).

As World War II drew to a close, the United States faced the most severe housing shortage it had ever experienced. Millions of soldiers were returning home to America, but homebuilding had decreased dramatically during the Great Depression and the war years. When my father was released from the Ordnance Corps in 1945, he and my mother could not find a home for themselves and their new baby anywhere near the new soap company's headquarters in upstate New York. Consequently, they moved in with Catherine's parents in New Haven, Connecticut; and Werner spent weekends there and weekdays living with his parents in Preston Hollow, New York. (This continued for two years, until Werner and Catherine were able to rent a house in nearby Oak Hill, New York.)

Once Werner and August were settled in Preston Hollow and ready to start work, my uncle Herb left Yale to move in with his parents and join the fledgling firm. Werner was 24 years old at the time, and Herb was only 18. The three men rented one room in an old wooden storage building owned by a lumber company. To access this room, they had to climb an outdoor wooden staircase; their only source of heat in the winter was an unvented kerosene stove—certainly not great for their lungs!

Armed with some old formulae from J.D. Stiefel, they engaged Hewitt Soap Company (a subsidiary of Procter & Gamble) to sell them unwrapped bars of about 30 different soap formulations. (Hewitt was a contract manufacturer—a company that made a profit by making products for other companies.) Werner and Herb wrapped these soap bars by hand, while (quite appropriately) listening to soap operas on the radio. August served as the company's entire sales force, calling on almost every dermatologist in the United States. Living out of a suitcase, he traveled for months at a time, visiting the southern doctors in the winter and the northern ones in the summer; when he returned home, he always gave me interesting matchbooks acquired during his travels. (Alas, my matchbook collection, like so many baseball card collections, failed to survive the relentless onslaught of maternal house-cleaning endeavors.) Amazingly, my grandfather covered this enormous territory as Stiefel's sole sales representative for the next fifteen years!

August, Werner and Herb managed to get their fledgling company off the ground, but they encountered an immediate problem.

Throughout its history, Stiefel always had a policy of allowing any customer to return unused merchandise at any time, for any reason, for a full refund. So as soon as August tried to get pharmacies to stock a few bars of the new company's soap, he was handed some old J.D. Stiefel products, along with a request for a refund. Even though some of these products were one or two decades old and sold by a different company, the three Stiefels nevertheless gave these customers a full refund. Consequently, in the early days, returns exceeded sales, and the company struggled to stay afloat.

In 1946, the two brothers and their father decided they should try to raise money to build their own soap factory. By eliminating the contract manufacturer from the equation, they could better control production schedules and (hopefully) reduce costs. Werner's best friend at Yale was a gentleman named Bob Appleton, whose sister Lucy had just married a man who worked at the Franklin B. Kirkbride private equity firm in New York City.

Werner hitchhiked from Preston Hollow to Manhattan to meet with Franklin Kirkbride himself. The first thing Mr. Kirkbride did was hand my father $200 in cash and tell him never to hitchhike again! (He never did.) The Kirkbride firm then agreed to invest $100,000 at 2 percent interest, with no principal payments due for 15 years. As part of the deal, however, Franklin B. Kirkbride Incorporated also received preferred stock representing ownership of 49 percent of Stiefel Medicinal Soap Company.

The Kirkbride connection kept the tiny soap company alive, and the three Stiefels immediately moved forward with their plan to build a new soap factory. All they could afford, however, was a beat-up old creamery in Oak Hill, New York. They purchased some antiquated machinery and, after some modest renovations to the two-story creamery building, were ready to start production. The factory layout was far from ideal, since the manufacturing equipment and shipping area were downstairs, while the soap wrapping table (all the soap was wrapped by hand) was upstairs.

Creamery building (center), Oak Hill, New York

Always the innovators, they modified an old hay bale elevator to carry the naked soap bars upstairs through a hole in the ceiling and set up an old wooden slide to carry the wrapped bars of soap back downstairs. (I remember as a kid thinking it was great fun to go to the office with my dad on a weekend so that I could slide from one floor to another!)

Dividing all the labor among the three of them, August handled Sales; Werner handled Research & Development, Finance and Administration; and Herb handled Production and Logistics. There was not enough money available to hire a secretary, maintenance person or anyone else to help run the company's daily operations. Herb took correspondence courses in engineering, business and economics for six years to make up for the Yale education he was missing. And, as is often the case in life, the school of hard knocks played perhaps the most important role of all.

While my father, uncle and grandfather were laboring to get Stiefel Medicinal Soap Company off the ground in the United States, August's brother Ferdinand was becoming a very successful architect and contractor in Germany. Proud of his J.D. Stiefel soap heritage, Ferdinand decided in 1948 to build a small soap factory in Offenbach to honor his grandfather and keep Johann's legacy alive in Germany. Ferdinand built his factory, but unfortunately passed away the following year. His son Anton (August's nephew) was a trained engineer who took over his family's successful construction business; and Anton shared his father's desire to pay tribute to Johann. Consequently, Anton kept the resurrected soap company alive, running it primarily for the sake of tradition. Three years after the Stiefel family soap business had ceased to exist, there were two different Stiefel companies on two different continents rising like the mythical phoenix from the ashes.

CHAPTER SIX

LOSING CONTROL

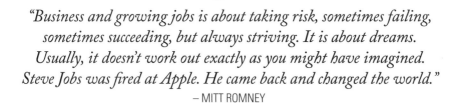

"Business and growing jobs is about taking risk, sometimes failing, sometimes succeeding, but always striving. It is about dreams. Usually, it doesn't work out exactly as you might have imagined. Steve Jobs was fired at Apple. He came back and changed the world."
— MITT ROMNEY

S tiefel Medicinal Soap Company, Inc. adopted a fiscal year ending March 31, an accounting practice that continued throughout its corporate existence. In its first full year of business (April 1, 1946 – March 31, 1947), sales were $20,598 (this was the actual total, not a number with zeroes omitted!), and instead of earning a profit, the company lost $16,097. The results for the second year were almost identical, and the third year was even worse. In 1950 (the year I was born), sales were $32,614, and losses were $14,075. So, for those people who might assume that I was born with a silver spoon in my mouth, please think again! My childhood years, while very happy, were extremely frugal times for our family.

These times were so frugal, in fact, that we could not afford "regular" milk. We mixed powdered milk with water in a gallon jug. And when my dad's white shirt collar became too frayed, my mom would cut it off with scissors, turn it inside out, iron it, and sew it back on. While we did not go hungry, there was never an abundance of food. Dessert every night consisted of two plain vanilla cookies, which were consumed by my siblings and me with great alacrity! Virtually all of my clothes were hand-me-downs from my two older brothers. My family could not afford our own home until I was in high school.

My father supplemented his meager income by performing electrical work at the boarding house across the street (he had somehow found time to obtain his electrician's license); my mother contributed to the family finances by playing the piano at other local boarding houses. My Uncle Herb, a very talented singer, helped feed his family by singing at weddings and other events.

The new Stiefel company lost money the first seven years of its existence, and the first year that it eked out a modest profit was 1954. How, you might wonder, did this company possibly manage to stay alive and support three households? The answer is that the good people at the Franklin B. Kirkbride firm believed that these three workaholic Stiefels would someday be successful, and in 1948, Kirkbride invested additional money in the business (and invested still more in 1953). But no astute businessman would make such high-risk investments without getting something valuable in return. Each time August, Herb and Werner received a cash infusion, it was necessary for them to give up more stock as part of the deal. By the end of 1953, the Stiefel family owned only 32 percent of Stiefel Medicinal Soap Company.

Private equity firms typically help their portfolio companies in many ways beyond merely serving as a source of cash. Their business expertise, analytical skills and industry contacts can be invaluable to any company—particularly a small company with inexperienced managers. Hence, the Franklin B. Kirkbride firm did much more for Stiefel than merely invest money—Kirkbride and his colleagues served as the life preserver that kept little Stiefel afloat. Kirkbride had many valuable connections, and they enlisted one of these connections, a creative New York dermatologist named Herman Sharlit, to consult for the struggling soap company.

Dr. Sharlit immediately suggested three new products—a moisturizing soap containing peanut oil, a detergent soap and a tar soap for psoriasis and eczema. Werner Stiefel loved Dr. Sharlit's ideas, but he decided to expand upon the tar soap concept. Dr. Sharlit had suggested a peanut oil extract of crude coal tar, but Werner Stiefel thought that the product would be more effective if he added pine tar, juniper tar and a coal tar solution known as LCD (liquor carbonis detergens).

The company launched all three products, naming them Oilatum® Soap, Acne-Aid® Detergent Soap, and Polytar® Soap respectively. These three products quickly became important products for Stiefel, and all three were recommended by dermatologists for several decades. Werner also formulated a tar shampoo utilizing the same four active ingredients that were in the tar soap; over time, several other formulations were launched as part of the Polytar® family of products.

The Stiefel family loved making and selling soap, but the sad reality was it was very challenging for them to earn meaningful profits in the soap business. Their soap products were all sold over the counter, which meant patients whose dermatologists had recommended these soaps were required to pay the full price themselves, with no insurance reimbursement. Even though Stiefel soaps were medicinal, there was nevertheless a limit as to what a patient would be willing to pay for a mere bar of soap. Consequently, Herb, Werner and August could not price their soap products aggressively; given the relatively high cost of manufacturing these products, the profit margins on Stiefel soaps were significantly lower than profit margins on most other pharmaceutical products.

Another long-standing issue was that most pharmacies were only willing to stock these soaps behind the pharmacy counter rather than on the store shelves. (We learned over the years that a pharmacy shelf is like a premier apartment in Manhattan—it cannot be occupied unless you are willing to pay dearly!) This meant consumers seeking to purchase a Stiefel soap at the local drugstore would rarely find the product unless they asked the pharmacist for help.

Some pharmacies refused to stock Stiefel's merchandise at all, stating they would order a product from the wholesaler if, and only if, a patient specifically requested it. A few pharmacists were particularly frustrating and aggravating; not wanting to take the time to special-order a product from the wholesaler, these pharmacists would lie to the consumer and assert Stiefel had discontinued that product. Not only would Stiefel lose that particular sale (because these pharmacists would recommend an alternative product), but the frustrated patient would then go back to the dermatologist and complain that this particular soap was no longer on the market. So, all of August's hard work convincing this dermatologist to recommend a Stiefel soap in the first place would go, like so much soap lather, down the drain!

Perhaps most normal people would have concluded this grandiose dream of building a major company was simply not working out, and it would be much more sensible for the three Stiefels to walk away and start new careers. But entrepreneurs are a unique breed; they perceive the world differently than most other people. In 1953, with their tiny business still in the red, Werner, Herb and August decided that it was time to expand operations beyond the United States! Sales at the time were only $77,000, but they were fortunate to find the perfect partner to start selling Stiefel soaps in Canada.

Morris Goodman, a brilliant and ambitious young entrepreneur who was just graduating from pharmacy school, had recently formed a company called Winley-Morris; his objective was to become the Canadian distributor for several foreign pharmaceutical companies. Winley-Morris did not yet have any major clients, and Stiefel did not yet have any major products; but the agreement they reached was the beginning of a long and mutually-beneficial relationship. Winley-Morris successfully marketed Stiefel's product line in Canada for more than two decades.

Recognizing the difficulties associated with marketing nothing but soap products, Herb, Werner and August made another major decision in 1956—they decided that it was time to diversify their product line and offer dosage forms other than soaps. To reflect this philosophical evolution, they changed the name of the company from Stiefel Medicinal Soap Company, Inc. to Stiefel Laboratories, Inc.

Werner Stiefel, who was still acting as a one-man research and development department, redoubled his efforts to identify new product ideas in the field of dermatology. Helping him in this endeavor was a brilliant dermatologist named Eugene Farber, chairman of Stanford's Department of Dermatology. Dr. Farber consulted for Stiefel for many years; his expert advice played an important role in helping Stiefel identify and develop products that were both safe and effective.

Notwithstanding the many challenges and frustrations, Stiefel Laboratories sales gradually inched higher. The first significant sales breakthrough came in 1958, when the company launched its first major non-soap product—Brāsivol®—for the treatment of acne. Brāsivol® was an abrasive cream that contained tiny sand-like particles of aluminum oxide. The patient would gently scrub their face and any other acne-prone areas with this cream and then rinse it off. The cream itself was essentially soft soap (true to the Stiefel soap tradition); and the product worked by simultaneously cleansing the skin and exfoliating dead skin cells to help unclog congested pores.

The concept for this product was conceived by a Los Angeles dermatologist, Rose Saperstein, who wrote about her discovery in a dermatology journal. When Werner read about this invention, he immediately called Dr. Saperstein and flew to Los Angeles to meet with her the following week. An agreement was quickly negotiated whereby Stiefel would obtain exclusive rights to Dr. Saperstein's invention in exchange for a royalty on sales. Brāsivol was an immediate hit with dermatologists; within a few years, it became the company's first million-dollar product. As an added bonus, Werner Stiefel and Rose Saperstein became lifelong friends.

The Kirkbride group was impressed with the initial success of Brāsivol, and they astutely recognized that this new product would propel Stiefel to a new level. Consequently, they decided that it was an opportune time to cash out their investment, and in December 1959, they negotiated a contract to sell Stiefel to an outside buyer for the sum of $558,300. Under New York corporate law, a sale of the company required an affirmative vote by the owners of more than two-thirds of the outstanding shares. Kirkbride owned more than enough stock to approve the sale; there was nothing the Stiefel family could do to stop the sale and retain ownership of their company.

Werner, still filled with the aforementioned entrepreneurial spirit but recognizing that he probably would not be allowed to compete in the field of dermatology, quickly incorporated a new company, Martyn Pharmaceutical Company (Martyn was my mother's middle name). He envisioned this company specializing in ophthalmic products. But lo and behold, the buyer insisted on a provision in the sales contract whereby a condition of closing was "the Buyer and each of the following: A. C. Stiefel, Werner Stiefel and H. A. Stiefel shall have entered into an employment agreement mutually satisfactory to each of the parties to each of such agreements." All three Stiefels refused to sign these employment agreements, so the sale fell through.

Kirkbride had been a great partner, however, and knowing he wanted to cash out, the Stiefels focused their energy on raising enough money to repurchase all of Kirkbride's stock. In 1960, Werner negotiated a loan with the New York Business Development Corporation, and when the loan proceeds were combined with some money invested by a few wealthy individuals, there was enough cash available to buy out the entire Kirkbride interest. Incidentally, one of these individual investors was our Canadian friend, Morris Goodman, who invested $20,000 in return for approximately 5 percent of the company stock. Morris also agreed to join the corporate Board of Directors. In his autobiography, *To Make a Difference*, Morris explains why he chose to invest: "One of the lessons I learned early in life was to invest in companies with strong leaders such as the Stiefels, who had both the vision and the passion to build for the future."

As Stiefel was always a privately-held company, with no public market for its shares, most shareholders were continually pushing to sell some or all of their stock. Morris, however, chose to retain almost all of his shares, despite having several opportunities to sell. His patience and astuteness were rewarded when the company was sold in 2009—Morris received more than $220 million for his stake in Stiefel Laboratories! A philanthropist as well as an entrepreneur, Morris promptly made a large donation to McGill University in Montreal to endow the Rosalind & Morris Goodman Cancer Research Center. Morris is living proof that the old adage "nice guys finish last" is simply untrue.

CHAPTER SEVEN

LOTIONS, POTIONS AND AMBITIOUS NOTIONS

"The entrepreneur always searches for change, responds to it, and exploits it as an opportunity."
— PETER DRUCKER

Throughout my years in the pharmaceutical industry, I encountered many companies that impeded their own growth because of what is known as the "NIH" (Not Invented Here) syndrome. Ralph Katz and Thomas J. Allen of the Sloan School of Management at M.I.T. wrote about this syndrome in a 1982 article published in the journal *R&D Management.* They defined NIH as "the tendency of a project group of stable composition to believe it possesses a monopoly of knowledge of its field, which leads it to reject new ideas from outsiders to the likely detriment of its performance."

NIH can afflict any group or department in any field, regardless of how diligently one endeavors to suppress it. I cannot claim I never saw the NIH syndrome raise its ugly head at our company, but NIH was not an issue at Stiefel (at least not in the early years when Werner Stiefel was a one-man R&D department). In fact, the Stiefel family always actively solicited the ideas of outside dermatologists; throughout its corporate history, many of Stiefel's best products were formulated as a direct result of inventions or suggestions by these dermatologists.

You have already read that Stiefel's first major non-soap product, Brāsivol®, was invented by a dermatologist. In the case of Stiefel's second major non-soap product, it was, to quote the late, great Yogi Berra, "déjà vu all over again." Cleveland White was a creative Chicago dermatologist who, in 1959, patented a super-absorbent foot and body powder that absorbed six times its own weight of moisture without caking. The key ingredient in this powder was a pure, starch-free cellulose derived from corn cobs.

Dr. White had published an article describing his invention in the prestigious dermatology journal *Lancet* in 1955; two years later, he and Werner Stiefel signed an exclusive licensing agreement. Do you remember learning about binomial nomenclature (genus, species, etc.) in high school? Everyone remembers that human beings are *Homo sapiens*, but you may not know that the scientific name for corn is *Zea mays*. Since Dr. White's invention consisted of an absorbent powder derived from *Zea mays*, Werner named this new product Zeasorb® Powder.

After the product was launched in 1960, the company began giving away corn cob pipes at the annual meetings of the American Academy of Dermatology to remind dermatologists of this unique aspect of the Zeasorb® formulation. A few years later, the formulation was refined to make it whiter in color, and Zeasorb® Powder is still sold in pharmacies today.

After working with dermatologists for over three decades, I can unequivocally state that dermatologists possess extraordinary expertise in the diagnosis and treatment of skin disorders. If anyone reading this book ever develops any type of skin condition, I strongly urge you to see a dermatologist immediately. It could actually save your life, not only because so many systemic diseases exhibit skin manifestations, but also because there are a number of serious and even life-threatening dermatological disorders—melanoma representing only one of many. Dermatologists possess an intellectual curiosity and research orientation that is truly unique. They desperately want to heal their patients, and if existing products are not helping adequately, they are not afraid to experiment with new therapies that might work better. One such dermatologist was Dr. William Pace, a Canadian doctor from London, Ontario.

In 1963, after years of research and experimentation, Dr. Pace presented a paper to the Canadian Dermatological Association describing a compounded cream containing benzoyl peroxide and sulfur that was effective in the treatment of acne. Dr. Pace's discovery was a major breakthrough in acne therapy; with his input and cooperation, Stiefel Laboratories developed and patented the first stable acne composition containing benzoyl peroxide. This product, which combined 5 percent benzoyl peroxide and 2 percent sulfur, was launched in 1966 and was named Sulfoxyl® Lotion.

Stiefel also launched a similar product, Benoxyl® Lotion, that did not contain sulfur; and we subsequently developed and launched alcohol-based and water-based gels containing benzoyl peroxide under the Panoxyl® trademark. These products worked so well in comparison to older remedies that many other companies launched similar products of their own. Five decades later, benzoyl peroxide is still widely used, not only in prescription products, but in popular consumer products such as Proactiv®. Stiefel pioneered this therapeutic revolution, but we never could have done so without our dermatologist friend Bill Pace, who was designated by many of his colleagues as "the Father of Benzoyl Peroxide."

Unfortunately, not all interactions with inventors have happy endings. Many individuals and companies are so enthralled with their inventions that their expectations are totally unrealistic. I was always wary when an inventor would walk into my office and proclaim their new product would cure not just one, but several different skin diseases and should easily generate enormous sales.

My dad called such an individual an EIH—entrepreneur in heat—and warned me no matter how much time and money a company might invest to promote an EIH's invention, the EIH would never be satisfied.

Even inventors who were realistic about their product's potential often conceived of product ideas that were either impractical, too difficult or expensive to manufacture, not sufficiently safe and effective, unlikely to achieve FDA (Food and Drug Administration) approval, or already patented by someone else. Consequently, although we diligently strived to avoid the NIH syndrome, we nevertheless turned down the vast majority of product ideas submitted to us by third parties. We hardly ever had cause to regret a decision to reject a product idea; but every once in a while a product declined by us would become very successful in the hands of another company. One tragic example of this involves the unusual story of Neutrogena® Soap.

In the early 1950s, a Belgian cosmetic chemist named Dr. Edmond Fromont visited my father's office in Oak Hill, New York. Fromont had patented an amber, translucent soap bar made from glycerin; since Stiefel was specializing solely in soaps at the time, he logically wondered if we might be interested in licensing his invention, Neutrogena®, for the United States. Werner Stiefel was intrigued by this aesthetically-pleasing product, but because the company was focusing primarily on medicinal soaps, he politely declined the opportunity to market what he perceived to be more of a consumer product than an ethical one. (In our industry, using the word "ethical" in this context has nothing to do with ethics—instead it is utilized to describe a promotional strategy that entails calling on physicians and trying to convince them to prescribe or recommend your product.)

A year or two after his visit to Oak Hill, Dr. Fromont struck a deal with Emanuel Stolaroff, who owned Natone, a California-based cosmetics company. The novel translucent soap bar became so successful in the United States that in 1962, Natone officially changed its company name to Neutrogena Corporation. Emanuel Stolaroff's daughter, Jo Anne, was married to a brilliant and charismatic businessman named Lloyd Cotsen. Under Cotsen's leadership, Neutrogena grew rapidly, expanded its product line and was eventually sold to Johnson & Johnson in 1994 for $924 million.

Unfortunately, it is nearly impossible to conduct business in corporate America without occasionally upsetting someone, whether it be an employee or a third party. We all recognize that business disputes of this nature can sometimes lead to litigation and hard feelings, but they almost never lead to murder. In 1979, while Lloyd Cotsen was traveling on a business trip in New York, a tragedy took place at his home in California. According to a 1981 UPI report, "Police said a gunman wearing a ski mask invaded the Cotsen home in Beverly Hills and tied up Mrs. Cotsen, her 13-year-old son, Noah, and his friend, Christopher Doering, before shooting them in the head." The report went on to note that the Los Angeles police believed they had identified the murderer as Erich Arnold Tali, who was then managing the Belgian company founded by Neutrogena's inventor, Dr. Fromont. A 1992 article in *Fortune* described Erich Arnold Tali as "a Belgian business rival who had feuded with Cotsen over rights to the Neutrogena trademark." According to the 1981 UPI report, "Tali was found dead in his home in Brussels, Belgium on October 15, 1979, the day he was to be questioned by Beverly Hills detectives."

I knew Lloyd Cotsen for many years, and I considered him to be an extremely nice person, an honest person, and a person of the utmost integrity—attributes which make these horrible murders even sadder and scarier to me. Apparently, the killer did not share my opinion about Lloyd, but how could anyone execute an innocent woman and two innocent children? We will never know for sure if Mr. Tali was the killer, nor will we fully understand the killer's motive. I just shudder to think that if my dad had entered into that deal to market Neutrogena® in the United States, then perhaps my mom would have been murdered, along with one or more of my siblings.

As noted in the last chapter, the Stiefel business lost money the first seven years of its existence, and the first year that it made a modest profit was 1954. Sales that year were less than $100,000, but the three Stiefels had ambitious notions and decided they needed more space to accommodate the growth they hoped to achieve in the future. An old, abandoned hotel next door to the manufacturing plant in Oak Hill, New York, was listed for sale at a bargain price, so the company purchased it and promptly converted it into a storage area. This decrepit hotel had no heat or air conditioning, so only items that could withstand severe temperature extremes (such as packaging materials) were warehoused there. Sales slowly edged higher and still more space was needed, so the company constructed a small pole barn on the other side of the plant. The Stiefel "campus" now consisted of three adjacent buildings in the downtown area of the quaint little hamlet of Oak Hill.

Stiefel soaps grew increasingly popular among dermatologists, and soon more manufacturing capacity was needed. To address this need, the company purchased 75 acres of vacant land on Route 145, about two miles from the existing Oak Hill buildings, and a new, state-of-the-art factory was constructed. Through the years, this facility was expanded multiple times, and it remains open to this day manufacturing toothpaste for GlaxoSmithKline. Throughout its history, that plant has served as one of the largest employers in the entire region. (Photos of this new Stiefel Oak Hill plant and several other Stiefel facilities around the world are bound near the center of this book.)

My former law partner, Hon. George J. Pulver, Jr., used to opine that "nothing in life is ever as good or as bad as it seems at any one point in time." The first time he offered me this advice, I suspected that he was simply in a cynical mood; but I learned over the years that he was sharing the type of wisdom that can only be acquired

August and Werner Stiefel at groundbreaking ceremony
for new Oak Hill manufacturing plant.

through life experiences. In fiscal year 1965, Stiefel Laboratories enjoyed sales exceeding one million dollars for the first time ever. There was a big party to celebrate this milestone; with the new manufacturing plant on Route 145 already undergoing expansion to accommodate this sales growth, everyone at the company was happy and filled with optimism. Then, out of nowhere, fate dealt a cruel blow.

In January 1967, there was a massive fire in downtown Oak Hill. I awoke that night to the terrifying sounds of fire sirens wailing and my parents running through the house. Everyone jumped into the family car, and time seemed to stand still as we raced to the scene of the inferno. Overcome with stunned disbelief, we watched helplessly as the fire raged—its mammoth flames seeming to reach the sky. Before the night was over, both the downtown Oak Hill factory and the pole barn were gone forever; and all of the machinery, equipment and other contents of both buildings had been completely incinerated. In one terrible night, years and years of hard work went, quite literally, up in smoke. I was 16 years old, and it was the first time I ever saw my dad cry.

Oak Hill factory after 1967 fire

CHAPTER EIGHT

GLOBAL EXPANSION ALL OVER AGAIN

"Those who do not remember the past are condemned to repeat it."
– GEORGE SANTAYANA

T he primary reason Stiefel went out of business during World War II was its reliance on the factory in Germany as its sole source of supply. With Brāsivol enjoying a rapid increase in popularity in the early 1960s, August, Herb and Werner Stiefel determined not to make the same mistake twice. They wanted a manufacturing plant outside of Oak Hill, New York; and after careful consideration, they determined that the next factory should be in Puerto Rico. There were many factors that influenced this decision. As a territory of the United States, Puerto Rico recognized US patents and trademarks. Furthermore, the island utilized US dollars as its currency, thereby obviating any issues relating to foreign exchange transactions. And perhaps most importantly, both the US government and the government of Puerto Rico were aggressively incentivizing US companies to do business there.

Working closely with Fomento, the local business development agency, Herb Stiefel negotiated to lease a building in an industrial park in Mayaguez; it was confirmed that the company's operations in Puerto Rico would not be subject to any income taxes for ten years! In 1962, Herb, his wife, Peg, and their four daughters moved to Mayaguez, where Herb personally supervised the establishment of the factory. The entire family learned Spanish, the primary language of the island, and Herb's fifth daughter was born there. There were many challenges, but with the help of a loyal and skilled workforce, the challenges were overcome.

Two years later, with the factory running smoothly and efficiently, Herb and his family moved back to Oak Hill. Herb offered the position of General Manager (the title given throughout the years to the senior executive in every Stiefel subsidiary) and a huge salary increase to a valued employee named Juan de Jesús. It is unusual, but not unheard of, for an employee to turn down a promotion; but Juan's reason for doing so was truly unique. Leaving his wife, his child, and all his worldly possessions behind, Juan moved to a retreat in the mountains to devote himself to the teachings of Rosicrucianism!

While Herb was busy in Puerto Rico, Werner and August were trying to find an agent to represent the company in Germany. Werner purchased a copy of a German dermatology journal and proceeded to visit every single company that advertised in it. Unfortunately, not one of these companies was interested in representing insignificant little Stiefel Laboratories. With nowhere else to turn, Werner reached out to his first cousin, Anton Stiefel (Ferdinand's son), who was busy running a successful construction business in Offenbach while simultaneously keeping alive the last vestiges of the original J.D. Stiefel soap company.

Anton was initially reluctant to take more time away from his construction business, but ultimately the cousins reached an agreement whereby Anton agreed to sell his J.D. Stiefel soap business to Stiefel Laboratories and manage the company's business in Germany. In the early 1900s, Stiefel had been a German company with operations in the United States. A few decades later, like a reflection in the mirror, everything was reversed. Stiefel was now an American company with operations in Germany. And with Canada and Puerto Rico already up and running, the new Stiefel—just like the old Stiefel—had become a multinational company. But don't be too impressed—worldwide sales of this particular multinational had not yet reached the million-dollar threshold.

In September of 1964, my grandfather, August C. Stiefel, passed away unexpectedly while on a business trip. It was two weeks prior to his 75th birthday, and it was halfway through the fiscal year when company sales finally reached the million-dollar mark. Sadly, August did not live to take part in that celebration; but I know that he was proud the US operation he founded was beginning to enjoy modest success. Right until the end, he kept a smile on his face and a cigar in his mouth. To honor his memory and his many contributions, the company opened the August C. Stiefel Research Institute ("SRI" for short) in 1967. Adjacent to the factory in Oak Hill, SRI developed and tested dermatology products for the next four decades.

The sudden death of their father took a toll on Herb and Werner. Reminded of their own mortality, my father and uncle typed up a short agreement whereby each gave to the other a right of first refusal in the event one of them wanted to sell any Stiefel stock—and this agreement provided that it would continue to be binding "in the event of the death of either of us." But more importantly, August's death dramatically changed the dynamic of the company. With three senior executives, all of them major stockholders, running the company, the implicit willingness of all three to abide by a majority vote virtually eliminated the potential for managerial deadlock. Now there were just two brothers, both of whom were strong-willed and opinionated. Both were willing to work feverishly to help the company grow and prosper, but what would happen if they were to disagree? What did August's demise portend for the future?

The first major corporate decision after my grandfather's passing was to continue expanding outside the United States by opening a subsidiary in the United Kingdom. It was agreed that Herb would undertake this project. So, in 1965, Herb and his family moved once again—this time to London. You might wonder why Herb chose London, given that the cost of living in a major city is almost always higher than in a smaller one. Two primary factors influenced his decision—the Ministry of Health was located there and most of the influential dermatologists practiced there. Working within a very tiny budget, Herb rented a small, empty room on the third floor of a decrepit old building with no heat or elevator. The building was in the Covent Garden district, home of the Royal Opera House; Covent Garden is now a popular tourist destination teeming with shops, bars, restaurants and theaters. In 1965, however, Covent Garden was the home of the wholesale fruit and vegetable market. Work in this market began well before dawn, and Herb wrote that by the time he arrived at the office each morning, the street was littered with spoiled or discarded fruit, cabbage leaves and broken crates.

Getting a telephone was a painful experience that took almost three weeks; and trying to obtain heat for the office was a separate ordeal. Herb walked to the local hardware store and purchased a space heater, only to find when he returned to the office that it had no plug. He walked back to the store to explain this oversight, only to be told that there were nearly sixty different plugs, and Herb needed to specify which one he wanted. He returned to the office again to inspect the wall socket and then walked back to the hardware store for the third time. This time, he purchased the correct plug, and after wiring it to the space heater himself, the office finally had heat. Since London in January is quite cold, this was an important achievement!

Trying to see the dermatologists presented another significant challenge. Herb found his way to the office of an important dermatologist but discovered the office door had no doorknob! He rang the bell, and when he told the lady who answered the door he wanted to see the doctor, he was informed that he needed to write for an appointment. In this era of e-mails and text messages, writing for an appointment might entail merely a minor delay. But for Herb, it meant that he needed to purchase the stationery and stamps, write letters to all the dermatologists himself, and walk to the post office to mail the letters.

Realizing that he could no longer perform every single office function personally, Herb hired a secretary and ran a newspaper ad for the position of Managing Director. He received fifty handwritten letters in response to his ad, and in Herb's own words, "decided I would see every one of them because I could learn how business was done in this strange country." Embarrassed by his dreary office, Herb rented a room at the Hilton and scheduled appointments with all fifty applicants at half hour intervals from Friday through Sunday. He placed a chair in the hall, taped a clock to the door of the hotel room and conducted the interviews. The person he eventually selected was a gentleman named Dennis Love, whom Herb had interviewed at eight o'clock Sunday morning. Dennis stayed with Stiefel for many years and did a great job. When asked years later why he had bothered to show up on that fateful Sunday morning, he replied that he simply had to meet the person who had the gall to schedule an interview at that ungodly hour!

Herb and Dennis Love divided the UK in half, with Dennis seeing all of the dermatologists in the eastern part of the UK and Herb calling on everyone in the western part. They were a good team, and sales grew steadily. But like any pharmaceutical company, Stiefel UK needed more products. Herb observed that baths were much more popular in the UK than they were in the United States; with his second London winter approaching, he had the idea that a therapeutic bath additive to help control dry skin and eczema could potentially become an important product.

Stiefel's biggest competitor in the US at that time was a company called Westwood; and Westwood had developed an excellent bath oil called Alpha Keri®. Herb really liked the Alpha Keri® formulation and wanted to develop and launch a very similar product in the UK. Werner, however, lived in the US, where more people preferred to shower rather than take a bath; and he also disliked the idea of validating a competitor's product portfolio by imitating one of their products. Consequently, Werner was vehemently opposed to Herb's idea. Werner and Herb were the two largest stockholders in the company, as well as the two top executives. How could this deadlock be resolved without threatening the viability of the company? The compromise that Herb and Werner reached would dramatically impact the future of the company for the next four decades.

CHAPTER NINE

CUTTING THE BABY IN HALF

"No person will make a great business who wants to do it all himself or get all the credit."
— ANDREW CARNEGIE

You have probably all heard the biblical story about the ancient Israeli King Solomon, who was once approached by two women, both claiming to be the mother of a certain infant. King Solomon, known for his wisdom, asked for his sword and informed the women that the only fair solution was to cut the baby in half and give half to each woman. When one of the two begged him not to do this, but instead to give the child unharmed to the other woman, Solomon knew immediately that the one trying to save the infant's life was the true mother. Problem solved!

Obviously, Stiefel Laboratories was not a baby; but after two decades of blood, sweat and tears, both Werner and Herb loved the company and viewed it in some ways as their baby. Unlike a baby, however, a company can sometimes survive and flourish even if cut in half, which is precisely what the Stiefel brothers decided to do. After much productive discussion, they typed up a short agreement that they both signed in November 1966. No lawyers were involved—the two brothers negotiated every word of this document themselves. The very first paragraph specified that the agreement was being "entered into for the purpose of giving HAS (Herb's initials) autonomy in the management of the foreign subsidiaries of Stiefel Laboratories, Inc., and WKS (Werner's initials) the same autonomy in the management of Stiefel Laboratories, Inc. and its domestic subsidiaries."

The agreement set forth how overseas operations would be funded in the future, and it further stipulated foreign earnings could not be repatriated to the US without Herb's consent. Herb was given the power to handpick the corporate boards of all foreign subsidiaries, and it was agreed that Herb would thenceforth receive an annual bonus based solely upon the profitability of foreign operations.

The company had experienced many changes between 1960 and 1964. The Kirkbride group's stock had all been repurchased, there were some new stockholders who had invested significant sums of money, and August Stiefel had passed away. Partially due to these changes, and partially to prepare the company for the future, Stiefel Laboratories amended its certificate of incorporation in early 1966 to make two important revisions.

Firstly, every share of "old" common stock was replaced with twelve shares of Class A common stock and eight shares of Class B common stock. Secondly, and perhaps more importantly, there were to be seven members of the corporate Board of Directors—four of whom would be elected by the Class B shareholders and the other three by the Class A shareholders. After this amendment, Werner and Herbert Stiefel each owned a substantial number of shares of both classes of stock. But as part of their November 1966 agreement, Herb transferred all of his Class B shares to Werner in exchange for an equal number of Werner's Class A shares. Herb thus became the company's largest Class A stockholder, and Werner gained ownership of a majority of the Class B stock— meaning that Werner could thereafter single-handedly elect four of the company's seven directors.

So, who do you think got the better end of this deal between brothers? On one hand, Stiefel was a US company, and Werner received the power to run the US Division of this company without any interference from Herb. At the time this agreement was signed, sales within the United States represented more than 95 percent of the company's total worldwide sales. On the other hand, Herb received virtually absolute power to run the entire International Division of Stiefel Laboratories as he deemed best, without any interference from his older brother. And although International sales were very small in 1966, there are a lot of countries in the world, many of which offered excellent potential for a pharmaceutical company. Viewed through the lens of history, I believe their 1966 agreement was an excellent deal for both men. They both received the freedom to spread their entrepreneurial wings; and throughout the years, each man seemed very happy with the choice he had made.

One fact relevant to this agreement causes me to be very proud of both my dad and my uncle. The agreement specified that it would not terminate until one of the men died; which did not occur until 2006, when, by sad coincidence, the two brothers died within six months of each other. In the four decades this "cut the baby in half" arrangement was in effect, corporate sales increased by 50,000 percent, and the corporate structure became infinitely more complex. Yet there was not one time that either man failed to live up to his word. Herb and Werner did not always agree, and neither one was shy about expressing his opinions to the other. But ultimately, each man respected the authority of the other granted by their 1966 agreement, and neither ever made any effort to evade or countermand this agreement.

I've often reflected on whether cutting the Stiefel baby in half was good or bad for the company. On the positive side, it gave both men the opportunity to be totally entrepreneurial. Furthermore, it allowed Herb to concentrate all his efforts on the International

Division, whereas Werner could focus solely on the US Division. But in my opinion, the most important positive factor was basic sibling rivalry—the sense of competition and jealousy that frequently develops between two siblings. Both Werner and Herb told me on many occasions how much respect each felt for the other's intellect and abilities. Neither one ever expressed to me a secret desire to outperform the other. But even if the sibling rivalry was subconscious, I believe that it existed quite strongly; I further believe it contributed enormously to the growth and success of Stiefel Laboratories.

As you can probably imagine, however, there were also several negative aspects associated with cutting the Stiefel baby in half. Operating one company as if it were two separate businesses necessitates a lot of extra paperwork and reports. It costs twice as much money to employ two senior executives—one for the US Division and one for the International Division—rather than one to preside over every corporate function. At some dermatology conventions, there were two separate Stiefel exhibits, which entailed both higher costs and greater potential for confusion. And there were many more inefficiencies, particularly when computer technology began to advance exponentially in the latter part of the twentieth century. Obviously, it made no sense for the US and International to expend precious capital on hardware and software platforms that could not effectively communicate with each other. This, however, is precisely what happened.

Some might opine that since Stiefel was sold for an enormous amount of money in 2009, cutting the baby in half obviously must have been good for the company. But we all have 20/20 hindsight. How do we know whether or not the company might have been worth even more if it had not been divided in half? Clearly, we will never know. But as my mother always used to say, "Things have a way of working out for the best."

CHAPTER TEN

ADVENTURES WITH SIDE VENTURES

"Success is not final, failure is not fatal:
it is the courage to continue that counts."
— WINSTON CHURCHILL

S ubsequent to cutting the Stiefel baby in half in 1966, Werner Stiefel began to investigate various avenues whereby he could supplement the income of the US Division. One such avenue involved the August C. Stiefel Research Institute, Inc. ("SRI"), which had been created as a wholly-owned Stiefel subsidiary to honor Werner's father. Initially, the mission of SRI was simply to handle Stiefel's research effort, which at that time entailed developing and testing new products and attempting (if necessary) to obtain FDA approval for them. I state "if necessary" only because most dermatological products marketed at that time did not require FDA approval. None of Stiefel's array of soaps, for example, required FDA approval, nor did any product classified by the FDA as a cosmetic. Only new drugs required approval— "drugs" being defined by the Federal Food, Drug and Cosmetic Act as "articles intended for use in the diagnosis, cure, mitigation, treatment, or prevention of disease" or "intended to affect the structure or any function of the body of man or other animals." And even many drug products could be marketed without undergoing any approval process—for example, nonprescription drugs that complied with a written FDA Monograph, and prescription drugs that were deemed to be "grandfathered."

As SRI grew, so did the number of talented people working there, leading Werner to the realization that other companies (particularly smaller ones with insufficient research capabilities of their own) would gladly pay for access to SRI's expertise. Consequently, Werner changed the mission of SRI, converting it to a profit center rather than a cost center. Pursuant to this new business model, SRI would bill Stiefel at cost for the work it performed on Stiefel's research projects, but it would also work on projects for other companies—invoicing at cost plus a moderate markup. Daniel Nicolai, a pharmaceutical industry veteran, was recruited to lead SRI. Dan guided SRI successfully for many years—providing excellent service to both Stiefel Laboratories (including its subsidiaries) and outside customers. Keeping both the internal and external customers happy was a difficult endeavor because everyone wanted to be SRI's top priority, but Dan was always up to this challenge.

Werner was very enthusiastic about SRI's evolved business mandate for a variety of reasons. Firstly, SRI earned a profit on this outside business. Secondly, SRI's personnel could enhance their breadth of experience by working on interesting projects for third parties. And finally, SRI's calculation of "cost" included an overhead factor; thus, the more outside projects SRI tackled, the more overhead that was absorbed. This overhead absorption was quite significant to Werner, because it is very expensive to operate a pharmaceutical laboratory that complies with all regulatory standards and provides a healthy work environment.

Some customers engaged SRI to perform straightforward microbiology or analytical chemistry testing, while others wanted assistance with product development or regulatory affairs. Many clients requested several different services, and a few wanted SRI to do everything necessary to develop a product, test it, and obtain FDA approval. One client, the New York State Police, awarded SRI the contract to manufacture ampoules containing chemical solutions for use in the breathalyzer machines utilized to test suspected drunk drivers. This police contract was financially rewarding for several years until criminal defense lawyers, trying to get the charges against their clients dismissed, began to subpoena our scientists to explain exactly how the ampoules were manufactured and tested.

There was nothing wrong with our procedures, and I am virtually certain that the defense attorneys knew this. But it was extremely disruptive and expensive for us to send our personnel to courts all across the state to testify—and the State Police did not have the budget to pay us for all of the time that was wasted away from the office. For defense lawyers, it was the quintessential legal loophole, but for us, it was the classic Catch-22 scenario. If one of our scientists did not appear in court, the charges against the drunk driver would be dismissed; but if we did appear in court, we lost money on the police contract. So, with regret, we were forced to give up the ampoule business.

In 1966 (the year that the U.S. Division was created), Werner incorporated another wholly-owned subsidiary he called Durham Pharmacal Corp. ("Durham"), named after a small community near Oak Hill. Durham's original mission was to market over-the-counter skincare products directly to the consumer—in contrast to Stiefel, which marketed only through healthcare professionals. Werner did not want Stiefel to undertake consumer marketing itself, because he knew some dermatologists became angry if they noticed a product being promoted in their offices was also being advertised in print media or on television. And since Stiefel Laboratories owed its very existence to dermatologists, we were always extremely careful to avoid offending anyone in the dermatology community. Throughout the years, Durham developed several excellent consumer products, including Students Choice® acne products; Tinamed® Wart Remover; Respite® Lotion for dry, itchy skin; and Capsagesic®, a topical analgesic containing capsaicin.

Although Durham's original mission was simply to sell skincare products directly to consumers, two other Stiefel side ventures were eventually merged into Durham. In 1965, Stiefel had acquired a tiny California company called Moreba Laboratories. Moreba's business was to package and sell vitamins and a few other miscellaneous products. Stiefel's brief foray into the vitamin business was unsuccessful, however, and we learned the hard way that selling vitamins is very different from selling skincare products. (Many years later, we learned further that marketing any product directly to the consumer was not our sweet spot—what we did best was ethical promotion to the dermatologists.) So, in 1967, Moreba changed its focus and entered the private label soap business.

Stiefel was always very proud of our expertise in the field of soap production. We were the first company in the United States to install a completely automated soap-making line manufactured by Mazzoni, a company near Milan, Italy, that was the world's largest producer of soap machinery. (As an aside, Mazzoni sent its own personnel to install their equipment in our Oak Hill manufacturing plant. As I recall, the lengthy presence in rural Greene County of a crew of handsome, sophisticated Italian men generated a high level of interest—particularly among the local young ladies.)

Another firm with an excellent reputation as a soap manufacturer was the John T. Stanley Company; Werner successfully recruited two top people from Stanley—Eduardo Matosis to manage all of our soap production and Thomas Jaeger to manage Moreba's sales and marketing. Moreba sold bags of soap that looked and smelled like lemons, similar bags of strawberry soap, as well as several other great-smelling items (such as lavender soap and rosewater

& glycerin soap) in gift boxes. I loved Moreba's soap-on-a-rope, which you could hang around your neck while showering. Moreba also manufactured some high-end soaps for other companies, such as Jean Nate´ Soap and Erno Laszlo Sea Mud Deep Cleansing Bar. The Erno Laszlo product was a beautiful black bar, and some of the sea mud came from the banks of the Dead Sea. But one of my first jobs at Stiefel, when I was still a college student working summers, was to drive to the banks of the Hudson River and shovel additional sea mud into 55-gallon drums. This Hudson River mud then underwent an extensive straining and sterilization process before it was used to supplement the Dead Sea mud in the product.

Another Stiefel side venture was our House Accounts Division, which utilized Stiefel's equipment to manufacture products for other companies. The business concept was very similar to that of SRI—by engaging in contract manufacturing, we could profitably utilize excess capacity in our Oak Hill manufacturing plant, while simultaneously absorbing overhead. The House Accounts Division manufactured a wide variety of popular consumer products, including Oxy® Lotion, Wart-Off® and Cortizone 10®.

As you have probably noticed, the business models of Durham, Moreba and the House Accounts Division were similar, so ultimately the latter two groups were moved under the Durham umbrella, with one management team handling all of this outside business. The leader of this management team was my longtime friend, Kevin Reeth, who possessed superlative sales skills, as well as an extremely creative marketing mind. Most of the Durham products to which I referred earlier were conceived by Kevin.

Durham engaged in a significant amount of private label manufacturing, selling store brands of popular topical products (products applied to the surface of the skin) to chain pharmacies such as CVS, Walgreens and Rite Aid. These store brands were basically copies of the brand (sort of like over-the-counter generics) and were usually placed right next to the brand on the pharmacy shelves in similar packaging. Walk into any chain drugstore today and you will see dozens of store brands. Right next to Zantac® Maximum Strength heartburn tablets, for example, you can find CVS Acid Reducer Tablets Maximum Strength, with both products containing 150 mg. of ranitidine. And in case a consumer misses the point, the CVS box suggests that one "Compare to the active ingredient in" the Zantac product.

Store brands are good for consumers, because they are sold for less money than the brand, but there was a bit of a controversy at Stiefel when Durham was asked to supply a private label copy of Stiefel's successful acne product, Benoxyl® Lotion. Does it make good business sense to knock off your own brand? After much internal debate, we decided to move forward, based upon the rationale that if CVS wanted a copy of Benoxyl, it would have one; and if Durham refused to supply CVS, there were many other companies that would happily do so. By giving Durham the green light, at least the company retained some of this business.

Ultimately, however, we exited the private label business entirely because the lack of customer loyalty made it too unpredictable. Durham might reliably supply a customer for several years, but if the buyers had the opportunity to save a penny by moving to a different supplier, they were quite likely to do so. Furthermore, we aspired to be a premium-price company, not a high-volume, low-margin company.

Not all of Stiefel's side ventures were owned by Stiefel. Parachem Corporation was an innovative company that sold metal soap-leaf dispensers filled with soap. These patented metal dispensers were placed in public or business washrooms, and when someone pressed down on a lever, one individual rectangular soap leaf was dispensed into the hand. Each leaf was as thin as paper and approximately three inches by four inches—intended to be the optimum size for one thorough hand-washing. Parachem wanted to offer a sanitary alternative to liquid or bar soap, and their product enjoyed considerable popularity for several years. They lacked, however, the infrastructure to manufacture the soap leaves themselves, so they entered into an arrangement whereby they placed their manufacturing equipment in our Oak Hill plant and purchased the soap leaves from us. The leaf-making machine was a very long, rectangular-shaped metal contraption that always fascinated me. After several years of a mutually profitable partnership, Stiefel and Parachem went their separate ways.

Dermatologics for Veterinary Medicine, or DVM, was a Miami-based company started by two brilliant entrepreneurs named Steve. Steve Smolev was an attorney who managed all of DVM's administrative, sales and marketing functions; Steve Mandy was a dermatologist who, in addition to his busy private practice, managed the company's research and development. DVM's 16-year relationship with Stiefel began in 1976, when Steve Mandy called Werner Stiefel to advise that one of our acne products, Panoxyl® Gel, worked not only on human skin, but animal skin as well.

Smolev and Mandy traveled to Oak Hill to meet with Werner, and a deal was negotiated whereby Stiefel would give a credit to DVM of $100,000, which DVM could utilize to purchase Stiefel's product development and manufacturing services. DVM was still in start-up mode, so this credit was very valuable to them; consequently, Stiefel received 10 percent of their stock in exchange. DVM was a pioneer in developing dermatology products for pets, and their business grew steadily. When their credit from Stiefel was exhausted, they switched to a different contract manufacturer, but SRI continued to handle their product development work. The two Steves built a great company, which they sold to Ivax in 1992 for $20 million. And Stiefel Laboratories was happy to walk away with $2 million, which represented more than 20 percent of our worldwide profit that year.

Alas, not all Stiefel's side ventures were as successful as our relationship with DVM. Shortly after the company divided into two divisions, Werner befriended a talented and prolific inventor named Thomas B. Noble. A very nice gentleman, Mr. Noble invented an interesting assortment of products that worked incredibly well. I recall being quite skeptical when I first saw a bottle of his Tearless Shampoo, so I intentionally left my eyes open while washing my hair with it. Unbelievably, this shampoo did not sting my eyes at all! And as newlyweds in 1972, my wife and I loved his Cold Water Wash, which enabled us to do the laundry successfully without using any expensive hot water. Another interesting innovation was his Beer Foam Hair Set and Conditioner. Regrettably, even though the Thomas B. Noble product line was excellent, Stiefel's expertise was confined to dermatology; thus, we were unable to market a laundry wash, a consumer shampoo, or any of Mr. Noble's other interesting inventions successfully.

Another joint venture was with Hermal, a company headquartered in Reinbek, Germany, which (like Stiefel) chose to focus on dermatology. Since there are a relatively small number of pharmaceutical companies that concentrate on the dermatology sector, it is fairly common for the senior executives of these companies to develop cordial relationships with one another. Werner Stiefel was friendly with Hermal's chairman, Dr. Kurt Herrmann, who felt that it was important for Hermal to build a successful subsidiary in the United States—the largest pharmaceutical market in the world.

Hermal's US operation was established in Elmsford, New York in 1976; but after three years, it became apparent that it was not cost-effective for the US company to import its products from Germany. (Does that sound familiar?) Consequently, Werner and Dr. Herrmann agreed to enter into a joint venture, with Stiefel Laboratories purchasing a one-third interest in Hermal's US subsidiary. Hermal moved its US headquarters to Stiefel's campus in Oak Hill, and for the next several years, Stiefel manufactured Hermal's dermatological products, provided regulatory and human resources services, and distributed promotional materials to dermatologists on Hermal's behalf. Stiefel billed Hermal for all of this work at fair market value. But the single most important service we provided to Hermal involved its patch test kit.

Allergic contact dermatitis is an itchy red skin condition caused by an allergic reaction to a substance (an allergen) that comes in contact with the skin. It is important for the patient to learn which allergen caused the reaction, so products containing this allergen can be avoided in the future. To solve this mystery, dermatologists will often engage in patch testing, whereby several small patches, each containing a well-known allergen, are affixed to the skin— typically the upper back. Patch testing is so important that for several years, the American Academy of Dermatology (AAD) distributed an official patch test kit to dermatologists who wanted to purchase it.

This kit was originally supplied to the AAD by Johnson & Johnson; but when they lost interest in this business, Hermal jumped at the opportunity. The only problem was that a great deal of regulatory work was required in order to bring the kit into compliance with the rules of the FDA's Bureau of Biologics (biologics are medical products derived from living sources). Stiefel Research Institute was retained to perform all of this work on Hermal's behalf, with Stiefel's Director of Regulatory Affairs, Bill Carr, personally spearheading this effort. One well-known patch test expert disagreed strenuously with Bill Carr's regulatory strategy and vocally outlined how he thought this work should be undertaken. Ultimately, however, the FDA approved all of the allergens in the patch test kit; so Bill's strategy was vindicated, and the officers of the AAD were extremely grateful.

As an aside, I attended my very first annual meeting of the AAD in 1982, and since I knew virtually no one, I was somewhat nervous. Just as I was clipping my registration badge to my suit jacket for the very first time, I was aggressively confronted by the aforementioned contact dermatitis expert, who angrily stuck his finger in my face while loudly warning me that "Your Bill Carr is out of control!" and he would personally see to it that Stiefel Laboratories would never again be allowed to exhibit at an AAD meeting. I was totally shocked! I had never before even met this gentleman, and I wondered how he even knew my name—until I realized that it was written on my registration badge. I tried to explain that Stiefel had merely been hired to help Hermal, and we were trying our very best, but he abruptly turned around and stormed away. I will never forget those few seconds. There I was, trying to develop cordial relationships with the physicians who prescribe our products ... and *that* was my first encounter.

Fortunately, the vast majority of dermatologists I have met since then have turned out to be extraordinarily personable; I am honored to count many of them as close personal friends. It is fascinating how relationships evolve as circumstances change— years later, after I became Stiefel's CEO (and after Stiefel had grown into a dermatology powerhouse) that enraged allergen expert not only began treating me very nicely, but even invited me to his home. (In case you are wondering, I politely declined—I can forgive, but I never forget!)

Stiefel and Hermal enjoyed an excellent relationship for several years, until both companies could foresee that conflicts of interest were likely to develop. To resolve these potential conflicts, Stiefel sold its one-third ownership interest back to Hermal, and Hermal moved its headquarters to nearby Delmar, New York. But for several more years, Stiefel continued to do contract manufacturing for Hermal, and the friendly relationship continued. Several years later, after Kurt Herrmann passed away, Hermal's corporate parent lost interest in dermatology, and the company was sold.

Another interesting company with which Stiefel partnered was Clientele, a South Florida cosmetics company founded in 1976 by a youthful entrepreneur named Patricia Riley. Pat had just graduated from the University of Florida, where she had studied chemistry, nutrition and food science. Early in her career, Pat developed a friendship with an innovative dermatologist named Victor Witten. Dr. Witten suggested several new product ideas to Pat, but Clientele did not yet have the infrastructure to formulate these products. Knowing of Stiefel's formulation expertise, Dr. Witten introduced Pat to Werner, who was very impressed with Dr. Witten's ideas, as well as Pat's enthusiasm and scientific vision.

Clientele was initially funded by Pat's parents, who were very nice and interesting people in their own right. Francis "Frank" Riley, as a member of the US Army Air Forces in World War II, had flown 168 missions over "the Hump"—the nickname given by Allied pilots to the Himalayan Mountains. Dreadful weather, extreme turbulence, and attacks by Japanese fighters were the norm on these flights; and he was awarded the Distinguished Flying Cross three times, as well as the Chinese Medal of Honor, for his bravery. After retiring from the military, Frank probably thought that he was finished with perilous flights; but in May 1961, Captain Frank Riley of National Airlines became the first American pilot to be hijacked to Cuba at gunpoint.

Stiefel Laboratories purchased 12 percent of Clientele for the sum of $60,000 and thus began a close relationship. Stiefel developed products and manufactured them for Clientele for many years until, eventually, the two companies parted as friends. When Clientele was threatened with a nasty lawsuit—one with which Werner did not want Stiefel to be associated—Werner transferred Stiefel's 12 percent ownership interest back to Clientele. Ironically, it turned out that the allegations against Clientele were completely false, and the threatened lawsuit never materialized. Clientele continues to operate profitably to this day. I asked Pat in March of 2016 what aspects of Clientele made her the proudest; she replied that Clientele was the first company to develop an oil-free moisturizer, the first to launch a topical product containing antioxidants, and the first to talk about the importance of free radicals.

Stiefel's most profitable side venture ever was its investment in Albany Molecular Research, Inc. ("AMRI"), a chemistry-based drug discovery, development and manufacturing company. Headquartered in Albany, New York (not far from Oak Hill), AMRI was founded in 1991 by Thomas D'Ambra and Chester Opalka, two chemists who had worked together at pharmaceutical giant Sterling Winthrop (maker of Bayer® Aspirin and Phillips'® Milk of Magnesia). Stiefel's Director of Product Development, Karl Popp, knew the two founders from his own time at Sterling; shortly after AMRI commenced doing business, Karl described how AMRI's expertise could benefit Stiefel and suggested we might want to consider investing in this new company.

Stiefel excelled at formulating dermatology products, but we lacked the ability to synthesize active ingredients—an undertaking AMRI could perform extremely well. We were so impressed with Albany Molecular's capabilities, we quickly became one of their customers; we also purchased 11.8 percent of the company's shares for approximately $3 million. AMRI became increasingly successful; in 1999 they decided to go public, with their shares trading on NASDAQ. By then, our AMRI stock was so valuable we decided to liquidate our holdings and utilize the proceeds to invest in our core dermatology business.

We owned so much stock we could not sell it all at once without negatively impacting the trading price, but we wanted to lock in the significant profit we had realized on paper. Consequently, we entered into several stock collar transactions with our banks, whereby we purchased AMRI put options while simultaneously selling call options. This strategy protected us against a significant decline in the stock price, but in exchange, we gave up some of the potential future upside—which did not concern us, as our profit was already so substantial. Having thus protected ourselves, we gradually sold our Albany Molecular shares over the next couple of years for nearly $50 million!

CHAPTER ELEVEN

AN EXTRAORDINARY LAWYER AND FRIEND

"To me, a lawyer is basically the person that knows the rules of the country. We're all throwing the dice, playing the game, moving our pieces around the board, but if there is a problem the lawyer is the only person who has read the inside of the top of the box."
— JERRY SEINFELD

For better or for worse, attorneys play an integral role in modern business. If you are not particularly interested in legal matters, you may wish to skip this chapter and go directly to Chapter 12. (And you should definitely skip the Epilogue!)

A lot of people distrust lawyers. There are probably more jokes about lawyers than about any other profession. Even one of Shakespeare's characters (Dick the butcher in *Henry VI, Part 2*) suggested, "The first thing we do, let's kill all the lawyers." As a lawyer myself, I concede that my viewpoint may be somewhat biased. In my lifetime, I have encountered a handful of lawyers who epitomize the word "sleazy," but I would characterize the overwhelming majority of attorneys as honorable, trustworthy and diligent. One of the most intelligent and skilled lawyers I have ever known is Richard M. Sandler, who co-founded the prestigious firm Lowenstein Sandler in 1961.

A graduate of Harvard University and Harvard Law School, Dick Sandler was a brilliant strategic thinker and an expert in corporate law and securities law throughout his career. He served as Chairman of the Securities Law Symposium, as well as the Corporate and Business Law Section of the New Jersey State Bar Association, and he helped build a firm possessing expertise in all major areas of the law. Early in his legal career, Dick developed a close friendship with Werner Stiefel; for more than three decades, Dick and his colleagues helped Stiefel Laboratories with virtually every significant corporate action. He also served as a mentor to me, although before I joined the company in 1982, his advice was always delivered via my father.

My earliest recollection of hearing Dick's name was in early 1966, when he handled our corporate restructuring to create two classes of common shares—Class A (which elected three directors) and Class B (which elected four). Years later, Dick told me he had modeled Stiefel's corporate structure after that of another client, Bergen Brunswig Corporation. Bergen Brunswig was a giant drug wholesaler which, like Stiefel, had been run by two brothers—Emil and Robert Martini; by coincidence, Bergen was one of Stiefel's most important customers for many years. As you may recall from an earlier chapter, it was this corporate structure, coupled with the 1966 agreement between Werner and Herb, that enabled Werner to elect a majority of the company's Board of Directors.

In 1975, I graduated from law school, and Dick offered some advice about my career options. Because I was valedictorian of my class, I had the opportunity to choose between two coveted judicial clerkships—positions whereby one works closely with one or more judges and thereby gains priceless insight into how the justice system works. One of these clerkships was in Albany, New York at the Appellate Division of the New York State Supreme Court, and the other entailed working in Manhattan for the Honorable Henry F. Werker, a federal judge in the Southern District of New York.

Dick advised my father that a clerkship with a federal judge was very prestigious, and if I were to choose this option, I would almost certainly receive job offers at the end of my clerkship from several of the top New York law firms. He strongly recommended I work with Judge Werker. At that time, however, my wife and I had no savings, and I was loaded with debt from my student loans; so we could not afford to live in New York City. Consequently, I accepted the job offer in Albany and never looked back. It was the only time I ever failed to follow Dick Sandler's advice.

Werner Stiefel always possessed an uncanny ability to foresee what might happen in the future; he also hated to pay a penny more in taxes than he was legally required to pay. Consequently, in 1973, even though the company's profits barely topped $300,000, Werner envisioned his Stiefel stock becoming extremely valuable someday, and he retained Sandler's firm to develop a comprehensive estate plan. The result of this plan was a Delaware holding company named D'Anconia Corporation (after the character Francisco D'Anconia in the novel *Atlas Shrugged,* one of Werner's favorite books).

Following Sandler's advice, Werner immediately transferred all his 24,680 Class B Stiefel shares into this new company, thereby making D'Anconia the largest shareholder in Stiefel Laboratories. D'Anconia Corporation was incorporated with three classes of stock—common, voting preferred and non-voting preferred. Each of the 500 common shares was granted one vote when deciding any corporate matter, so in total, the common shareholders could cast 500 votes. The 2400 non-voting preferred shares had no voting power at all; but the 100 voting preferred shares each had the power to cast 200 votes, for a total of 20,000! Consequently, whoever owned these so-called "super-voting" preferred shares could single-handedly outvote all of the common shareholders and control D'Anconia.

The value of the non-voting preferred shares was fixed in the corporate charter at $571 per share, for a total value of $1,370,400. Each voting preferred share had a fixed value of $100 per share, for a total value of $10,000. Thus, the total value of all the D'Anconia preferred stock was fixed at $1,380,400, which (by no coincidence) was exactly equal to the appraised value at that time of the Stiefel stock owned by D'Anconia. As a holding company, D'Anconia conducted no business of its own, so its value was always equal to the value of the Stiefel stock it owned. This Stiefel stock was worth $1,380,400, and the two classes of preferred stock were also worth a total of $1,380,400; thus, the common stock initially had a value of zero. Since the value of the preferred stock was fixed, or "frozen", any increase in the value of the underlying Stiefel stock would accrue to the sole benefit of the common stockholders.

When D'Anconia was formed, Werner owned all of its shares, but as part of Dick Sandler's master plan, Werner immediately gave all of the common stock equally to his five children; and since this stock was theoretically worthless, no gift tax needed to be paid. He also gave away as many non-voting preferred shares to family members as he could every year without exceeding the annual exclusion defined in the federal gift tax laws. He retained the voting preferred shares for himself because by voting these shares, he could elect a majority of Stiefel's Board of Directors. Within a few years, the end result was Werner managing to transfer (tax-free!) virtually all of the value of his Class B Stiefel stock to his family, without sacrificing any voting power at all.

Herb Stiefel established exactly the same type of holding company as part of his estate plan. Herb's company, called Bacamachli (created by using the first two letters of each of his five daughters' first names), was equally effective as a tax planning tool; the Stiefel brothers were thus able to save millions of dollars in estate taxes. Thanks very much, Dick Sandler! If any of you readers like the idea of forming your own so-called "freeze corporation" like

D'Anconia or Bacamachli, alas, it is not to be. In the eternal battle between the IRS and innovative estate planning attorneys, the IRS frequently changes the rules of the game to eliminate clever tax-avoidance (not tax-evasion, which is illegal) techniques such as freeze corporations. Fear not, however—estate planning experts are always devising creative new ways to save taxes for their clients.

In 1975, Dick Sandler's firm helped Stiefel Laboratories establish an Employee Stock Ownership Plan (ESOP) for its US-based employees. The requirements for creating and maintaining an ESOP had been set forth the previous year in the Employee Retirement Income Security Act of 1974 (ERISA), and Dick immediately advised Werner Stiefel about this new law and described how an ESOP would work at Stiefel. After considering the pros and cons of this type of plan (particularly the tax advantages), Werner decided to move forward. A trust was created for the employees, and every year the company would contribute either cash or Stiefel stock (or a combination) to this trust. All adult US employees with one year of service were automatically enrolled in the Plan, and the contributions to the trust were allocated to employee accounts based upon salary and seniority. After five years in the Plan, an ESOP account would become fully vested; when employees left the company for any reason (or became disabled), they were entitled to receive a distribution of the cash and stock in their accounts. Since Stiefel's stock was not publicly traded, the Plan's trustee would engage an independent appraiser every year to evaluate how much one share of Stiefel stock was worth; and employees were given the absolute right to "put" their shares back to the company at the most recent appraised price.

There were several positive features of this new ESOP. Firstly, employees did not have to pay any income tax when the annual contributions to the trust were made, nor did they owe tax as their accounts increased in value over the years. All taxes were deferred until the employee took a distribution upon leaving the company, and even then, this distribution could be rolled over, tax-free, into an IRA or other qualified retirement plan. Secondly, owning a piece of the company would (hopefully) cause US employees to feel happier and more motivated. And finally, Stiefel Laboratories received a tax deduction for its annual contributions to the Plan—even though most years the company donated stock. This was an important factor for Werner, as CEO, because the company could receive the benefit of the tax deduction without negatively impacting cash flow.

There was one very negative downside of the ESOP: Stiefel stockholders who weren't employees became very jealous of the put option given to employees leaving the company. The company had several dozen stockholders who were not Participants in the ESOP, and since Stiefel Laboratories was privately held, these shares were very illiquid. Many of these individuals continually wanted to sell some or all of their Stiefel stock; they deeply resented the fact that employees were given the right to force Stiefel to redeem their shares, whereas the non-employee shareholders possessed no such right.

A few of these disgruntled stockholders constantly pressured Stiefel either to go public or to purchase their shares; one such stockholder, Albert Musher, threatened to bring a lawsuit forcing the company to purchase his shares. In a panic, Werner called Dick Sandler, who immediately assured him that the company had no obligation to redeem anyone's shares. Dick telephoned Albert Musher's lawyer and calmly encouraged him to go ahead and "bring your suit." Werner was initially a bit disconcerted by Sandler's aggressive challenge, but his concern turned into elation and admiration when the threats of litigation were withdrawn.

A few months later, Musher called Werner and tried another tactic. He threatened to increase the number of Stiefel stockholders to over 500 by giving one share of stock to as many individuals as necessary. He informed Werner if the 500-shareholder threshold were exceeded, then the federal securities laws would force Stiefel to go public. Once again, Dick Sandler instantly reassured Werner and placed a phone call to Musher's attorney, warning him if Albert were to embark upon this gifting program, then the company would immediately engage in a ten for one reverse stock split—which would mean Musher would no longer own a sufficient number of shares to effect all of his threatened gifts. Another crisis was averted, thanks to the creative mind of Dick Sandler.

As the company's sales and profits increased, however, the underlying issue Albert Musher and others had legitimately identified became more and more problematic. There were always dozens of people wanting to sell, but virtually nobody willing to buy. My siblings and I faced the exact same problem as everyone else—although our stock had significant value on paper, it had no practical value whatsoever in our everyday lives. We could not use our stock to pay bills, buy groceries, or make a down payment on a house.

In fact, the D'Anconia stock we owned created a huge estate tax problem for us, because if we were to die, the IRS could potentially place a very high value on this stock—so high the resultant estate taxes could exceed the value of all of our other assets combined. If this scenario were to occur, then our life savings would be wiped out by taxes, and our children would receive nothing. We began to think of our D'Anconia stock certificates as worthless pieces of paper that did nothing for us except cause estate tax problems. Consequently, my wife Daneen and I changed our wills to provide that our children would inherit as much of this stock (if any) as possible without incurring federal estate tax, and that all the rest of the stock would be transferred to the American Cancer Society. I sent a copy of this provision to my four siblings, who wanted to add similar provisions to their wills to protect their own children.

Bequeathing virtually all of our stock to charity ameliorated our estate tax problems, because no tax was payable on charitable bequests. There was a huge problem associated with this strategy, however. It ensured that virtually none of the stock Werner had given to his children would ever be passed down to his grandchildren. Herbert Stiefel's children faced the same problem, as did every other major Stiefel shareholder. And while our smaller shareholders might not have been worried about estate taxes, they nevertheless hungered for the opportunity to monetize the value of their holdings. We needed to find a way to allow our stockholders to sell some shares, and as always, Dick Sandler devised a solution to our problem. His recommendation was that the company engage in a series of tender offers. A tender offer is a limited-time invitation by a corporation or third party extended to every shareholder of the corporation. During this time, shareholders can place some or all of their shares for sale at a specified price.

Dick suggested the first tender offer, in 1985, be made by the ESOP, because there were tax advantages to handling the transaction in that manner. The ESOP borrowed $1,000,000 from the company's bank and then offered all Stiefel shareholders the opportunity to tender whatever number of shares they desired. The price per share specified in this tender offer was the exact same price per share that had been determined by the independent appraiser who performed the stock valuation each year. If more than $1,000,000 worth of shares were tendered to the ESOP, then the number of shares to be purchased would be prorated.

The response to this tender offer was overwhelmingly positive, with the tenders received by the Plan dramatically exceeding the million dollars available. The only negative was many stockholders were dissatisfied with the number of shares they were permitted to sell; several voiced the suggestion there be another tender offer immediately. In 1990, as soon as Stiefel felt that its cash position was adequate, a second tender offer was indeed made, this time by Stiefel Laboratories; and an additional million dollars was budgeted. Once again, the number of shares tendered for sale exceeded the money set aside to redeem shares; so another proration was necessary. There were still a few complaints, but the pressure on the company was reduced—at least temporarily.

I joined Stiefel Laboratories as General Counsel in 1982, and as Werner did not particularly enjoy getting pressured by shareholders demanding to sell, he placed me in charge of shareholder relations. I engaged Lowenstein Sandler to ensure I handled this responsibility as fairly as possible, and Dick taught me a great deal about securities law. When we decided to move forward with the first tender offer, Dick prepared a thick package containing detailed information about Stiefel, its business operations, its future prospects, and what could go wrong. A copy of the most recent stock appraisal prepared for the ESOP was also included; this package of information was mailed to every stockholder in the company.

I asked Dick why a private company needed to send such detailed information; Dick replied it might not be absolutely required, but it was better practice for us to comply with the tender offer rules that applied to publicly-traded companies. I then asked Dick if we needed to provide this type of information to Participants in the ESOP who were selling their shares back to Stiefel, and Dick was very emphatic with his response—absolutely not. He pointed out there was a huge difference between a tender offer, where the company was actively soliciting people to sell their shares, versus an ESOP Participant exercising a put option, where the company was legally required to purchase these shares—whether it wanted to or not. Dick stated that not only was Stiefel not required to furnish detailed company information to retiring employees, but his advice was that Stiefel should never provide any confidential information at all to employees in the ESOP.

Dick noted that every single year, there were numerous confidential developments within the company that a retiring employee might consider material; we could not disclose just one of these developments without disclosing them all. It would be very difficult, as well as time-consuming, to pinpoint every single piece of information someone might later argue should have been revealed. Disclosing just one fact without disclosing everything would not only be unfair to the employees, but also legally hazardous to Stiefel. Learning one fact in a vacuum, with no context, can be very misleading. And because Stiefel was a private company, Dick informed me we had no duty to disclose anything.

Even after the two tender offers, stockholders were constantly contacting the company with offers to sell shares, so I solicited Dick Sandler's advice as to whether Stiefel could accept one of these offers without giving every other stockholder the same opportunity to sell. His advice was very interesting. All shareholders needed to be treated equally, so the company could not offer to purchase shares from one stockholder without offering the same deal to all; in that event, the tender offer rules would need to be observed. But there was an important distinction between making an offer and responding to an offer. If a stockholder contacted the company and made an offer to sell at a specific price, the company could legally accept that offer without needing to reach out to anyone else.

Dick pointed out there was no market for Stiefel shares, so it was very beneficial to the person wanting to sell to be afforded the opportunity to do so, but other shareholders might complain that they received no corresponding benefit. He proceeded to observe that if someone sold a Stiefel share at the appraised price, there was no benefit to the other shareholders—their percentage ownership of the company would increase slightly, but the value of the company would be correspondingly reduced by virtue of the company having less cash. On the other hand, if someone were to sell at a price below the appraised value, that would be financially beneficial to all the other stockholders. In that event, everyone would win. People selling shares at a discount would be happy because Stiefel had accepted their offer to sell, thereby giving them the liquidity they desired. Likewise, the non-selling stockholders would be happy because the value of their investment would have increased as a result of this stock redemption.

Consequently, Sandler's ultimate advice was Stiefel could, and should, accept offers to sell, but only if these offers were at a discount to the annual appraised price. Stiefel Laboratories followed Dick's advice and started a practice, after the 1990 tender offer, of periodically accepting offers to sell at a discount if sufficient cash was available. If a small block of shares was offered, the company would typically expect a discount of 10 percent or sometimes slightly more, but for larger blocks (where the negative impact on cash flow was more dramatic), the company would expect significantly higher discounts. The only ones who were thereafter able to sell at the full appraised price were the Participants in the ESOP.

Serving as Stiefel's liaison with its stockholders sometimes placed me in an awkward position, in which case I would always seek Dick Sandler's advice. On one such occasion, Herb Stiefel contacted me and asked if he could sell a significant number of shares every year, always at the most recent appraised price. I asked Dick if this was permissible, and he answered my question by asking if the company would be willing to allow every shareholder to do this. We both knew the company could not possibly give such a guarantee to every shareholder, because there was no way of knowing in advance whether or not the cash would be available to effect the purchase. Dick advised the company always needed to treat every stockholder equally; we could not do something for one shareholder unless we would be willing to do the same thing for all shareholders. He added we needed to be particularly careful not to afford special advantages to shareholders who happened to be family members or other corporate insiders. I shared Dick's comments with Herb Stiefel, who immediately withdrew his request and agreed with the logic of Sandler's advice. Like everyone else in the company, Herb had enormous respect for Dick Sandler.

Any business that interacts with outside customers is likely to disappoint a customer occasionally, and sometimes this disappointment can lead to the threat of litigation. Stiefel Laboratories owned several subsidiaries (as described in Chapter 10) that dealt with outside customers, and if such a customer were ever to commence a lawsuit, I wanted to ensure Stiefel's financial exposure would not be unlimited. We had no problem whatsoever with cheerfully offering a full refund to anyone who was unhappy with the work we had performed, but we did have a problem with placing the financial viability of the entire company at risk.

As always, Richard Sandler provided the solution to our dilemma. He drafted a clear and concise paragraph which very clearly limited our liability to a fair and reasonable amount and which expressly prohibited the customer from recovering punitive or consequential damages. Everyone within Stiefel management liked this paragraph so much that we immediately began including it on every quotation one of our subsidiaries sent to a prospective customer; we also included it in every contract with an outside customer. This paragraph was affectionately referred to as the "Sandler language."

I have interacted with many wonderful attorneys through the years, and I am grateful to all of them for the excellent work they performed on behalf of Stiefel Laboratories. But no other attorney ever had a more profound and positive influence on our company and our family than Richard M. Sandler.

CHAPTER TWELVE

WERNER

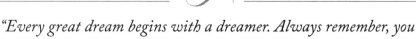

"Every great dream begins with a dreamer. Always remember, you have within you the strength, the patience, and the passion to reach for the stars to change the world."

– HARRIET TUBMAN

How can I best describe my father, Werner K. Stiefel, to you? He was a visionary, a dreamer and an intellectual. He was enthusiastic, entrepreneurial and driven. Having grown up during the Great Depression, he was very fiscally conservative. My Uncle Herb declared to me frequently, "Without your dad, there would be no company." To Werner, working at Stiefel Laboratories was not just a job—it was his passion, his hobby and even his identity. While many individuals are a bit depressed about returning to work after the weekend, my father frequently wore a tie stating, "I Love Mondays." To relax after a long day at the office, he would play the piano or read the latest issue of *Scientific American*.

During the Cold War, he recognized that Russia could prevail, in which case the Russian language might become the most commonly-used language in business—just to be prepared for this eventuality, my dad learned Russian! He loved to swim, and he was an avid chess player. While at Yale, a professor assigned everyone in the class the task of writing an aphorism using iambic pentameter. I have always loved what my father wrote: "The hardest part of any job is done,/ When once the start is o'er and you've begun." Even towards the end of his life, weakened by cancer, he would respond to inquiries about how he felt with a hearty "Great!" or "Couldn't be better!" He was always positive, upbeat and eternally confident that Stiefel would grow and prosper.

My dad and my mom, Catherine, had seven children together— five boys followed by two girls. My oldest brother, John (nicknamed "Jay"), an actuary by training, enjoyed a long and successful career as a senior executive at Aetna. An excellent trumpet player in his youth, he is now regarded as one of the best bridge players in the world, having earned the highest possible ranking of Grand Life Master and having won several international bridge tournaments. Jay served on the Stiefel Board of Directors for many years.

The next son born after Jay was Edward, who unfortunately died after living only two days. When another son followed, my parents also named him Edward to honor the infant they had lost. My brother Edward (nicknamed "Ned") was an extremely talented drummer, and his amazing performance in winning our county talent show inspired many youngsters in the area to take up the drums. He and I played in a dance band together for several years, and Ned always made even the most difficult drum solos seem easy. After completing law school, he became a partner in the Catskill, New York law firm of Bagley, Chadderdon, Pulver & Stiefel. Ned also served faithfully on the company's Board of Directors for many years.

I was the next child born to Werner and Catherine, followed by my younger brother Richard. Richard and I shared a bedroom growing up, so we were always very close. He was my best man when Daneen and I married in 1972. He had a wickedly funny sense of humor, and he was an amazing musician. I had the pleasure of substituting a few times in his dance band, and he was the best drummer I've ever heard in my entire life. He also became an accomplished guitar player, so after high school, he matriculated at Syracuse University as a music major. Tragically, the Hodgkin's lymphoma that he had successfully battled in his early youth recurred aggressively, and he died at the age of 18. I think about him often and will never stop missing him. Daneen and I named our firstborn son in his honor.

After five consecutive boys, my parents were thrilled when their first daughter arrived. Joan excelled at both singing and dancing, and like my father, she possessed a strong aptitude for science. After earning an undergraduate degree in biochemistry and a master's in microbiology, she went to law school and became a patent attorney. Through the years, she served Stiefel Laboratories in several different capacities, most notably as the founder and President of Webderm, our online sales platform, and as a member of our corporate Board of Directors.

Ten years after Joan was born, along came Stephanie, my youngest sibling. Steffi was a talented dancer, but she particularly excelled at singing. Encouraged by her voice teacher to enter the Miss New Haven pageant, she not only entered, but won. Next was the Miss Connecticut pageant, and I remember feeling awestruck listening to Steffi perform "Musetta's Waltz Song" from Puccini's *La Bohème*. She not only won the pageant and was crowned Miss Connecticut, but she swept the talent, swimsuit and congeniality awards. More than just another pretty face or talented singer, she also possesses a brilliant mind. She became an attorney, specializing in insurance defense work; and she served for many years on Stiefel's Board of Directors.

In 1974, after 32 years of marriage, my mom and dad divorced; shortly thereafter, my father married Marie Caruso, the widow of his best friend from college. Marie served on Stiefel's Board of Directors for several years. She and my dad were married for 31 years, until his death in June 2006. Marie and Werner had one child together, whom they named Lili in honor of Werner's mother. Lili earned both her bachelor's degree and her master's degree in religion at Yale.

As noted previously, Werner and Herb essentially separated Stiefel Laboratories into two independent companies in 1966. After this separation, both the US Division and the International Division began to grow steadily. During Werner's 35 years as the company's CEO, sales of the US Division grew from $1.4 million in 1966 to $72.6 million in 2001—an increase of more than 5000 percent. In fact, in 32 out of Werner's 35 years in office, yearly sales increased from the previous year. These annual increases were not the result of any single product or technology, but were the consequence of consistent effort every single year to provide safe and effective products for dermatologists and their patients.

During this same period, the sales performance of the International Division was even more remarkable. In 1966, International sales were just $70,000—less than 5 percent of total company revenues. By 1979, however, non-US sales had surpassed domestic sales; International's percentage of the total grew steadily higher every year. Working together, yet independently, the two brothers revitalized the prestige of the Stiefel brand in dermatology. It had taken 119 years for the company to reach the sales milestone of $1 million in a single year. It took only 10 additional years to surpass the $10 million mark (in 1976).

Achieving a tenfold sales increase is a formidable challenge, particularly as the numbers grow larger, but in 1993, the company's sales exceeded the $100 million mark for the first time. Total sales that year were $105.5 million, 80 percent of which originated overseas. Could the company multiply its sales by ten one more time? To do so would require us to attain a seemingly impossible goal—selling more than one billion dollars-worth of our products in a single year. No company specializing in dermatology had ever reached this milestone.

Immediately, Werner established a new corporate slogan: "The Big B by 21 C," which reflected his new dream of reaching the one-billion-dollar sales mark by the 21st century. A few people scoffed at this dream, but Werner politely opined that there was nothing wrong with setting a lofty goal; if the company were to attain that goal a few years after, rather than before, the turn of the century, he would nevertheless be extremely happy. He also was quick to remind everyone they should "never underestimate the power of compounding."

My dad detested hypocrisy. Not long after I joined the company in 1982, the CEO of a company with which we had worked for years terminated the relationship very abruptly; additionally, he refused to pay Stiefel the money Werner felt was clearly owed. Several acrimonious letters were exchanged, and, ultimately, my father accepted partial payment to avoid the expense of litigation. That December, lo and behold, Werner received a Christmas card from this individual—just as he had for the past several years. I will never forget my dad's response. He wrote a terse note expressing his amazement that someone who had just acted so shamefully and unprofessionally would nevertheless pretend nothing had happened by sending a holiday card. My dad ended his rebuke with this quote from "To A Louse", by Robert Burns: "O wad some Power the giftie gie us/ To see oursels as ithers see us!/ It wad frae mony a blunder free us,/ An' foolish notion." To this day, I remain a big fan of Robert Burns!

As Stiefel's Chief Executive Officer and Chairman of the Board, my father's duties extended far beyond merely running the US Division. Stiefel Laboratories, Inc. was a United States corporation, so Werner was tasked with ensuring that Stiefel's entire worldwide organization was operating in compliance with all federal and state statutes and regulations. Some US laws regulate how business can be conducted outside the United States—so even though Herb was in charge of foreign operations, adhering to these extraterritorial laws was a responsibility shared by the two brothers.

An unfortunate byproduct of being an American company was that complying with US laws would sometimes place Stiefel at a competitive disadvantage versus local companies. The Foreign Corrupt Practices Act of 1977 (FCPA), for example, prohibits US companies from bribing foreign officials in order to obtain or retain business. As a fundamental principle, Stiefel refused to offer bribes in order to win business anyway, but the FCPA has been interpreted very broadly; several pharmaceutical companies have been charged under the FCPA for conduct local competitors might consider to be normal business practice in their particular country. Taking a doctor who works for the government out to dinner, for instance, has been deemed a bribe; so has offering employment to a relative of a government official.

The list of pharma companies that have been charged under the FCPA reads like a veritable *Who's Who*, including such prestigious names as Novartis, Bristol-Myers Squibb, Pfizer, Eli Lilly, Johnson & Johnson, and Schering-Plough. Many years ago, Stiefel was encountering difficulty getting a product approved for sale in Italy, and I asked our General Manager in Milan what our local competitors would do in this situation. He replied very matter-of-factly that it was commonplace to bribe either the Vatican or the Mafia to influence the Italian government, but "the Mafia is much more reliable!" His face looked a bit wistful, giving me the strong impression he wished this option were available to him.

During Werner's tenure as CEO, several wealthy individuals chose to invest in the company. I have already told you about Morris Goodman, who was not yet wealthy when he purchased his Stiefel stock (but who subsequently made a fortune). I have also referred briefly to a gentleman named Albert Musher. Although Albert and my father continually locked horns about whether or not the company should go public, Albert was a brilliant businessman who helped Stiefel Laboratories not only by serving on our Board of Directors, but also by suggesting several interesting new product ideas.

The son of a Russian immigrant, Albert earned his first fortune through the Musher family's ownership of Pompeian Olive Oil, which grew to become the largest olive oil company in the world. In 1945, Albert and his younger brother, Sidney, founded another company, which they called Aveeno®. The name Aveeno is derived from the scientific name for the common oat, *Avena sativa*; colloidal oats or oatmeal extracts were the key ingredients in all Aveeno products. The company enjoyed noteworthy success; in 1963 it was acquired by Cooper Tinsley Laboratories, which subsequently became Cooper Laboratories. Now owned by Johnson & Johnson, the Aveeno product line continues to expand and remains a popular consumer choice for a variety of skin conditions.

Albert Musher and I became very friendly after I joined the company in 1982, and he frequently shared stories about his business career. A prolific inventor, Albert was issued more than 50 patents in the pharmaceutical and food industries. Ironically, although he was always lobbying my father to sell the company or go public, Albert often expressed regret about his own decision to sell Aveeno. Eventually, he donated much of his Stiefel stock to Columbia University, where he and his wife of 53 years endowed the Willma and Albert Musher Chair for the Betterment of Life through Science and Technology.

A warm and generous man, Albert never forgot the years when he and his family were virtually penniless. Although he happily donated millions of dollars (not only to Columbia, but to a number of Jewish charities), Albert lived his personal life very frugally. I will never forget the time I met him in a Manhattan restaurant for coffee. Albert asked the waiter to bring him just a cup of hot water. When this cup arrived at the table, Albert reached into his jacket pocket, unfolded a stained old napkin, and took out a used teabag—which he then immersed into the hot water for two or three minutes. When he removed this old teabag from the cup, I assumed that he would discard it; instead, he calmly rewrapped it in the napkin and placed it back into his pocket for future use! In many ways, Albert's frugality reminded me of my dad, who likewise never forgot his years of poverty. While most doctors and pharmaceutical people like to dine in nice restaurants when attending dermatology meetings, my father would invariably seek out the nearest McDonald's®.

Another stockholder group with which Werner forged a close alliance was the Huisking family. Over a period of several decades, Charles L. Huisking & Co., Inc. and its wholly-owned subsidiary, Glyco Chemicals, developed an excellent reputation as suppliers of drugs, essential oils, botanicals and other raw materials. During World War II, the company became the primary source of cod liver oil in the United States; Charles Huisking's successful efforts to keep the price affordable resulted in him being knighted by the King of Norway. Huisking became the sole American source of the anthelmintic drug santonin, which became vitally important for use by the US military in the Middle East and Asia.

In addition, the Huisking group became a major producer of camphor and menthol (two active ingredients that are still widely used in dermatology); and like the Stiefels, they branched out into soaps and other topical products. With similar interests as well as a cordial business relationship, it was natural that the Stiefels and the Huiskings became close.

Werner was very happy when the Huisking family purchased stock in Stiefel Laboratories and when Charles's son William joined our Board of Directors. I first met Bill Huisking in the mid-1970s; and I admired him not only as an excellent businessman and board member, but also as the consummate gentleman. Coincidentally, my son Brent and daughter-in-law met as undergraduates at Notre Dame; and the Huiskings have for decades been passionate supporters of this university. Charles Huisking served for 17 years on Notre Dame's Advisory Council for the Colleges of Science and Engineering, and the family has endowed multiple professorship chairs. All five of Charles Huisking's sons attended Notre Dame, as have numerous grandchildren. To learn more about this interesting family, check out Charles Huisking's book, *Herbs to Hormones: The Evolution of Drugs and Chemicals that Revolutionized Medicine.*

One more Stiefel stockholder who invested because he believed in Werner was Lloyd Newcombe—considered by many to be the wealthiest man in Greene County, New York. Lloyd was a serial entrepreneur, and his many successful investments included an oil company, a restaurant, a marina and a Cadillac dealership. He also served in the New York State Senate and owned the largest yacht I have ever seen in upstate New York, so you might assume that he was arrogant and snobbish. But you would be wrong—I always found him to be extremely warm, gracious and down-to-earth. He initially purchased Stiefel shares as a favor to my father, at a time when the company really needed to raise money. A true friend, he patiently held this illiquid asset for many years; and happily, when he eventually sold his shares, he was rewarded with a very healthy return on investment.

Unlike Lloyd Newcombe, Jerry Hirschberg became a Stiefel shareholder not because of any need by the company, but because of Werner's personal financial situation. A former Chief Financial Officer for pharmaceutical company Purdue Frederick, Jerry started his first company, Corporate Development Specialists, in 1964. Jerry and his son, my good friend Andy Hirschberg, are highly intelligent finance experts with a unique ability to bring parties together to consummate deals. Jerry is now retired, but if you want to acquire or divest a product or company—particularly in the pharmaceutical industry—call Andy. The Hirschbergs made it a point to get to know virtually every senior executive in the dermatology sector, which greatly contributed to their success in effecting dozens of major business transactions. They are universally respected, not just for their honesty and integrity, but because they can explain the financial implications of any contemplated deal. I always emphasized to my wife and children that if I were to die and they ever needed to sell some of my stock or explore the sale of Stiefel Laboratories, they should call Andy Hirschberg. Obviously, my father possessed a similar mindset, because when he wanted to sell some shares in 1974, he phoned his friend Jerry. I asked Jerry about this telephone call, and he told me that Werner had explained that he needed cash because he was getting divorced, and had then asked if Jerry was interested in purchasing a few Stiefel shares. Jerry inquired about the price per share, and an agreement was quickly reached.

A year or two later, however, Werner called Jerry again, advising that the company had not been performing as well as he had hoped, and expressing regret that he had overcharged Jerry. Werner offered to return some of the money that Jerry had paid, but Jerry replied that there was no need for that—if Werner felt guilty, why not sell Jerry a few additional shares at a lower price? Werner was happy to oblige. Not long thereafter, Gavin Herbert, the founder and CEO of Allergan, offered to purchase Jerry's Stiefel shares; but Jerry felt that he should give his friend the right of first refusal. Werner was shocked at Allergan's offer, believing it to be way too high; so he urged Jerry to take the money and run! Jerry did so, pocketing a healthy profit in the process. But the story does not quite end there. Gavin Herbert was always a very astute businessman with a clear vision for what he wanted. In 1980, for example, he purchased an oceanfront estate in San Clemente, California—the so-called Western White House— from Richard Nixon. His purchase of stock in Stiefel Laboratories was obviously not as glamorous, but it turned out that Gavin did not overpay after all. When Allergan ultimately sold its Stiefel shares, it earned a profit of approximately $27 million!

Enduring the pain of losing virtually everything during the Great

Depression left a lifelong impression on my dad. I cannot imagine what it felt like for Werner, Herb and my grandparents to lose their family home because they could not afford the mortgage payments they owed the bank. As a consequence of this traumatic childhood experience, however, my father absolutely hated owing money; this deep-seated aversion to being in debt precipitated Operation ZD— an extended effort for Stiefel's balance sheet to reflect "Zero Debt." Most business experts would probably agree it is healthy for a company to carry a reasonable amount of debt on its balance sheet, because utilizing this financial leverage can afford the shareholders a higher return on their investment.

Let's look at an example. Company A purchases an asset for $1,000,000, using its own cash, and sells it one year later for $1,500,000—a 50 percent return on its cash investment. Company B also purchases an asset for $1,000,000 and sells it one year later for $1,500,000; but Company B utilizes only $100,000 of its own cash and borrows the other $900,000 from a bank. After repaying the bank from the proceeds of the sale (for purposes of this simple example, we will ignore the interest owed to the bank), Company B is left with $600,000, which represents a 500 percent return on its cash investment. So, Company B is obviously much smarter than Company A, right? Perhaps, but let's examine the opposite scenario, whereby the asset decreases in value to $500,000 before its liquidation. In this instance, Company A suffers a loss of 50 percent, but Company B's loss is far worse. After remitting all of its cash proceeds to the bank, not only has Company B lost every penny of the cash it invested, but it still owes an additional $400,000 to the bank; and if it is unable to do pay this sum, the company may go out of business. Financial leverage magnifies both the risks and the rewards of doing business; Werner preferred to give up the potential rewards in exchange for the security of avoiding the risks. After several years of concerted effort, Operation ZD was successful, and Stiefel's debt was reduced to zero.

What was the secret to Werner's success in business? In my opinion, there were many. First and foremost, he was an extremely hard worker—oftentimes he was the first to arrive at work in the morning and the last to leave at night. As a child, I recall many an evening when my father would come home for dinner, only to return to work immediately thereafter—typically with a smiling comment, "Back to the salt mines!" Another key to his success was he was very organized. Every business discussion ended with a clear designation of one or more individuals who were given the "action assignment" of taking the next steps. He insisted every document bear a date, as well as the name of the person who authored it; he asked that every communication be as concise and to the point as possible. He strived to hire very intelligent individuals at Stiefel, often commenting, "There is no substitute for brains."

No discussion of my father would be complete without mentioning his objectivist philosophy. Profoundly influenced by the author Ayn Rand, my dad often referred to her novel, *Atlas Shrugged*, as his "Bible"; he frequently gifted copies of this book to friends, family members and business associates. In 1968, disillusioned with American politics, Werner decided the only logical course of action was to form (like the heroes in *Atlas Shrugged*) his own country—a country to be named Atlantis— where reason, freedom and individual rights would be paramount. Using the pseudonym Warren K. Stevens, my father outlined his vision for this utopia in a 32-page book, *The Story of Operation Atlantis*, which was published by the recently-created Atlantis Publishing Company.

At first blush, the notion of founding a new nation might seem like an unrealistic fantasy, but such a sentiment fails to take into account my dad's unique intellect and determination. While simultaneously running Stiefel Laboratories, Werner spent more than three decades in pursuit of this vision, during which time he wrote a constitution, opened a bank (ATCOPS, an acronym for Atlantis Commodity Purchasing Service), created a flag, minted currency (silver coins called "decas"), recruited citizens, and made several serious attempts to acquire the appropriate territory outside the United States.

Ultimately, Operation Atlantis was unsuccessful, primarily due to my dad's declining health, but he came much closer than anyone could have envisioned. The full story of this endeavor is beyond the scope of this book; but anyone interested in the details should search online for the June 19, 2006 article by Spencer Heath MacCallum entitled "Werner K. Stiefel's Pursuit of a Practicum of Freedom." Eleven days before this article was written, on June 8, my father passed away at the age of 85. To honor my dad's lifetime of dedication to the treatment of skin diseases, the company made a major contribution to the Dermatology Foundation to endow in perpetuity the "Werner K. Stiefel Lectureship," which is delivered annually by a distinguished speaker at the foundation's clinical symposium.

CHAPTER THIRTEEN

HERB

*"The visionary starts with a clean sheet of paper,
and re-imagines the world."*
— MALCOLM GLADWELL

I n some respects, my father and uncle were very much alike; in other respects, they were polar opposites. Both men passionately loved Stiefel Laboratories and worked tirelessly to make it larger and more profitable. They shared a strong intellectual curiosity, and both were voracious readers. But whereas Werner tended to be somewhat soft-spoken and reserved, rendering it difficult at times to perceive what he was thinking, Herb was the quintessential big personality. He was very extroverted, extremely blunt, and never hesitant about telling someone exactly what was on his mind. Endowed with a booming baritone voice, Herb could often be heard late at night singing "Ol' Man River," "Danny Boy," or some other old favorite in the hotel bar after a long day of meetings in some foreign country.

In matters of compensation, Werner was very frugal and conservative, while Herb frequently quoted the old adage, "If you pay peanuts, you get monkeys." Both men were likable visionaries with strong leadership skills, but their styles were uniquely their own. As someone who loved and admired both individuals, I would suggest that Werner was more tactful and dignified, while Herb was more open and charismatic. Although my father was six years older than my uncle, Herb passed away only a few months after Werner in 2006.

Herb and his first wife, Margaret (Aunt Peggy to me), had five daughters together—Barbara, Catherine, Mary, Christine and Linda—and all of them are highly intelligent and insightful. Fluent in German, both Barbara and Linda helped the company grow in Europe by serving stints as medical sales representatives in Germany. Mary Stiefel, an expert in accounting and finance, worked for several years as the Chief Financial Officer of Stiefel International. Chris Stiefel and her husband, Bob Caiola, both spent an extended period of time in Singapore (managing the company's operations in Asia) before ultimately returning to the States to assume senior marketing positions in the International Division. A bright and gregarious friend to all, Bob tragically passed away in 2005 after battling a serious kidney disorder for several years. He was only 51. My cousin Cathy was never employed by Stiefel, but she served on our Board of Directors from 2006 until the company was sold in 2009. A gifted CPA, Cathy spent nearly a decade at Deloitte & Touche before joining Science Applications International Corporation, a multi-billion dollar publicly traded company, where she rose to the position of Vice President in charge of corporate accounting for all acquisitions, divestitures and investments. When Cathy joined the Board in late-2006, Stiefel was in the process of finalizing its first major acquisition transaction, so it was very beneficial for the company to have Cathy's expertise in the boardroom.

I mentioned in Chapter 8 that Herb and his family moved to Mayaguez in 1962 to establish our operations in Puerto Rico and then moved to London in 1965 to form our UK subsidiary. By late-1966, however, Herb was back in the United States, because the company could not afford the significant investment that would be required to open any additional overseas subsidiaries. We observed back in Chapter 2 that the cost of contracting with an agent in any given country is much less than the cost of opening a subsidiary. Consequently, following the same logic employed by Anton and Ferdinand Stiefel nearly a century before, Herb embarked upon a program of negotiating deals whereby agents in other countries would add Stiefel's dermatological product line to the product lines of the other pharmaceutical companies they already represented. The anticipated profits from these distributorship arrangements were relatively modest, but at least Stiefel Laboratories would be represented in these foreign markets; and the value of the Stiefel brand would be enhanced.

Furthermore, this was a way to introduce our products to dermatologists in new countries, thereby reducing the risk of failure if we eventually determined to open our own subsidiaries in these countries. Over the next five years, Herb traveled extensively around the world, interviewing prospective agents and choosing the ones that he felt would work the hardest for a tiny company like Stiefel. Herb started in Latin America, where he visited Venezuela and then five Central American countries within a span of eight days. The trip to Venezuela was successful and eventually resulted in an agreement. But the first agency contract actually signed was in Nicaragua by a gentleman named Raul Estrada.

After negotiating mutually satisfactory terms in Raul's office, Herb sat down at Raul's typewriter and typed out a one-page contract on a piece of stationery from the hotel he had just left in Caracas! Both parties immediately signed it (nope, no lawyers were involved), and Herb received his first order on the spot. Raul Estrada represented the Stiefel product line very successfully for several years, until the Sandinista revolution broke out in 1978 and Raul found himself on the losing side.

Shortly after returning from Central America, Herb resumed his globe-trotting, visiting prospective distributors in Asia, Australia, Africa, Europe and Mexico. Everywhere he traveled, he learned how business was conducted in that particular part of the world (knowledge that served him well throughout his career), and he also met lots of interesting and unique individuals. One such individual served as our agent in Mexico for several years; one evening, Herb thought it would be nice to invite this gentleman and his wife out to dinner. Since the man had been born in America, Herb casually inquired what had prompted him to move to Mexico. The man replied that, while still living in the States, he had done extensive research and had painstakingly compiled a list of the ten wealthiest Mexican families that had daughters eligible for marriage. He then moved south of the border and immediately made an unsuccessful effort to marry the daughter who was number one on his list. Undaunted, he proceeded to court the number two daughter on the list—whereupon, pointing to his wife, he announced that "here she is." Assuming that this was simply a bad joke, Herb turned to the wife and asked her if this story was actually true; and she answered quietly with just one word, "yes." Talk about awkward moments, right? In any event, Herb continued to travel extensively, signing up distributors for our products everywhere he went. By 1972, he had successfully negotiated fifty agency deals around the world, vastly expanding our global reach.

Having a presence all across the globe provided many benefits beyond the obvious increase in sales and profits. For example, while serving as a medical sales representative in the UK, Herb became friendly with a brilliant Scottish dermatologist, Professor Mary H. Bunney. A pioneer in wart research, Dr. Bunney conducted several important clinical trials, authored numerous papers, and even wrote a textbook on the treatment of viral warts. One of her papers, published in 1976 in the prestigious *British Journal of Dermatology*, reported the results of eleven comparative wart treatment trials involving 1,802 patients.

Through our connection with Dr. Bunney, we had already learned about one of the safest and most effective wart treatments described in this article—a "paint" containing lactic acid and salicylic acid. Consequently, in 1975, Stiefel launched its product Duofilm®, which contained 16.7 percent of each of these active ingredients in flexible collodion. Duofilm was a major success for us in many countries, but particularly in the United States, where it soon became the number one prescription product for warts.

Nothing lasts forever, however, and in 1990, the FDA issued a rule entitled "Wart Remover Drug Products for Over-the-Counter Human Use; Final Monograph," which would have required us either to discontinue Duofilm or market it as an OTC product. Some companies are very skilled at marketing directly to the consumer, but Stiefel was not one of them; additionally, we had no experience with so-called Rx to OTC switches.

Therefore, after extensive financial analysis, we reluctantly determined that it would be in the best interests of our stockholders if we were to sell Duofilm to Schering-Plough, which had made us a generous offer. Schering-Plough already owned the Dr. Scholl's product line, so they had considerable experience with this type of product. Duofilm is still on the market today, positioned by Schering-Plough as the "#1 Family Doctor Recommended Brand."

In addition to gaining access to some of the world's best dermatologists, Herb's travels allowed him to learn plenty of business lessons from around the world. One such lesson Herb learned from his new business contacts was that ofttimes "know who" is just as important as "know-how." With this in mind, Herb instituted a policy in the International Division that the General Manager of every Stiefel subsidiary should always be a national of that particular country. It was very important to him that the person in charge be intimately familiar not only with local customs, traditions, laws and business practices, but also with the individuals who could best help the company grow and prosper.

In 1971, Herb decided to start a subsidiary in Brazil and moved to São Paulo for six months; one of his first moves was to retain Mario D'Almeida, a local accountant with plenty of both "know-how" and "know who." Mario was affiliated with one of the "Big 8" global accounting firms, Coopers & Lybrand—which is now part of PricewaterhouseCoopers, one of the "Big Four" remaining firms (as a college basketball fan, I prefer the term "Final Four").

Our initial office was in an old house needing significant renovations, and one of Herb's first priorities was to get a telephone. He went to the local telephone office to obtain the government-mandated license, but after dutifully waiting in a very long line, he was told to complete and submit some lengthy forms, after which he would have to wait about two years! Herb sought advice from Mario, who suggested that he simply buy a phone by responding to one of the many ads in the local newspaper. Herb expressed concern that this practice might be against the law, to which Mario responded, "Of course it is, but everyone does it anyway." Unable to conduct business without a phone, Herb took Mario's advice, answered an ad, and paid the outrageously high price of $4000 ... for a telephone! However, the phone was installed the next day, thereby illustrating why some businessmen facetiously suggest that "Brazil is the country of the future—and it always will be!"

While living in Brazil, Herb became close friends with Dr. Sebastião Sampaio, whom Herb affectionately called "Sam." Widely considered to be the father of Brazilian dermatology, Dr. Sampaio trained an entire generation of dermatologists; his sage advice and status as a thought leader (now more commonly referred to as a key opinion leader, or "KOL") significantly helped spur our growth in that market. Gregarious by nature and fluent in English, German and Spanish, Herb developed similar friendships with important dermatologists all over the world; and these individuals were always extremely generous with their counsel about product ideas, as well as their insights about trends in dermatology.

Meanwhile, back in Brazil, Stiefel's new subsidiary was almost ready to launch. Import restrictions and other local regulations rendered it cost prohibitive for us to manufacture products for this market at our plants in New York or Puerto Rico. Consequently, Herb had to negotiate a supply agreement with a local contract manufacturer, after which he hired a General Manager. Fortunately, none of our American dermatology competitors had any presence whatsoever in Brazil when we opened our subsidiary in 1972—a key reason why we were able to grow rapidly. Before long, we were the leading dermatology company in Brazil, with our sales there even exceeding our sales in the United States! This was an astonishing accomplishment, given the United States market has long been by far the leading market in the world for pharmaceutical products.

By the time Stiefel opened its subsidiary in Brazil, we had agents throughout Central America and South America, as well as in Mexico and several of the countries in the Caribbean islands. Herb could not personally supervise all the individuals responsible for these myriad countries, so he placed a small ad in the *New York Times*, seeking an "Area Manager" for this vast region. One of the applicants for this position was a young man named Otto Fuentes, who had just escaped the Castro regime in Cuba. Otto already had a job in New York City, and during the interview, he learned that the Stiefel job was based out of our plant in upstate New York (farm country) where virtually no one spoke his native language, Spanish. He learned further that Stiefel's entire Latin American "Area" (which included Spain and Portugal at that time for language reasons— eventually we decided these countries could more efficiently be managed by our European executives) enjoyed sales of only $50,000, and he would need to travel extensively away from his wife and young child.

As fate would have it, Herb and Otto bonded instantly; when Herb offered him the job, Otto readily accepted. The two men became lifelong close friends, and under Otto's outstanding leadership, our sales in Latin America grew more than a thousand-fold. In fact, this market rapidly became so important to us that Werner decided to move our corporate headquarters from Oak Hill, New York to Coral Gables, Florida in 1977. His reasons were threefold: firstly, to be near a major international airport; secondly, to be closer to the Latin American market; and finally, because Werner read an article in the *Harvard Business Review* that listed Coral Gables as one of the best three cities in the world to be the global headquarters for a multinational corporation. (We subsequently heard that the Coral Gables Chamber of Commerce may have played a role in getting their city on that list!)

Thinking about Otto compels me to digress a bit and mention Herb was an HR executive's worst nightmare. There was not a mean or prejudiced bone in Herb's body, and everyone who really knew him understood this fact. But sometimes he would, quite innocently, say things that made everyone around him cringe. When Otto retired from the company, for example, we held a farewell party for him at our Coral Gables, Florida, headquarters; Herb gave a brief speech praising Otto's many achievements over more than three decades of service. At the conclusion of this glowing tribute, Herb added, "Not bad for a wetback!" Otto burst out laughing, but there was stunned silence among the other attendees, most of whom were Hispanic. There were a handful of complaints to Human Resources, but when HR tried to explain to Herb why this remark was inappropriate, he was bewildered that anyone could take offense to a comment that he felt was so obviously a joke. Furthermore, he explained, "Otto is Cuban, and everyone knows that the term "wetback" refers to Mexicans!"

All of Herb's colleagues had a collection of "Herb stories," and one of my personal favorites took place in Coral Gables one Halloween, when we invited all employees to dress in costume for a luncheon in our main conference room. One lady in our office had recently undergone breast enhancement surgery; she sat down next to Herb dressed as a pirate girl wearing a very low-cut blouse. Herb glanced over to say hello and then did an immediate double take. Staring directly at the pirate girl's breasts, Herb commented, "Wow, they're nice! Are they real?" A complaint to HR ensued, and, once again, Herb was confounded as to why this lady had taken offense. "But her top was so low-cut, she obviously wanted everyone to look," he explained. "What's so wrong about paying her a compliment?"

Another time, Herb wrote a memo to our head of HR, Matt Pattullo, copying me. In this well-intentioned memo, he noted that there were quite a few seriously overweight employees in our Coral Gables office; he suggested the company offer a free program to help these people lose weight and lead more healthy lifestyles. It was a very kind idea, but Matt and I winced at the brutal title of the memo: "FATTIES." Herb genuinely loved people, and he frequently opined that "getting along with folks" is a critical component of being successful in business. But political correctness was a concept that simply eluded him.

Dermatology products do not travel well. Compared to most oral medications, topical formulations are relatively heavy, so shipping by air is not cost-effective. Shipping by sea in large freight containers, on the other hand, often subjects the products to temperature extremes, potentially causing emulsions (such as creams and lotions) to separate and become runny. Furthermore, shipping products halfway around the world is quite expensive, and some countries restrict imports or impose costly duties. In light of the foregoing, Herb decided to construct manufacturing plants in relatively close proximity to every country in which we conducted business.

In 1975, Herb negotiated a deal with the Irish Development Board—if we would build a manufacturing facility in the northwestern town of Sligo, the Irish government would contribute one million dollars towards the cost of construction.

Our worldwide sales that year were only $8.7 million, so this construction grant was enormous for Stiefel. But more importantly, the company would not be taxed on the Sligo plant's profits for a period of fifteen years! In those days, the Republic of Ireland was aggressively trying to create local jobs by attracting the pharmaceutical industry to the Emerald Isle; they were willing to offer key incentives in order to do so. Their strategy was extremely successful; today, approximately 120 overseas pharma companies have plants in Ireland, including nine of the ten largest pharmaceutical companies in the world. (Might there be an economics lesson to be learned here, folks?)

Incidentally, once Stiefel's facility in Sligo was completed, we hosted a grand opening party, with many dermatologists, politicians and local dignitaries present; this occasion provided an opportune circumstance for Herb once again to display his unique and uninhibited sense of humor. Standing at the podium to deliver the keynote address, Herb spent the first thirty seconds swaying, slurring his words, and generally doing his best to act like he was in a drunken stupor. It was a very convincing performance, prompting one dermatologist to whisper to Gabriel McGlynn, "Is he fond of the booze?"

Before Gabriel could answer, Herb straightened up and delivered a clear and rousing speech, drawing an appreciative round of applause. Despite this unusual dedication ceremony, our manufacturing plant in Ireland proved to be so beneficial to Stiefel that the International Division subsequently built manufacturing facilities in Brazil, Singapore (also a tax haven), Mexico and Pakistan in accordance with Herb's philosophy (photos of a few of our facilities are in the center of this book).

Herb was fond of saying that starting a company from scratch and building it to $1,000,000 in annual sales requires a unique set of skills, but growing the company from $1,000,000 to $10,000,000 (and beyond) requires entirely different capabilities. In a start-up situation, an entrepreneur can be personally involved with every action and decision; whereas in a larger company, the leader must learn how to delegate and how to recruit, motivate and retain top talent. Herb opined it was a rare individual who possessed all of these skills—one who could successfully get a start-up business off the ground and then adapt as the business continued to grow. One such exceptional person is the aforementioned Gabriel McGlynn, my friend and former colleague.

Gabriel started his career with Stiefel in 1976 as our only salesman in Ireland. When we subsequently started a marketing subsidiary in Dublin (not to be confused with our manufacturing plant in Sligo), Gabriel was tapped to be the General Manager. Continuing to excel in his new position, he was then asked to supervise our activities in more and more countries, until eventually he assumed responsibility for all of Stiefel's operations in Europe, Africa, Asia and Australia! He was so instrumental to our success that, in 2003, Herb invited him to join our corporate Board of Directors. (As noted previously in this book, Stiefel's Class A and Class B stock structure enabled Herb to elect three of our directors and me to elect the other four.)

My Uncle Herb was a very complex person. Notwithstanding his big personality, he was very cerebral and a voracious reader—accumulating a huge library of books and reading the *Wall Street Journal* and the *Financial Times* every day, and the *Economist* every week. He was also an excellent singer, touring New England with the Yankee Male Chorus every summer, and shocking a British Gilbert & Sullivan troupe by joining them onstage and singing a perfect rendition of "When I Was A Lad." Like many visionaries, including his brother Werner, Herb initiated several programs designed to ensure the company's goals were achieved.

The first of these initiatives he christened the "Tablet of Stone"—a name that clearly conveyed his message that the tenets set forth therein were not particularly flexible! Originally intended to impress upon his managers the negative impact of excess inventory and accounts receivable on a company's cash flow, this detailed financial model resulted in two firm business policies for the International Division: firstly, no product would be marketed if its cost of goods was more than 30 percent of its selling price; and secondly, the budget for sales and marketing would never exceed 25 percent of forecasted total sales in any given year. (Werner liked these policies so much he adopted them for the US Division as well, albeit with a fair amount more flexibility.)

Another one of Herb's major initiatives he named the "Tier Program," which established guidelines for launching subsidiaries in new countries. Essentially, if our forecasted first-year sales in a particular country exceeded $500,000, then we would commence operations in that country with a full management team. In countries with lower forecasts, if we opted to start a subsidiary at all, it would be with minimal personnel—often just a General Manager. With such a modest investment, the negative financial impact would be tolerable if we later decided to revert back to an agency arrangement in that country. Thanks to Herb's "Tablet of Stone" and "Tier Program," the International Division grew rapidly and in a very disciplined manner.

In Chapter 6, I mentioned that Morris Goodman's company, Winley-Morris, became Stiefel's agent in Canada in 1953, and the two companies enjoyed an excellent relationship. In 1971, however, Winley-Morris was acquired by ICN, a large multinational company founded by a charismatic entrepreneur named Milan Panic (who, as an aside, later became Prime Minister of Yugoslavia). Werner and Herb had felt very comfortable being represented in Canada by a Canadian company; but they were concerned that Stiefel's small dermatology products would be a low priority for ICN. They expressed this concern to Morris Goodman and tried to convince him to leave ICN and join Stiefel, but Morris was not interested in this offer.

Consequently, in 1976, when the agency agreement with ICN expired, Herb approached Morris's right-hand man, Richard "Dick" MacKay, and offered him the presidency of what would be a new subsidiary, Stiefel Canada. Dick was a rising star at ICN, so to induce him to make such a risky career change, Herb offered him 24 percent of the stock of this new Canadian company. At first blush, this might sound like an overly generous offer, but remember that, as a start-up company, Stiefel Canada had zero sales and zero assets; so this large block of stock initially had no value whatsoever. Dick, however, felt confident he could build a significant business—and happily for both Stiefel and Dick, he was right.

Stiefel Canada grew rapidly and became very profitable, always ranking as one of our top subsidiaries in the world. Furthermore, Dick's clever marketing campaigns were shared with the rest of the Stiefel world through what Herb dubbed our "cross fertilization" program—a program whereby the sales and marketing materials developed by each subsidiary were shared with all our other subsidiaries—and sales aids and journal ads created in Canada were often copied by smaller Stiefel units. The fact that Dick owned stock in Stiefel Canada rather than Stiefel Laboratories created some issues, however, because sometimes a proposed course of action that would be best for the company as a whole might have an adverse impact on Stiefel Canada—which would be unfair to Dick.

To resolve this problem, Dick entered into an agreement with the two Stiefel brothers whereby he would swap all of his Stiefel Canada stock in exchange for 5 percent of the stock in the parent company. This agreement was a win-win for everyone, with Dick eventually selling his Stiefel stock for approximately $190 million! During Dick's lengthy tenure at Stiefel Laboratories, he and I became good friends; I tried to emulate the professional manner in which he conducted business. Herb also greatly respected Dick; or as Herb used to phrase it, "I have a lot of time for him."

A chronic workaholic, Dick always maintained a hectic schedule and made a point of knowing every single dermatologist in Canada personally. He eventually suffered a heart attack, but despite my frequent urging that he curtail his grueling travel schedule and work fewer hours, he was soon working just as diligently as ever. He was such an important part of our senior management team that when Herb invited Gabriel McGlynn to join our corporate Board of Directors in 2003, he likewise invited Dick MacKay.

Finally, in 2007, Dick decided to step down from running the day-to-day operations of Stiefel Canada. To thank and honor my friend and colleague for his years of service, I appointed him to a newly-created position—Vice Chairman of the Board of Directors.

My Uncle Herb had greatly enjoyed living in the UK in the mid-1960s; so once he finished establishing our Brazilian subsidiary in 1972, he moved back to England and lived there happily until 1985. In fact, the only reason he left the UK at all was because his solicitor (lawyer) warned him if he stayed any longer, he would be subject to British inheritance taxes. His return to the United States lasted only a year before he moved once again—this time to Singapore for two years. He enjoyed Singapore as well, but found he could not work efficiently from there given the thirteen-hour time difference from company headquarters.

Finally, in 1988, Herb returned to the US for good, although he continued to travel tirelessly to increase sales, open new subsidiaries and upgrade others. In Offenbach-am-Main, Germany, where Stiefel had been founded so many years earlier, my cousin Claus (who had taken over his father Anton's successful construction business) erected a beautiful new three-story building to house all of our German operations (see photo). In other countries, our sites were considerably more modest. In Brussels, for example, we initially rented some first-floor space in an old building, only to learn subsequently that there was a brothel upstairs! By 1996, more than 80 percent of Stiefel's worldwide sales were from outside the United States. By the time

Herb retired at the end of our 2006 fiscal year, Stiefel's products were being sold in over 100 countries, more than 30 of which were wholly-owned subsidiaries; and Stiefel was #1 in dermatology in Brazil, Canada, Chile and the United Kingdom.

Under the able leadership of Herb's two hand-picked research chiefs (Jeff Corne and Dave Matkin), the company opened major research centers in Maidenhead, UK and just outside of São Paulo in Guarulhos, Brazil. Our Brazilian campus had the distinction of being the world's largest dermatology research center south of the equator. Parenthetically, we erected no sign at our Maidenhead campus indicating that it was part of Stiefel Laboratories, because any facility identified as a "laboratory" was likely to be a terrorist target of the very aggressive UK animal rights activists. I always found this to be ironic, given we never maintained an animal colony at any of our research facilities; essentially the only animal testing we conducted was to satisfy the legal requirements of the various health ministries around the world.

Stiefel Germany, built by Claus Stiefel

A quick story about my Uncle Herb and my friend Morris Goodman is in order. In 2005, with both gentlemen getting on a bit in years, Morris came to visit me at Stiefel's world headquarters in Coral Gables, Florida. While Morris and I were chatting in our main conference room, the door opened and Herb (having heard that Morris was visiting) walked in. After a hearty handshake and a brief exchange of pleasantries, Herb started to leave but paused in the doorway and asked if I would mind stopping by his office after Morris left. As soon as Herb had closed the door behind him, Morris turned to me with a shocked look on his face and said, "Oh my God, Herb looks terrible!" I replied something vague about all of us getting older, and shortly thereafter, Morris bade me farewell. Before returning to my office, I stopped to see Herb; exhibiting a look of serious concern, he immediately exclaimed, "My God, man, Morris looks terrible!"

I mentioned earlier in this book that Herb left Yale during his freshman year to join the family business. I never asked if it bothered him not to have an advanced degree, but I was nevertheless thrilled when the University of Bradford in the UK recognized his lifetime of achievement by bestowing upon him an honorary doctorate. As Herb's retirement date loomed near, I struggled to devise a fitting way for the company to recognize his six decades of leadership. The perfect opportunity presented itself quite serendipitously.

For several years, the International Society of Dermatology ("ISD") had been operating a dermatology regional training center in Moshi, Tanzania, and I knew several dermatologists who had spent time there as volunteers. There was a desperate need for dermatological care in this impoverished area of Africa; patients walked for miles and miles, often barefoot, to seek treatment for leprosy, albinism, skin cancers, cutaneous ulcers, skin manifestations of HIV, and other serious skin disorders.

Herbert A. Stiefel

Stiefel Laboratories had been supporting this center for years by donating products, and most of the ISD board members had become personal friends of mine. Consequently, when Canadian dermatologist David McLean, M.D. approached me about the ISD's desire to construct a dermatology wing at the medical center in Moshi, I immediately thought of Herb, and David and I quickly agreed upon a win-win scenario. Stiefel made a large grant to sponsor construction of this hospital wing, which the ISD was very pleased to name the "Herbert A. Stiefel Dermatology Ward." In my opinion, this was a fitting tribute to a man who dedicated his entire adult life to dermatology.

CHAPTER FOURTEEN

LEARNING THE HARD WAY

*"Success consists of going from failure to failure
without loss of enthusiasm."*
– WINSTON CHURCHILL

S tiefel Laboratories made so many mistakes throughout our history I sometimes marvel we somehow managed to survive. But each mistake rendered us a little bit wiser—and hopefully stronger—as we endeavored never to make the same mistake twice.

One of our more embarrassing blunders occurred in 1982, when we developed a very effective lotion for the treatment of pruritus. The product contained three active ingredients—camphor, menthol and phenol—each in a concentration of 0.5 percent. We wanted a trademark for this product that would suggest how cooling and soothing it would be when applied to inflamed, itchy skin; several ideas were considered and rejected before one of our marketing people decided to look up the word "itch" in an English-Spanish dictionary. The translation he found was "sarna," which sounded quite soothing to the group, and Sarna® Lotion was successfully launched.

A few months later, we received our first complaint. A

dermatologist had recommended our product to a Spanish-speaking patient, and the patient had taken offense. Much to our dismay, we learned that the variation of Spanish in our marketing person's dictionary was Castilian Spanish—used primarily in certain parts of Spain. In the Western Hemisphere, however, the Spanish translation of "sarna" is "scabies" or "mange," so Hispanic patients were understandably upset when their dermatologists recommended a product clearly intended for a mangy dog!

Naturally, our Latin American subsidiaries could not use the name "Sarna," so they utilized an alternate trademark, "Prurix®," which seemed to me to be a much better name for a pruritus product. We seriously considered adopting this name in the United States, but the costs of discontinuing and relaunching this very successful product were much higher than the revenues we thought we might be losing because of the trademark. We continued to receive periodic complaints for the next 27 years, but the total number was always manageable, and Sarna Lotion remains on pharmacy shelves to this day. We learned, however, to exercise extreme diligence when selecting a trademark—a lesson that many larger companies have also learned the hard way.

I mentioned a few chapters ago that part of Stiefel Research Institute's business model was to provide a variety of services to outside customers. One such customer (let's call it "Company X" to avoid embarrassing anyone) was a start-up company that engaged SRI to develop a cream formulation for a new dermatological product. Developing a topical formulation is analogous to creating a recipe—it often takes numerous attempts to achieve an excellent outcome—and SRI so informed Company X. Having limited funds, however, Company X declared that it would pay for three (and only three) tentative formulae and would then select whichever of these three it liked best. SRI reluctantly agreed and (a few weeks later) sent Company X some tubes containing the three alternatives.

SRI was not happy with any of these initial attempts and recommended the client allow them to engage in further product refinement. Company X, however, wanted to test its product in a clinical trial immediately; it selected one of the prototypes and asked SRI simultaneously to conduct stability testing and manufacture enough tubes of this product to start a trial. Stiefel Laboratories (SRI's parent company) would never have commenced a clinical study in human beings before being absolutely certain that the product in question was both physically and chemically stable, but SRI's customer insisted on moving forward urgently, notwithstanding SRI's warnings.

Living by the old adage that the customer is always right, SRI reluctantly manufactured the clinical supplies, and Customer X commenced the clinical trial. As the stability testing proceeded, however, it became clear the product was not physically stable (specifically, the oil and water phases of the emulsion began to separate, causing the cream to be watery in the tube). As a result, the clinical study had to be discontinued, and the owner of Company X was furious—threatening to sue Stiefel Laboratories (not SRI) for millions and millions of dollars, even though Stiefel Laboratories had not even been aware of any of these discussions.

In an effort to resolve this unfortunate situation, my father and I met with Company X's owner at a meeting of the American Academy of Dermatology; I will never forget that meeting. This person yelled at us, told us the incompetence of our product development people had caused a months-long delay of a blockbuster product, and accused us of intentionally sabotaging the development of his product. He completed his tirade by angrily proclaiming that, after he won his lawsuit, "I will own Stiefel Laboratories!"

My father sincerely apologized for what had happened and offered to refund every penny Company X had paid SRI, and he then rounded this figure up to $50,000—a very substantial sum for us at that time. This settlement offer was instantly and angrily rejected; oddly enough, however, the threatened lawsuit was not filed. For the next several years, every time I encountered this individual, he would hiss at me the suit was forthcoming and the statute of limitations had not yet expired. But he never did sue. To this day, I have no idea why he would leave $50,000 on the table and then walk away without taking it—but that is precisely what he did.

As an odd postscript to an odd tale, this same obnoxious individual wrote to me two decades later, hoping Stiefel (which by then had grown into a significant force in dermatology) would make an investment in his company. Suffice it to say that I thoroughly enjoyed not reading any of the accompanying materials before politely declining to invest!

Stiefel's entire unfortunate experience with Company X was very disconcerting, but the lessons I learned were priceless. Firstly, never burn bridges in life. As my son Brent likes to say, "What goes around comes around." Secondly, always be true to your own standards of excellence and never compromise them for anyone. Thirdly, the customer is not always right! Every business should bend over backwards to delight its customers, but ultimately a CEO must act in the best interests of the shareholders, not necessarily the customers. And finally, there are certain individuals with whom one should never, ever conduct business—no matter how attractive a potential deal might appear. Even a hundred-page contract cannot adequately protect you from someone who is inherently dishonest or untrustworthy.

Speaking of lengthy contracts and sleazy individuals, I am happy to report one potential mistake we did not make. Stiefel was negotiating a contract with a prospective customer and marked-up drafts were being sent back and forth. Finally, the two sides reached a meeting of the minds, and the other party sent us a final signature copy for us to sign and return. When we compared every page of this signature copy to the final draft, however, we were shocked to discover our would-be business partner had removed the seventh page of our agreement and substituted a completely different page containing terms that had never even been discussed! It was an egregious breach of ethics, as well as a gross deviation from time-honored business practice. Needless to say, Stiefel never conducted any business with that company.

We have all heard the old adage if something seems to be too good to be true, then it probably is. Our failure to abide by this warning caused Stiefel Laboratories to be dragged down the rabbit hole into the seedy world of drug diversion. If you have never heard of drug diversion, you are definitely not alone. When I joined Stiefel as General Counsel in 1982, none of our employees (including yours truly) was familiar with this term either. Basically, drug diversion is the practice of acquiring pharmaceutical products at a special price (or even free of charge) by misrepresenting their intended use and then reselling these products to the pharma company's own customers at a higher price.

One example might be a relief organization that asks a pharma company to donate drugs they claim will be used to help poor people in third world countries, but instead sells these donated drugs to McKesson, a giant wholesaler. This seriously harms the pharma company, because every unit McKesson buys from the drug diverter represents a lost sale. But, you might logically wonder, wasn't the company donating that unit anyway? The answer is yes, but what the company *thought* it was donating was the cost to manufacture that unit, whereas what it lost was the unit's selling price—which typically would be much, much higher. How Stiefel was victimized by diversion is a more complicated story.

In 1982, Stiefel was being operated as if we were two independent companies, and US export orders were booked by personnel in England. One day, a company (let's call this company "Shyster", just for fun) based in Long Island contacted our UK export office and placed a small order for products to be sold in Burma (now

Myanmar). We had never before dealt with Shyster, nor had we even heard of them, but since we did not have an agent in Burma, our export office readily accepted this order—viewing it as sort of a windfall. After all, how often is one afforded the opportunity to make a profit without expending any effort whatsoever? Shyster specified, however, we could not fulfill this order utilizing any of the packaging we used in other nearby Asian countries. Instead, the packaging must be the same as what we used for products marketed in the United States, supposedly because the Burmese people (according to Shyster) considered US products to be of the highest quality.

The prices Shyster offered to pay for these products represented a huge discount off Stiefel's published price list; but this was necessary, Shyster explained, because the Burmese people were very poor and could not afford to pay US prices. Finally, Shyster noted, we should not ship these products to an address in Burma, but rather to Shyster's warehouse in Long Island; Shyster would take care of the rest. Does any of this sound suspicious to you? The head of our UK export group was very experienced, and red flags may have arisen in his head, if not for the fact that the order was so small. Consequently, Shyster was approved as a new customer, and the order was shipped.

One month later, Shyster placed a second order, twice as large as the first; but since he was already an approved customer, this order was shipped with virtually no scrutiny whatsoever. A third order followed, which was twice as large as the second, and once again the order was shipped. No US executives were even aware this was happening, because the UK export office was part of the International Division. (As previously noted, there were a lot of disadvantages associated with running Stiefel as two separate companies.) Shyster's fourth order was twice as large as his third—eight times the size of the first order—and fortunately, this order was so large our shipping department was astute enough to raise a question with US management. This fourth order was immediately placed on hold pending an investigation, which I (as General Counsel) was asked to spearhead.

My first action was to write to Shyster, alert him his latest order was being reviewed, and request answers to several questions. I asked how he was able to import our products into Burma, given they were not registered there. He responded by saying his company did not personally import the products—they were transferred to a ship in Rangoon harbor and then smuggled into the country! I asked what promotional activity in Burma generated demand for our products, to which he replied advertising and distribution within Burma were handled by the smugglers. These two answers alone were sufficient to convince me we should immediately stop doing business with Shyster. The question remained, however, as to what had actually happened to the products we had sold him.

I turned to my friend Larry Pickering for advice. Larry was running dermatology operations at Johnson & Johnson at that time, and Larry introduced me to his corporate head of security. As a giant company, J&J took security extremely seriously, even to the point of sweeping their board room for hidden microphones on a daily basis. Their head of security was extremely helpful, and he warned me about how pervasive drug diversion had become in the United States. He then introduced me to Phil Robinson, a leading diversion expert who was doing work for the Manhattan District Attorney's office.

I retained Phil as a consultant, and after reviewing our customer list, he instantly flagged several customers as drug diverters. Phil taught me all about diversion, opining that (in many instances) the practice was not illegal, but it was almost always fraudulent. He informed me most of the major drug wholesalers purchased "grey market" products from diverters, euphemistically referring to this practice as "alternative source buying." He noted further that executives within some companies intentionally dealt with diverters—either to earn bonuses based on sales or (in the case of public companies) to hit their quarterly targets.

Phil also knew all about Shyster, warning me this company was a notorious drug diverter and part of what he called the "Israeli Mafia." There was absolutely no doubt in his mind the Stiefel products sold to Shyster had been diverted and sold to our customers in the United States. I asked if there was any possible way that we could prove this in court, and he asked me to give him a few days to ponder this question. True to his word, Phil called me later that week and confided the Manhattan District Attorney's Office and the US Attorney's Office for the Southern District of New York were conducting a joint criminal investigation of Shyster, and an undercover operative had infiltrated the Shyster organization.

Under cover of darkness, I met with this operative a few nights later at a secret location in downtown Manhattan, and we furtively passed envelopes to each other. My envelope contained $1000 in cash (big money for Stiefel back then); his envelope contained copies of Shyster shipping documents proving that Shyster had sold our products to a drug wholesaler in New Jersey! There were just two provisos: firstly, I would testify against Shyster if criminal charges were brought; secondly, I would subpoena these documents from Shyster rather than let anyone know that I already possessed them—otherwise, they emphasized, the undercover operative's life could be in danger. After accepting these conditions, I immediately commenced a civil lawsuit against Shyster under the RICO (Racketeer Influenced and Corrupt Organizations) Act, seeking treble damages—all of the profits Shyster had cost us multiplied times three.

Apparently, Shyster did not want any of his secrets revealed in court, because shortly after our suit was filed, he agreed to pay us the treble damages in full, if we would agree to waive interest and court costs. I readily agreed, and a couple of weeks later, we received our check. To my knowledge, no criminal charges were ever filed against Shyster, and I never heard another word from him or about him after our court settlement. From Stiefel's perspective, we were relieved our serious lapses in judgment had not cost us any money, but we recognized the significant opportunity cost associated with investing so much time to recoup our losses. On the positive side, we had learned some extremely valuable lessons; thenceforth, we were much more selective in choosing the customers with which we were willing to do business.

I have always felt it is extremely important for an organization to be able to perceive its strengths and weaknesses with a high level of accuracy. Every leader should consider the question, "What core expertise does this organization possess that should enable us to be successful—to outperform our competitors?" On three separate occasions, Stiefel Laboratories answered this basic question too broadly, and in each instance, the result was a substantial loss of both time and money.

In the early 1980s, Stiefel acquired two companies in Europe: a French cosmetics company called Maussion and a British men's toiletry company called Aegis. At that time, our International Division believed that our core expertise was the skin, so we should be successful marketing any products that were applied to the skin, hair or nails. We learned the hard way, however, that we knew very little about products utilized solely for grooming or beautifying the skin. Our sales and marketing people were experts at selling products for diseases of the skin, but novices when it came to color cosmetics and men's toiletries—which involved different promotional strategies, different channels of distribution, and a different competitive set. Some corporate executives might have expended promotional dollars on these product lines for years, hoping desperately to recoup our initial investment. My Uncle Herb was very pragmatic, however, and he recognized the money we had paid to acquire these companies was a sunk cost; so he quickly decided to cut our losses and exit these new markets. As Kenny Rogers sang in "The Gambler", "You've gotta know when to hold 'em; Know when to fold 'em;" and I believe that the applicability of this advice extends far beyond a mere poker hand. From that time onward, the International Division viewed our primary expertise more narrowly and determined to focus on products for skin disease rather than for the skin in general.

Unfortunately, the lesson learned by our International Division did not prevent the US Division from making a similar mistake. Werner Stiefel agreed with Herb that Stiefel should focus on products for skin disease—but not necessarily skin disease in humans. In Chapter 10, I described to you the story of our successful investment in DVM, a company focused on skincare products for small animals—particularly cats and dogs. Not long after DVM was acquired by Ivax in 1992, the idea arose within Stiefel's US Division that perhaps we could repeat DVM's success by starting a company that would develop and market products for the treatment of skin diseases in large animals, particularly horses.

When I first learned of this idea, I volunteered my opinion; the concept was worthy of consideration, but we should conduct some market research before entering a new market about which we knew very little. It turned out, however, Werner was extraordinarily enamored with this concept and had already made the decision to move forward immediately. The idea evolved into reality in 1994, when our new subsidiary Vetgenix® was incorporated. With considerable input from a West Palm Beach veterinarian who possessed vast expertise in the equine market, we succeeded in developing several excellent products. What Stiefel had not sufficiently considered, however, was that horses are enormous animals; and to treat a skin disease in a horse requires a very large dose of product.

One of our human products, for example, was a shampoo, but whereas a typical bottle size for Stiefel's product Polytar® Shampoo was 250 ml, we needed to market the Vetgenix equine shampoo in gallon jugs! Our high-speed packaging lines in our Oak Hill manufacturing plant were not designed for packages this large; making matters worse, the low initial demand for Vetgenix products meant that Oak Hill was asked to produce only a small number of units in each packaging run. The cost to set up and take down a packaging line is the same, whether you are manufacturing 1000 units or 100,000 units, so unfortunately, we were unable to manufacture the new equine products at competitive prices. In fact, even after demand for Vetgenix products began to grow, our cost of goods per unit continued to exceed our selling price.

There is an old expression stating if you initially are losing money on a product, you can "make it up on volume," and sometimes this can actually be true. But it was not true for Vetgenix; as the years passed and our sales gradually increased, our losses grew higher and higher. I will never forget sitting in a meeting about Vetgenix in 1997 with my father and Richard Fried, our Chief Financial Officer. Richard was a very astute CFO, and he was never afraid to broach sensitive subjects, but when he opined Stiefel should begin formulating an "exit strategy" for Vetgenix, Werner became uncharacteristically angry and chastised Richard for suggesting we "give up."

Consequently, the company continued to bleed money for four more years. Please understand that I do not relate this story to criticize my father. I loved and respected my dad, he was my mentor, and very few individuals could have built a company from scratch the way he did. On the contrary, the point of this anecdote is to acknowledge sacred cows can cloud the judgment of even the most logical and brilliant minds. We all have issues about which we feel passionately, and it is important that we recognize when personal passion or bias may be distorting our thinking. When I succeeded Werner as CEO in 2001, one of my first actions was to close Vetgenix.

All mistakes tend to render one "sadder but wiser," and Stiefel's

Vetgenix venture was no exception. We had lost a considerable amount of time and money, but we had learned two vitally important lessons. Firstly, Stiefel's core expertise was developing, manufacturing and marketing products for the treatment of skin disease in humans. And secondly, leaders should never fall so deeply in love with an idea they are unwilling to consider rational advice from colleagues who are being paid to render such advice. Sacred cows must be meticulously avoided.

CHAPTER FIFTEEN

FUN WITH THE GOVERNMENT

"If you put the federal government in charge of the Sahara Desert, in 5 years there'd be a shortage of sand."
— MILTON FRIEDMAN

For better or for worse, we live in an era of intensive governmental regulation. Stiefel Laboratories did business in more than 100 countries, and it was often very tricky to comply with the laws of all of them. We sold products throughout the Middle East, for instance, including in Israel and several Arab countries. Israel had no problem with our selling products in Arab nations, but sadly, the reverse was not true. Many Arab League nations had been boycotting Israel since 1948, and they frequently requested representations from companies assuring the products they were importing had not been manufactured in Israel.

Since Stiefel never operated a manufacturing plant in Israel, you might think that such a representation would present no problem for us, right? Wrong. It was a violation of US law for American companies or their foreign subsidiaries to cooperate in any way with the boycott of Israel; making such a representation of origin was considered to be a form of illegal cooperation. Stiefel was just a small company trying to sell skincare products to everyone who might want them, but we found ourselves in a situation whereby this became impossible. Ultimately, we decided to stop conducting business in several countries that insisted on these illegal boycott representations.

It is difficult enough to observe all national laws throughout the world, but to make matters even more complicated, many countries comprise a number of states or provinces with local laws of their own; we needed to observe all these rules as well. In order to comply with the laws of Quebec, for example, all the instructions and other labeling on our products were required to be in French, but since more Canadians speak English than French, the practical solution was to sell bilingual packages throughout the entire country.

As we grew, we learned business practices that were the norm in some countries were illegal in others, and the manner in which contracts were interpreted differed vastly from country to country. I mentioned earlier, for example, Stiefel had entered into agency agreements all over the world, but in some countries we could not walk away from these agents even after the agreement had expired. My Uncle Herb was always philosophical about some of these unpleasant surprises, stating that "if you tell me the rules, I can play any game." We sometimes learned these rules the hard way, but as Nietzsche once said, "That which does not kill us makes us stronger." As time passed, Stiefel grew not only stronger, but much more savvy. In some countries, you could meticulously obey all of the laws and finish the year with a nice profit, only to have the government deem your profit to be too high and "claw back" what it viewed as excessive.

In other countries, it was extremely difficult and expensive to terminate an employee—regardless of how valid the reason might be. When we launched our subsidiary in Argentina, we found a trademark pirate had recently registered most of our product names and even our corporate name! We tried unsuccessfully to win back these names in court, but the local court system sided with the pirate; and eventually we had to buy back our own trademarks—precisely what the pirate had wanted all along.

In some countries, we were prohibited from owning 100 percent of our own subsidiary, so we were forced to take on a local partner. In others, we were restricted from importing our products into the country, so we needed to manufacture locally. Prices were controlled by the government in a number of countries; more than once, the price designated for one of our products was so low we opted not to sell that product at all in that country. As noted earlier, Herb established a policy stating the General Manager in each of our overseas subsidiaries must be a citizen of that country, thereby insuring each country was led by someone familiar with all local laws and customs. Complying with the laws of more than 100 countries was definitely a challenge, but it was relatively easy compared to conducting business in the United States!

As a US company doing business in all 50 states, Stiefel was governed by a myriad of federal, state and local statutes. As the company's General Counsel for 15 years, I found many of the statutes themselves were straightforward and logical. My personal pet peeve, however, was that we were forced to interact with a significant number of federal and state administrative agencies. I have always felt administrative agencies possess far too much power—they typically promulgate regulations, interpret them and then enforce them; and if there is a hearing, it is usually before an administrative law judge who works for the agency! I have been involved in my fair share of these hearings, and it is very disconcerting when the attorney representing the agency works in the same office (and quite possibly has lunch every day) with the judge who is deciding the case. Since Stiefel was a pharmaceutical company, the agency with which we interacted most frequently was the Food and Drug Administration (FDA).

My first introduction to the FDA was early in my career, when the company filed a New Drug Application (NDA) for a topical product containing hydrocortisone and pramoxine. The product was formulated to treat inflamed, itchy skin; since hydrocortisone is an anti-inflammatory, while pramoxine is an anesthetic used for pain and itching, this combination seemed to us like it should be ideal. We conducted several clinical trials, and the results were outstanding—our product was statistically significantly superior to either active ingredient alone and to placebo. This would have been Stiefel's first ever NDA approval, representing a major step forward for our company; and the data we had generated were so strong that approval seemed like a slam dunk. Then the phone call came—not a letter, but a call from a high-ranking FDA official—informing us that this particular official had a personal bias against this combination of active ingredients, and that no such combination would ever be approved while he was at the agency.

We were shocked and very angry. We had met all the criteria for approval, so our product deserved to be approved, right? We talked to a law firm specializing in FDA matters, and we learned we had a fairly high probability of success if we were to sue the FDA. The critical question, however, was whether we really wanted to start a war with an agency holding virtually life-and-death power over our future. Our attorneys warned us many FDA staffers remain at the agency for years, and they tend to have very long memories. After anguishing over this issue for several days, we reluctantly resolved to accept the FDA's irrational decision and not commence a lawsuit. The pain of having been treated so unfairly gradually faded away as our scientists developed other products, but this anecdote does not have a happy ending. A few short years later, the FDA approved a competitor's product containing these exact two active ingredients!

Stiefel's second attempt to win approval of a New Drug Application fared somewhat better than the first, but we were once again confronted with the brutal reality that administrative agencies often make decisions that are arbitrary or political in nature. This time, our product was an acne gel containing isotretinoin as its active ingredient. Accutane®, a pill containing isotretinoin, was already on the market and was widely considered to be a miracle drug for patients with severe, cystic acne. Also on the market was J&J's highly successful acne gel Retin-A®, which contained tretinoin. Tretinoin and isotretinoin are isomers, having the same molecular formula but different chemical structures; so we expected our gel, which we named Isotrex®, to be at least as effective as Retin-A Gel.

As we hoped, our product worked very well indeed; the results of our clinical trials were published in the August 1987 issue of the prestigious *Journal of the American Academy of Dermatology,* which (because of its blue cover) we all called simply the "Blue Journal." Accutane had been invented by the Swiss pharmaceutical giant, Hoffmann-La Roche; when Roche learned that little Stiefel had developed a topical version of their blockbuster drug, their US subsidiary's CEO, Irwin Lerner, immediately hopped into a limousine and drove from his office in Nutley, New Jersey, to Oak Hill, New York, to meet with Werner. I was with my dad that day, and it was quite memorable, because most of us in Oak Hill had never seen a limo before!

Mr. Lerner was extremely professional, and he very nicely explained to my father and me that Roche would like to acquire Stiefel Laboratories. Werner replied by saying he was grateful and flattered, but he would prefer to keep Stiefel private and independent. Irwin then suggested Roche acquire just one product, Isotrex, and once again Werner declined. I knew that Stiefel could save millions of dollars and months (if not years) of time if Roche would give us permission to access all their Accutane toxicity data; so I suggested that perhaps our two companies should consider a joint venture. Werner and Irwin both liked this concept, and I (as General Counsel) was asked to negotiate with a top Roche attorney named Bernie Leon.

Bernie and I got along very well, and we successfully negotiated what he and I felt was a win-win deal for both companies. Stiefel was granted the right to access all Accutane data on a global basis; we had the exclusive right to market Isotrex everywhere in the world outside the US; in the States, we would co-develop and co-market Isotrex together with Roche, with all decisions to be made by committees comprised of people from both Roche and Stiefel. Despite the enormous disparity in the sizes of our companies, we worked extremely well together; and before long, the FDA sent us an "approvable letter" indicating our NDA would be approved as soon as the FDA successfully completed an inspection of our Oak Hill facility. We were overjoyed to receive this letter, but there was one piece of very bad news—the FDA had decided the Isotrex label must bear a black box showing that we had been assigned Pregnancy Category X, meaning that our product should never be used by pregnant women or women who might become pregnant.

Accutane had justifiably been assigned Category X, because it was well documented that this pill could cause birth defects. Retin-A, on the other hand, had been assigned the much more favorable Category C, which meant while risk to the fetus could not be ruled out, the potential benefits of the product may outweigh the potential risks. We submitted to the FDA test results demonstrating tretinoin and isotretinoin break down into similar substances on the skin, and our data showed no presence of these substances in the blood, even after application of twelve times the normal dose. All the Roche and Stiefel scientists agreed we had proven we deserved the same pregnancy category as Retin-A, so it seemed obvious the FDA's decision was totally political in nature.

In other words, given all the lawsuits and bad press associated with Accutane, the FDA would be subject to less criticism if it simply placed our topical gel in the same pregnancy category. The question we faced was what to do about FDA's position. Stiefel's and Roche's marketing people differed strongly on the question as to how much a Category X would hurt Isotrex sales. The Roche people felt a Category X black box would be devastating and would give Retin-A an insurmountable marketing advantage over us. The Stiefel people, on the other hand, felt dermatologists would understand why the FDA made its decision and would prescribe Isotrex just as readily as Retin-A. The Roche scientists were convinced they could generate more data that would convince the FDA to change its mind within two years; whereas we argued that since the decision was a political one, no amount of data, no matter how compelling, would ever make any difference.

The joint venture had reached an impasse, and there were only two ways to resolve it: either by pursuing legal options or by one company buying out the other's share of the joint venture. We had a very friendly relationship with Roche, so neither side wanted to engage in a legal battle. Instead, in 1992, we agreed to sell Roche all our rights to Isotrex in the United States for $15 million (a huge sum for us at that time), and we reluctantly walked away from what would have been our first ever NDA approval.

As a postscript to this story, the Roche scientists proceeded to generate some compelling data in support of their argument, but they never could persuade the FDA to change its mind. Isotrex was never approved in the US, and Roche eventually abandoned the project entirely. Every few years thereafter, I called Roche in an attempt to repurchase Isotrex, but they were never willing to sell. Outside the US, however, Stiefel successfully marketed Isotrex for many years; those sales, coupled with our $15 million, made this project a big win for us.

Shortly after Stiefel sold Isotrex to Roche, we started working on another topical acne product. More than a quarter of a century had passed since Stiefel had pioneered the use of benzoyl peroxide (BPO) in acne, but it was still very popular among dermatologists. And topical antibiotics—particularly erythromycin and clindamycin—

were also widely prescribed. We felt if we could combine BPO and clindamycin into one product, we would have a blockbuster. BPO is a powerful oxidizing agent, however, so it was a significant challenge to develop a formulation that would be both physically and chemically stable.

Our marketing people felt a gel would be optimal, and our product development people responded heroically by developing a stable and cosmetically elegant gel formulation containing 1 percent clindamycin and 5 percent BPO. To afford this gel adequate shelf life, we opted for a requirement that the product be kept refrigerated throughout its distribution cycle until it was actually dispensed by the pharmacist to the patient. This requirement increased our warehousing and shipping costs somewhat, but we felt that the enormous potential of this product justified these increased costs. We immediately decided to name this new product Clindoxyl® Gel, because the "oxyl" suffix enjoyed powerful name recognition globally.

Through the years, Stiefel had launched BenOxyl®, Sulfoxyl®, PanOxyl® and Brevoxyl®—all acne products containing BPO—so we felt dermatologists would recognize instantly that a product named "Clindoxyl" contained clindamycin plus BPO and was being sold by Stiefel Laboratories. We successfully registered this trademark with the US Patent and Trademark Office in 1994, and a different branch of the same office granted our patent application the following year. We conducted the required double blind clinical trials, and the results (published in the Blue Journal in October 1997) demonstrated our product was highly efficacious. Everything was moving forward without a hitch—it was almost too good to be true! Filled with hope and cautious optimism, we filed our third New Drug Application with the FDA in May of 1996. It is said that the "third time's a charm," right?

As fate would have it, Stiefel had purchased its clindamycin active ingredient from an Italian pharmaceutical company named

Biochimica Opos, a wholly-owned subsidiary of French pharma giant Roussel-Uclaf. Subsequent to our purchases, Biochimica Opos was accused of manufacturing some of its chemicals at plants unknown to the FDA and then falsifying records to hide where these chemicals were actually produced. Given these accusations, the FDA was understandably suspicious about any active ingredients produced by this company. Consequently, FDA inspectors visited our Oak Hill campus in February 1997 and conducted a comprehensive inspection that focused on the many lots of clindamycin that we had purchased from Biochimica Opos.

Fortunately, this inspection showed that all of these lots met all quality control specifications; so we breathed a huge sigh of relief and eagerly awaited our very first approval of a New Drug Application. But alas, it was not to be. On January 30, 1998, the FDA sent us a letter invoking their "Application Integrity Policy," meaning that our entire NDA lacked "integrity" because Biochimica Opos had broken some rules that were totally unrelated to Clindoxyl. Stunned, we struggled to comprehend the nightmare scenario whereby the FDA would not consider any of the data we had generated using Biochimica Opos material. After spending all that time and money, were we really back to square one?

Surely, we thought, there must be some way to salvage some of the work we had done. We already had a new source of clindamycin, so one of our many ideas was to conduct a so-called "bridging study" to demonstrate the Clindoxyl containing the new clindamycin was exactly the same as the Clindoxyl containing the Biochimica Opos material. We were eager to move forward as quickly as possible, so we requested a meeting with FDA to discuss our ideas and agree upon a path that might lead to approval. Much to our dismay, the FDA refused to meet with us! We were afraid to expend more time and money generating data without any prior input from FDA, so we pleaded with them to meet, but they steadfastly refused. My father lamented that each day of delay was costing Stiefel $100,000 in lost sales (it turned out to be much more than that); our situation was urgent. Since the FDA is a federal agency, I decided to seek a favor from an old friend in the federal government.

Gerald "Jerry" Solomon was a Marine Corps Korean War veteran and successful businessman who decided in 1978 to run for Congress in a district that included my home town in Greene County, New York. I was peripherally involved in politics at that time, serving as Assistant Greene County Attorney while spending most of my time as a partner in a local law firm. I met Jerry Solomon through a mutual friend and was immediately impressed with his candidness, integrity and military bearing. Jerry was from a different county, and since his campaign was in its infancy, he knew very few people in Greene County. Wanting to help him, I volunteered to serve as his campaign manager in my county; and a few months later, he was elected. Jerry remained in Congress for twenty years, eventually becoming Chairman of the powerful House Rules Committee, but I never saw or spoke to him again after I moved to Florida in 1982.

Would he still remember me two decades after I had supported his first Congressional bid? Stiefel Laboratories was desperate, and I could think of no other options, so in early February of 1998, I called Jerry's Washington office and (since Jerry was not there) explained our plight to one of his staffers. I emphasized that we were not seeking to influence the FDA's ultimate decision—we only wanted them to meet with us. The staffer made only two statements: firstly, she would explain our situation to the Congressman; and secondly, she was certain he would remember me. Amazingly, we received a phone call from the FDA the very next day, inviting us to a meeting the following week!

A productive meeting with FDA ensued, although our scientists were disconcerted by the fact they were receiving glares seeming to reflect pure hatred from one particular FDA employee. A course of action potentially leading to Clindoxyl's approval was mutually agreed upon, and the FDA promised to confirm our discussion in a letter. About a month later, we did indeed receive a letter, but it was unsigned and was marked "draft" in bold letters. What this portended was unclear to us, but we feared that the agency wanted the flexibility to disavow the contents of this letter in the future. Nevertheless, Stiefel proceeded to conduct all the additional work contemplated by this unsigned draft letter, and we dutifully submitted the new data.

In September of 2000, our application was rejected again. The only positive news was that OPDRA, the agency's Office of Post-Marketing Drug Risk Assessment, reviewed the name "Clindoxyl" and had no problem with it. So, if we could ever get our NDA approved, we had a trademark ready to go. Meanwhile, the regulatory dossier the FDA still deemed insufficient won us regulatory approval from the health ministries in both Mexico (1999) and Canada (2000). Much to our chagrin, a US competitor, Dermik Laboratories, submitted an NDA in 1998 for an acne product containing the same active ingredients in the same percentages; and their product (BenzaClin®) was approved in 2000. We had filed our NDA two years before Dermik, and they had beaten us to the market.

Undaunted, we continued to strive for approval in the United States, but there were many challenges. At one point, the FDA requested, in writing, we conduct a "study consisting of three arms: Clindoxyl Gel vs. clindamycin vs. benzoyl peroxide," with no placebo. Our clinical group resisted, fearing the absence of a placebo could unfavorably skew the results of the study—a fear ultimately proven to be very well-founded. Imagine our frustration, then, when an FDA staffer later criticized us for conducting a study with no placebo! We strongly believed our NDA deserved to be approved, so we decided to avail ourselves of the FDA's internal appeal procedure. A meeting was scheduled at FDA's offices in

Rockville, Maryland, and I suggested to our regulatory group we bring in some heavy artillery.

Dermatologist James Leyden, M.D. is one of the world's foremost acne experts, and I asked Jim if he would be willing to attend this meeting and offer some expert comments on our behalf. Jim was willing in principle, but his busy schedule rendered it unlikely he could travel from his office in Philadelphia to Rockville in time for our meeting. Desperate times call for desperate measures, however, and after chartering a small airplane, Jim landed safely at Montgomery County Air Park, where my sister Joan (who ran Stiefel's Webderm subsidiary) picked him up and whisked him to FDA headquarters in the nick of time. Jim has a big personality—he is outspoken, direct and ruthlessly honest. His comments at our meeting were so logical and practical the FDA folks in attendance could not help but agree with him. (And given Jim's unquestioned expertise, they were probably afraid to disagree!)

In common acne (acne vulgaris), there are two primary lesion types—non-inflammatory lesions, often referred to as blackheads and whiteheads, and inflammatory lesions, which are papules and pustules. The FDA's primary rationale for not approving Clindoxyl was it had not demonstrated sufficient superiority over benzoyl peroxide in treating non-inflammatory lesions. This objection seemed unfair and ironic to us, given the FDA statistician who reviewed Dermik's two clinical trials had concluded, "Neither study supports the statistical superiority of BenzaClin to Benzoyl Peroxide in regards to Non-Inflammatory Lesions." We felt that we were being held to a totally different standard, and the FDA did not deny this. But thanks to Jim Leyden, we were able to negotiate a compromise with FDA whereby they would approve Clindoxyl, but only for the treatment of inflammatory acne. Every other acne treatment on the market at that time (including Benzaclin) was indicated for acne vulgaris, which included both types of lesions, but we did not mind this labeling restriction at all because we knew dermatologists would be likely to prescribe our product primarily for their inflammatory acne patients anyway.

Our joy, however, was short-lived. In January of 2002, the FDA had formally reorganized its Office of Drug Safety, and OPDRA (which had approved the name Clindoxyl) had become DMETS—the Division of Medication Errors and Technical Support. You have probably already guessed why I am mentioning this administrative change at FDA. Well, you are correct—in May 2002, DMETS reversed OPDRA's earlier decision and decided that Clindoxyl was not an appropriate name for our product after all. The trademark we had registered eight years earlier and which had been blessed by the FDA two years earlier was suddenly not acceptable. Six years after we had submitted our NDA, the agency was finally ready to approve it, but there could be no approval unless and until there was an approved name for our product.

Everyone at Stiefel scrambled to think of alternate names, and one of the names I conceived was Duac®. I liked this trademark because it was short and easy for dermatologists to write on their prescription pads. I also hoped this name would suggest our product was "dual acting" or, with two active ingredients, it was a "duo for acne." Happily, DMETS had no objection to this name, and in August 2002, Duac was formally approved by the FDA. The path to approval had been protracted and arduous, but it was well worth it. Duac quickly became the top-selling acne product in many countries around the world, as well as the most successful product in the history of Stiefel Laboratories.

Not all of Stiefel's interactions with federal agencies were exasperating. During the first few years of my tenure at the company, I interacted several times with the Interstate Commerce Commission, and I consistently found ICC personnel to be both pleasant and helpful. One of the ICC's responsibilities was to regulate common carriers (which included trucking companies) to ensure shipping rates were reasonable and nondiscriminatory.

Stiefel shipped virtually all of our products in the US by truck; in the early eighties, we were caught in the middle of a very confusing regulatory scheme. The Interstate Commerce Act had for many years required truckers to publish their rates in "tariffs" filed with the ICC, and both truckers and their customers were prohibited from deviating from these rates.

In 1980, however, Congress substantially deregulated the trucking industry via passage of the Motor Carrier Act of 1980, which dramatically increased competition and caused many truckers to start negotiating new, lower rates with their customers. These discounted rates were still required to be filed with the ICC, but sometimes (unbeknownst to their customers) the trucking companies neglected to do so. The legal problems arose when the combination of increased competition and lower rates caused many truckers to file for bankruptcy; these bankrupt firms (or their representatives) then commenced thousands of lawsuits all over the United States against their former customers. Stiefel Laboratories was the defendant in several of these cases, and the fact patterns were very similar in all of them.

Our shipping department had negotiated rates with various trucking companies for the shipment of our products, we were invoiced accordingly, and we paid all of these invoices on time and in full. The problem was some of these truckers had promised to file new tariffs reflecting these negotiated rates with the ICC but had failed to do so. The lawsuits against us demanded we pay not only the higher rates reflected in the tariffs most recently filed, but also interest and late charges for not paying these higher rates on time! It sounds very unfair, right?

But as General Counsel for Stiefel, I was very concerned about these lawsuits because courts had consistently held fairness was not relevant in these cases. You might think our shipping department was naive, but the list of companies named as defendants in these bankrupt shipper lawsuits reads like a veritable *Who's Who* of American industry. Hoping to avoid litigating all these cases, I called the ICC for advice and was connected to a staffer who was extremely knowledgeable and helpful. This gentleman told me the ICC, in an effort to stop this unfair (and sometimes fraudulent) practice by trucking firms, had recently adopted a Negotiated Rates policy. Pursuant to this policy, if a trucker negotiated a discounted rate with a customer, failed to file this rate with the ICC as required, billed the customer at the discounted rate and accepted payment, and then subsequently tried to collect a higher amount, this would constitute an unreasonable practice.

Armed with this immensely helpful information, I contacted the attorneys representing the truckers suing Stiefel and was able to settle all these cases for very little money. The timing of these settlements happened to be extremely fortuitous for Stiefel Laboratories, because in 1990, the Supreme Court of the United States, in the *Maislin Industries* case, struck down the ICC's Negotiated Rates policy, holding that it was inconsistent with the language of the Interstate Commerce Act.

As a postscript to this anecdote, Congress essentially overturned the *Maislin* decision by enacting the Negotiated Rates Act of 1993, and finally, in 1995, Congress abolished the Interstate Commerce Commission entirely. I was sorry to see the ICC disappear, because I have never found a governmental administrative agency to be so accessible and obliging.

Another agency with which I enjoyed a positive relationship was the New York State Department of Environmental Conservation (EnCon). Stiefel's Oak Hill manufacturing facility was located in a very rural setting, so we were not connected to a municipal sewer system. All of our manufacturing and packaging equipment needed to be thoroughly washed after each usage, so we generated a significant amount of wastewater. To ensure this wastewater was appropriately treated to remove all potentially harmful substances, we constructed a large wastewater treatment plant on our Oak Hill campus. EnCon regulated the engineering, design and performance of this plant. The agency staffers with whom I dealt were passionate about protecting the environment in New York State, but although they were tough, they were nevertheless willing to offer helpful advice.

Whereas some governmental agencies seem to hope you will make a mistake, so they can punish you, EnCon apparently believed the best way to fulfill their mission was by proactively providing direction to the industries they regulated. It was an extremely refreshing philosophy; with EnCon's guidance (and the help of an excellent engineering firm), the water we eventually discharged from our plant was cleaner and purer than the water we had originally pumped from our wells. Our efforts were so successful we were honored with an environmental award from a local conservation group!

Unfortunately, Stiefel's excellent track record with EnCon meant nothing to EnCon's federal counterpart, the Environmental Protection Agency. As bad luck would have it, there was an EPA inspector who worked in Manhattan but lived in close proximity to our Oak Hill plant. I would estimate this gentleman's daily round-trip commute entailed traveling approximately five hours—and undoubtedly much more than that in snowy weather. Perhaps by coincidence (you be the judge), during one significant snowstorm in the 1990s, this EPA inspector did not travel to Manhattan, but instead appeared by surprise at our front door, announcing he intended to commence a comprehensive audit of our entire Oak Hill campus—which included a manufacturing plant, a separate research building and a distribution center.

Rightly or wrongly, all of us at Stiefel believed he desperately wanted to find evidence of wrongdoing so he would have a legitimate reason to spend several weeks in Oak Hill rather than travel to Manhattan every day during that long, snowy winter. His operating assumption seemed to be we were lawbreakers; when he failed to find any problems initially, he called in additional EPA as well as EnCon personnel to join the audit team. The EnCon staffers knew Stiefel had an excellent compliance record, and we inferred they deeply resented this intrusion by the feds.

Ultimately, after being subjected to several days of intense scrutiny, we were vindicated. All those auditors could only identify one relatively minor paperwork issue, and we were left with the strong impression that this "audit" had actually been an abusive witch-hunt. I was very happy that we did not have very many additional interactions with the EPA.

I interfaced with a myriad of different federal and state administrative agencies throughout my career, and all of these agencies worked diligently to accomplish their objectives. Much like people, however, these agencies manifested their own unique personalities. Some, such as the Interstate Commerce Commission and the New York State Department of Environmental Conservation, were actually helpful. Others were more adversarial, but nevertheless fair and businesslike. The Internal Revenue Service, for example, audited our corporate tax return every single year, but we never really encountered a significant problem with the IRS. Sure, they were overreaching at times, but so was virtually every other tax authority in the world.

Alone at the extreme end of the agency personality spectrum sits the US Securities and Exchange Commission, or SEC, which (in my opinion) goes far beyond being merely adversarial to the point of being ruthlessly hostile. Of all the governmental agencies in the United States, the one for which I feel the least respect and the most antipathy is the SEC. My reasons for feeling this way are explained in the Epilogue of this book.

CHAPTER SIXTEEN

GLADES PHARMACEUTICALS

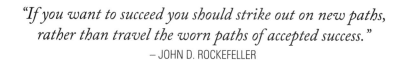

*"If you want to succeed you should strike out on new paths,
rather than travel the worn paths of accepted success."*
– JOHN D. ROCKEFELLER

would wager every single reader of this book has had a doctor's prescription filled with a generic drug. But this experience was not always as common as it is today. As recently as 1983, only about 10 percent of prescriptions written in the United States were filled with a generic. Today, this number exceeds 80 percent. The reason for this dramatic increase is straightforward—in 1984, a bipartisan piece of legislation (yes, younger readers, there was once a time when Republicans and Democrats actually worked together) called the Drug Price Competition and Patent Term Restoration Act (commonly referred to as the Hatch-Waxman Act) was passed by Congress and signed into law by President Ronald Reagan. This law made it simpler and easier for pharmaceutical companies to obtain FDA approval of generic drugs; it modernized the process of generic regulation in this country. In addition to this federal law, all 50 states enacted laws which encouraged generic substitution.

The first renowned prescription brand to go generic pursuant to Hatch-Waxman was Valium®, a popular tranquilizer which had been marketed by Hoffmann-LaRoche without generic competition for nearly 23 years. Valium quickly lost its status as one of the five best-selling drugs in the United States, and sales eroded steadily as the generics won ever-increasing market share. An FDA regulatory submission seeking approval of a generic drug is called an Abbreviated New Drug Application (ANDA), and as more and more ANDAs were approved pursuant to Hatch-Waxman, it was disconcerting for Stiefel to watch major prescription brands lose approximately 90 percent of their sales within one year after the generic entered the marketplace.

How could we protect our brands against generic competition, when even the largest and most powerful pharmaceutical companies could not do so? After much reflection, we decided to abide by the words of the old idiom, "If you can't beat them, join them." I broached to my father the concept of starting our own generic company, and Werner enthusiastically asked me to work on the idea. Brendan Murphy, who was then our National Distribution Manager, had considerable expertise getting our products stocked by the drug wholesalers and chains; I sat down with Brendan and I pitched the idea to him. Brendan shared Werner's enthusiasm, so in 1991, Stiefel embarked upon a new path by forming Glades Pharmaceuticals, with Brendan Murphy as its first President.

It was a risky career move for Brendan, since Glades had no products and zero sales, so to incentivize him to work hard and build this new business from scratch, I proposed to Werner that (in addition to his base salary) we offer Brendan a bonus package equal to 5 percent of Glades profits each year—with no cap. Werner pointed out Brendan could earn more money than even my father or Herb if Glades became successful, but I contended there could be no better motivator than offering someone the potential to actually get rich—as opposed to simply earning a comfortable living. Furthermore, I queried, wouldn't we be happy paying Brendan a $1,000,000 bonus if his entrepreneurial efforts brought Stiefel Laboratories an incremental $20,000,000 in profit?

Werner readily agreed, and Brendan was thrilled to accept this results-oriented bonus package.

It typically takes time to build a successful new business, and our Glades subsidiary was no exception. To help him move Glades forward, Brendan recruited two talented pharmaceutical veterans to join him, and in 1994, Jeff Thompson and Chris Schneider joined the Glades team. Both Jeff and Chris developed generic expertise so quickly that Brendan (with Werner's consent) offered them uncapped bonus programs similar to his own—only with a smaller percentage of Glades profits. The initial Glades strategy was two-pronged: firstly, to leverage Stiefel's expertise in developing and manufacturing skincare products by focusing primarily on generic dermatologicals; secondly, to pursue smaller brands the large generic companies were ignoring.

Let's look at a very simplified example. Suppose a minor dermatology product was selling 40,000 units annually at an average price of $100 per unit, which equals $4,000,000 in sales. The large generic companies were typically working on copying the brands with the most profit potential, so this small dermatology product would not (at least at that time) have been interesting to them. But if Glades could launch the sole generic alternative and capture 90 percent market share, then Glades could sell 36,000 units at a price of, let's say, $85 per unit—meaning this one product would add more than $3,000,000 annually to Glades sales.

Compared to Stiefel, which typically spent approximately 25 percent of total revenues on sales and marketing, Glades could successfully sell its products with relatively little promotional spend (which translated into a much higher percentage of sales hitting the profit line). Stiefel needed a large sales force to tout the advantages of Stiefel's brands to dermatologists, but Glades required only a small staff to get its generics stocked in the pharmacies. Once these products were stocked, state generic substitution laws mandated (or at least encouraged) pharmacists to substitute Glades products for the brand that had been prescribed; we quickly learned most pharmacists actually preferred to dispense the generic because (as counterintuitive as it might seem) pharmacies earned more profit selling the lower-priced generic. As a matter of fact, being in the generic business taught us a great deal that helped us in our core Stiefel brand business.

Our initial Glades strategy worked extremely well; both sales and profits grew steadily. Unfortunately, however, the rest of the industry began to take note of our increasing sales (most pharma companies purchase sales data), and before long, a number of generic competitors started focusing on the same smaller brands Glades was targeting. The way the generic marketplace functioned, if Glades were marketing the sole generic alternative to any given brand, that generic would typically be highly profitable. If there were two or three generic alternatives to that same brand, they could all still earn a modest profit, provided that the competing companies priced their generics in a way to allow everyone a reasonable share of the pie. This could be very tricky, because it is illegal (for antitrust reasons) for competitors to discuss price with each other, but experienced companies could signal their willingness to share the market without breaking the law.

For Glades, the worst-case scenario would entail multiple generics being available for the same brand, in which case prices would erode very quickly, rendering it virtually impossible to generate a profit. If a competitor undercut your price at a given account, the only way to keep that account might be to agree to a retroactive price decrease, whereby a sale already booked at one price is retroactively deemed to have been sold at a lower price— and you owe the account the difference. Stiefel had never dealt with issues like this, so it was a nightmare for our accountants and a genuine education for us! We decided our strategy needed to evolve, so we began targeting larger brands which, for formulation and regulatory reasons, were more difficult to genericize.

Brendan Murphy left Glades in 2003 to start his own generic company, River's Edge® Pharmaceuticals, but Jeff Thompson, Chris Schneider and Darren Alkins (who became President of Glades in 2006) continued to provide excellent leadership. (Jeff, incidentally, proved himself to be such a talented leader I promoted him to the position of Chief Operating Officer at Stiefel and asked him to join our corporate Board of Directors.) Johnson & Johnson had sold a very successful oral antifungal product called Grifulvin® for many years; and in 2005, Glades received the first ever FDA approval for a generic version of Grifulvin Oral Suspension. This griseofulvin (the generic name) product quickly became the best-selling Glades product of all time, with sales of nearly $22,000,000 the following year.

The generic marketplace can be cruel, though, and after the FDA approved another company's ANDA for griseofulvin oral suspension, sales of the Glades product dropped by two-thirds within a year. Total Glades sales, which had reached $73 million in the fiscal year that ended March 31, 2006, dropped to $49 million the following year. The level of competition was increasing dramatically, and we decided a further change in strategic direction was appropriate. Consequently, in March 2007, Glades sold nine of its marketed generic products in addition to four of its pipeline projects to Perrigo for $56 million in cash plus some additional consideration. The Glades business continued to thrive, but with a more limited and targeted scope. We retained, for example, all our authorized generic business. Pursuant to our typical authorized generic arrangement, the company marketing the brand would partner with Glades; the brand's exact formulation would be filled into Glades packaging; Glades would launch this new generic; the two parties would split the profits.

Are you perhaps wondering why any company would genericize its own product? The rationale is the authorized generic deal enables the brand company to reduce the negative financial impact associated with the brand going generic; customarily, the brand manufacturer would not consider such a deal until such time as some third party's generic approval was imminent. Essentially, the thought process is if someone is going to capture 90 percent of your sales anyway, you might as well own a piece of the action. One of the many ways Glades contributed to Stiefel's profitability through the years was to serve as the authorized generic distributor for all of Stiefel's prescription brands. Glades performed this function so expertly for Stiefel that other companies likewise enlisted Glades as their authorized generic partner. These partnerships were very beneficial for Glades, providing a quality source of new products while obviating the need to invest time and money seeking approval of an ANDA.

Stiefel's decision to strike out on a new path and enter the generic business proved to be an excellent one. Not only did our Glades subsidiary generate millions and millions of dollars in incremental profit, but it vastly increased our expertise and sophistication as a pharmaceutical company. In addition, the units manufactured for Glades helped absorb fixed overhead at our Oak Hill plant, thereby reducing the cost of the Stiefel products manufactured there. At the time GlaxoSmithKline (GSK) acquired Stiefel in July 2009, Prasco Laboratories, a company based in Cincinnati, Ohio, was marketing an authorized generic for at least one GSK product. The Glades team made a presentation to GSK, pointing out if GSK were to give Glades its future authorized generic business, GSK would no longer need to share some of that profit with a third party—all of it would belong to GSK through its ownership of Glades.

Sadly for the Glades team, GSK decided to dissolve Glades rather than utilize its authorized generic expertise. In December 2009, GSK announced an authorized generic deal with Prasco for Stiefel's product Olux® Foam, a product for which Glades had previously been selling the authorized generic. This announcement sounded the death knell for Glades. Eighteen years after its formation in 1991, Glades disappeared from existence. Good night, sweet prince.

CHAPTER SEVENTEEN

CHARLIE

"The best executive is one who has sense enough to pick good people to do what he wants done, and self-restraint enough to keep from meddling with them while they do it."
— THEODORE ROOSEVELT

I must confess writing a chapter about myself causes me to feel very uncomfortable. Including anything positive about myself might seem like bragging, but I hesitate to omit facts you, the reader, might consider germane. After a considerable amount of soul-searching, I have decided to include within this chapter the same material a biographer writing about someone else might include. I apologize in advance if anything I write strikes you as immodest.

From my earliest childhood days, I knew I wanted to work for Stiefel Laboratories someday. If someone back then had asked me why, I could not have explained it, but the feeling was nevertheless powerful. It certainly had nothing to do with the company's success. In 1967, the year I graduated from high school, the company had been in business for 120 years, yet global sales were still only $1,700,000. No, the lure of Stiefel Laboratories was never about money—it was all about tradition and family and my desire to help build the business to which my father, my uncle and their ancestors had dedicated their lives. My name and the company name were the same. From the very beginning, Stiefel was in my blood; and working there always seemed like my destiny.

I grew up in rural upstate New York, in the northern region of the Catskill Mountains. My early summers were primarily spent outdoors—playing Little League baseball, visiting my grandmother's farm, and volunteering as a Red Cross swimming instructor. I was also very active in scouting, becoming, at age 12, the youngest Eagle Scout in the history of my troop. As soon as I became old enough to obtain working papers (age 14 for non-factory work; age 16 for factory work), I landed my first job as the groundskeeper at a local boarding house. I mowed the lawns, raked leaves, picked up trash, and performed any other tasks the resort owner ordered (I once weed whacked her prize flowers, thinking they were weeds). I rode my bike to and from work six days a week, starting at 8:00am and ending whenever all the chores were completed. I earned $1.25 per hour (minimum wage), and it seemed like a fortune to me.

As soon as I turned 16, I asked my dad for a job at the local Stiefel facility. I worked one summer making soap, another in the laboratory at Stiefel Research Institute (SRI), and a third in the warehouse—all at minimum wage. It was hard work, but I loved it—at least most of it. Unloading boxes from the back of a tractor-trailer parked in the sun on a 100-degree day gave me a totally new perspective on what it meant to be hot! These jobs taught me a great deal about how products are developed, manufactured, tested, warehoused and shipped; I developed a lasting respect for the individuals who so expertly performed these tasks.

I also gained some valuable insights into how different workers perceive themselves and their colleagues. I wore a blue uniform during my two summers in the factory and warehouse, but I wore a white lab coat during my summer at SRI. I noticed a few of the blue-collar workers were jealous of the SRI employees, believing they had soft jobs sitting around in air-conditioned luxury all day. I noticed also the hourly workers, who punched a clock, often resented the fact our salaried personnel received superior fringe benefits. (Years later, as CEO, I implemented numerous changes to eliminate these disparities and equalize our employee benefit packages.)

I have always loved music, and if Stiefel Laboratories had not existed, I might have pursued a musical career. After one year of piano lessons, I became a woodwind guy, playing clarinet in high school and the Yale Marching Band, as well as bass clarinet in high school and a regional all-star band. When I was 15, an opening arose for a tenor saxophone player in a local dance band, the Catskill Mountain Hot Shots. I had never played a tenor sax before, but my experience on clarinet and bass clarinet made it very easy for me to learn. So that summer, in addition to my day job, I started playing with the Hot Shots four nights a week at various resorts in the Catskills. Every summer thereafter, for the next ten years, I played in one or more bands an average of six nights per week, in addition to numerous afternoon weddings and, of course, New Year's Eve. Not only was this job great fun, but it paid much better than my day jobs!

My home town, Oak Hill, was actually too small to be deemed a town, so officially it was considered a hamlet. I would not characterize Oak Hill as a poor area, so let us simply say it was economically challenged. Not one family I knew owned a swimming pool, so all of us swam in the local swimming hole, which was part of the Catskill Creek. It was at this swimming hole I met Daneen Cheryl Waldstein when we were both seven years old. She was with her parents, who owned a summer cottage at the top of the hill, and I was with mine; since there were a lot of kids swimming, we took no particular note of each other. Thirteen years later, however, both of us having completed our sophomore years in college, we started dating—and we have never stopped. We were married on August 20, 1972, just before I started law school, and she remains the love of my life.

Daneen supported us during my three years in law school, working as a child abuse caseworker for Greene County. After we moved to Miami in 1982, she became the assistant director of a nursery school and subsequently worked for a travel agency, eventually handling all domestic travel and meetings for Stiefel Laboratories. She ended her career as Vice President of Travel, Meetings and Conventions at Stiefel. But I digress...

Heading off to college, I faced a problem many children in middle-class families face ... we were not poor enough for me to qualify for financial aid, but my parents could not afford the high cost of sending me to Yale. Fortunately, our income was low enough I was offered the opportunity to work for the university during the school year. I sold class rings and Yale mugs to fellow students on a commission basis, but my primary job was at Yale's Payne Whitney Gymnasium, where I worked 20 hours a week for the next 3 ½ years. Why only 3 ½ years, you might wonder? The answer is my mom and dad were able to pay half of my tuition, but I was responsible for the other half, as well as books, travel and personal expenses. So, despite working two jobs every summer and borrowing as much student loan money as possible, I simply could not afford my last semester at Yale.

Fortunately, I had already accumulated enough credits to graduate early, so I left New Haven halfway through my senior year and went back to work at Stiefel—this time as part of an inventory reduction task force. I enjoyed working there so much I seriously considered skipping law school. But as much as I wanted to spend my career at the company, I wanted to do something else first and hopefully acquire some expertise that would make me more valuable as a future employee. Once again, Dick Sandler had some valuable advice. Law is a great background for business, he opined, but working too long in a law firm can cause one to become risk-averse, and the essence of business is to take risks.

So, in 1982, after six years of practicing law in a Catskill, New

York, firm, I left my law partnership behind and joined Stiefel Laboratories as its first ever General Counsel. Taking this job entailed relocating to Miami, where the cost of living was much higher, while simultaneously sustaining a significant cut in pay; so the next few years were very lean ones for Daneen, our two young sons and me. I remember installing ceiling fans in our new home in Miami because for the first two years we could not afford to run the air conditioning. But I was filled with excitement and anticipation as we made the long drive from New York to Florida, because my childhood dream of working for Stiefel Laboratories was finally coming true.

I had always loved and respected Werner Stiefel as my dad, but knowing how strong-willed he was, I was slightly apprehensive about what he would be like as my boss. As it turned out, this was never a problem at all. I accorded him the deference he deserved as our corporate CEO, and he respected my opinions on the company's legal matters. And there were always a great number of legal matters! Many of these matters involved specialized areas of law, so I served as Stiefel's primary liaison with whatever outside firms we retained to handle these matters.

Trademark law is very specialized, for example, so for many years we worked with Rob Kunstadt of the New York firm Pennie & Edmonds. (After more than a year of working together, Rob happened to be in my office in Coral Gables and noticed my Yale diploma on the wall. He walked over to see what year I had graduated, and imagine our surprise when we learned that we were classmates!) Patent law was also specialized, and our patent lawyer for several years was Bruce Collins of the New Jersey firm Matthews, Woodbridge & Collins. For specialized FDA matters, we retained Paul Hyman of Hyman, Phelps & McNamara. And, as you learned earlier in this book, for specialized corporate work, we always turned to Dick Sandler.

When we were sued, which unfortunately happened quite

frequently, we usually had insurance in place to cover any potential loss, and I would work with whatever firm the insurance company retained to represent us. Naturally, I was biased in favor of Stiefel, but I always tried to be objective and view the facts from the point of view of the plaintiff (the one suing us). On the rare occasions I felt that we were in the wrong (for example, if a Stiefel employee had driven a company car negligently and caused an accident), I would strongly urge the insurance carrier to offer a fair settlement to the plaintiff. The vast majority of these lawsuits, however, struck me as totally lacking in merit; at the risk of sounding cynical, it seemed to me that these plaintiffs were intentionally making baseless allegations in the hopes of winning what I dubbed the "litigation lottery." To illustrate this point, I will describe just three of the many, many unusual claims made against Stiefel through the years.

Stiefel Laboratories once developed a topical product for psoriasis which contained the active ingredient anthralin in a vehicle known as Lassar's paste. Our trademark combined the first three letters of the paste with the first two letters of "anthralin"; our product was thus called Lasan® Pomade. This formulation was very irritating when applied to normal skin, so naturally our label contained a number of warnings stating the patient should apply Lasan only to psoriatic skin and not to normal skin or (duh!) the eyes or mouth. Believe it or not, a gentleman from West Virginia sued us, alleging he had severely burned his eyes when he rubbed Lasan into them. Our attorneys pointed out we had specifically warned him not to do this, to which his lawyer replied he could not read the warnings because he was completely illiterate! We felt this unfortunate situation was entirely the plaintiff's fault, but our insurer insisted on offering him a modest settlement anyway; and he readily accepted.

Then there was the time one of our Los Angeles sales reps, driving his company car, accidentally bumped into the rear end of another car at an intersection. The driver of the other car was alone and uninjured, and our sales rep was likewise uninjured. Given the small dent in the other car's bumper, however, the two gentlemen exchanged insurance information. Imagine our surprise when, two months later, we were sued not only by the other driver, but by five of his friends who all swore that they had been in the car! All six plaintiffs were represented by the same lawyer, and all six were claiming that they had suffered very painful "soft tissue injuries," documented in detail by the same physician.

Clearly this was an insurance scam, and I was furious! But our insurance company calmly informed me this sort of fraud happens all the time, and since no accident report had been filed, it was our sales rep's word against six other individuals as to how many passengers had been in the other vehicle. The insurer's attorney further stated the crooked doctors and lawyers involved in perpetrating these insurance scams understand it is very difficult to disprove that a patient is experiencing pain associated with a soft tissue injury. Over my vehement objection, all six of these lying plaintiffs were offered modest settlements, and the lawsuit was withdrawn. The settlement money was paid by the insurance carrier, not by Stiefel Laboratories, but I was nevertheless outraged by what I considered to be a gross miscarriage of justice.

Another one of our sales representatives, an attractive young woman, liked to wear micro-miniskirts when calling upon her dermatologists. We received complaints from several doctors' offices about this practice, so the district sales manager informed this young woman about these complaints and counseled her about the importance of dressing professionally and projecting a positive corporate image. The sales rep replied by saying she was proud of her fashion sense, friends complimented her on her sexy legs, and the company did not have the right to tell her how to dress. She continued to wear very short skirts while working, and we received more complaints; whereupon the district manager issued her a formal warning. She defiantly refused to wear more conservative clothing while representing Stiefel in physician offices, so she was terminated.

Given how litigious Americans seem to be, we were not surprised when, almost immediately, we received a nasty letter threatening litigation. Her lawyer, a young man relatively new to the practice of law (yes, we looked him up), angrily demanded his client be reinstated immediately with back pay—otherwise, she would sue us for millions of dollars. We responded that his client had been fired for refusing to obey a very reasonable request from her boss, and we challenged him to (quoting Dick Sandler's words from years earlier) "bring your suit." He did not. In fact, we never heard from him again. Internally, we wondered what had inspired this lawyer to represent our sales rep in the first place: did he truly feel her claim was meritorious, or could he perhaps have been influenced by the micro-miniskirt she undoubtedly wore into his office?

One of my responsibilities as General Counsel at Stiefel was to negotiate and draft contracts on behalf of the company. Licensing or purchasing products or technology from a third party usually required a lengthy and complex contract, so as a logical extension of my legal duties, Werner asked me to serve as our company's first ever Director of Corporate Development. Wearing this hat, my job was to identify and acquire new products that would represent a good strategic fit for Stiefel—ideally, ones that would complement, rather than compete with, our existing product line. In order to undertake this exciting challenge, I first needed to take a crash course in dermatology.

I read several dermatology textbooks to learn about dozens of skin diseases and how they were being treated, as well as basic information about the structure and function of the skin (the largest organ of the human body). I took the same basic and advanced sales training classes all of our sales reps took, and this taught me about all the competing products being marketed by other companies. Stiefel subscribed to all dermatology journals currently being published, and I perused all of them faithfully. Some of the articles I read, particularly the ones in the *Journal of Investigative Dermatology*, were miles over my head scientifically, but I always learned something, even from the most esoteric papers. In addition, I paid attention to the names of the authors writing these articles, gradually gaining awareness of who the thought leaders were in each segment of dermatology.

Many of these thought leaders were members of a group called the Noah Worcester Dermatological Society, an organization formed to honor the author of the first American textbook on dermatology, published in 1845; I represented Stiefel every year at the Noah's week-long annual meeting. There were lectures every morning at these meetings, and I noticed that several of the pharma people would skip these lectures to play golf; while a few opted to attend every lecture. I was part of the latter group, and I learned a lot about both dermatology and the lecturers themselves by sitting there quietly in those darkened auditoriums. This also prepared me for my own 15 minutes of fame when, several years later, I was invited to address this distinguished group about a compound called pseudocatalase Stiefel was developing for vitiligo.

I thoroughly enjoyed my stint in business development. I traveled all over the world, meeting primarily with pharmaceutical companies that did not have a presence in the United States. Our marketing executives wanted a topical corticosteroid, so I negotiated a deal with Schering AG, a large German company, whereby Stiefel licensed US and Canadian rights to their successful product Nerisone® (generic name diflucortolone valerate). The marketing folks likewise wanted a topical antifungal, so I traveled to Milan and acquired US rights to a broad-spectrum antifungal called fenticonazole from mid-sized Italian company Ricordati.

Unfortunately, however, neither of these deals worked out the way I hoped. Both Nerisone and fenticonazole had been marketed all over the world for years, and the data overwhelmingly proved these products were both safe and effective, but the FDA would not approve either product based on these foreign data. Our regulatory people fought valiantly, but ultimately, they were unsuccessful. To this day, neither of these products has been approved in the United States. The only silver lining was the health ministry in Canada approved Nerisone relatively quickly, and this product family proved to be quite successful for Stiefel Canada.

One aspect of my job that was somewhat frustrating in the '80s and '90s was the fact large pharmaceutical companies typically would not even talk to us. Stiefel was simply too small to merit any of their time or attention. We had an idea, for example, that a topical version of the Merck antiparasitic compound ivermectin might work well in treating scabies—and possibly even rosacea, given the presence of significant numbers of *Demodex* mites in the faces of rosacea patients. (Many years later, it turned out that this idea was a fairly good one.) I wrote to Merck, offering them upfront cash plus royalties in exchange for topical rights to ivermectin; all we wanted from them was access to their drug master file for this compound. Merck did not reply to my letter, so I tried again; I also called several times leaving messages.

Apparently, my repeated efforts eventually began to annoy them, so finally someone called me to explain that their lawyers and corporate development people were far too busy pursuing large deals to take their time on a deal this small. I hated this response, but sadly, it made sense. From that day forward, however, I vowed that I would never turn down the opportunity to meet with a senior executive of any big pharma company. Typically, such a meeting would only be requested if a giant company wanted to acquire Stiefel; but even though we were not seeking to sell the company, I wanted to develop friendly relationships with executives who might be able to help us in the future. Plus, it never hurts to listen, right?

One deal that turned out really well for Stiefel was inked in 1991. Dermatologist Richard (Dick) DeVillez, MD was then at the

University of Texas, where he discovered benzoyl peroxide was less irritating to the skin when incorporated into a formulation containing dimethylisosorbide. Dick assigned his resulting patents to the university, so I quickly flew to San Antonio and negotiated a deal granting Stiefel exclusive worldwide rights under these patents in exchange for a modest royalty. Soon thereafter, Stiefel launched Brevoxyl® (also called Solugel® in some countries), which enjoyed significant sales for the next 2 ½ decades. In my opinion, the best deals are those that represent a true win-win, so I was very pleased when the University of Texas contacted me several times during the '90s to express their happiness with the royalties they were receiving.

In Chapter 11 of this book, I told you about Werner Stiefel transferring all his Class B Stiefel shares into D'Anconia Corporation; I also mentioned he retained personal ownership of the 100 voting preferred shares that could essentially control the company. Werner had divided his D'Anconia common shares equally among the 5 surviving children of his first marriage (he established a different holding company to benefit his second wife and their child), but after sharing control of the company with Herb throughout his career, he did not want to see control shared again in the next generation. He felt strongly that the most efficient operating structure entailed one person owning all the "super-voting" control shares; and when I joined the company in 1982, he promised me I would be that one person if we worked well together, and he would leave me his control shares in his will. His estate planning philosophy was to give his five children equal value, but not equal voting power.

Over the next few years, it became crystal clear my dad and I did indeed work well together; so in 1991 (the year he turned 70), he called me into his office for a serious discussion. He acknowledged his promise to leave me the super-voting shares in his will, but he expressed concern his will would be challenged in court; while such a challenge was pending, control of the company would be in limbo. What he preferred to do was sell me his control shares as quickly as possible for the sum of $100,000—payable over time, since I did not possess anywhere near that much money. Before transferring the stock, however, my dad asked me to make him two promises. The first was I would vote the control shares in accordance with his wishes until he either died or retired; naturally, I had no problem making and keeping this promise.

My father's second request was much more onerous. He began by stating something I already knew: he loved working and did not ever plan to retire. He recognized, however, his mental acuity might someday decline to the point where he was no longer fit to run the company; if that day ever arrived, he wanted me to tell him. He loved Stiefel Laboratories so much, he said, he preferred to retire rather than potentially harm the company by hanging around too long.

This entire concept made me extremely sad, and I confessed I was not sure I could ever do what he asked. I also argued he was still sharp as a tack, and in the unlikely event his mental faculties were to decline, he would recognize this himself without my intervention. With tears in his eyes, he noted that people are often unable to recognize changes in themselves that might be obvious to someone else; and that nearly everyone loses their edge eventually. "Please promise me," he asked again, "for the good of the company." Reluctantly, I agreed, genuinely believing I would surely never need to keep this promise. Sadly, I was wrong.

My father remained an intellectual giant for the next several years—advancing age could not diminish his genius. Then came the horrible news my dad had developed cancer. Chemotherapy takes its toll on everyone, but it can be particularly brutal when one is 80 years old. My dad's very first chemo treatment was extremely traumatic, and I noticed a drastic mental decline immediately thereafter. I had read articles about so-called "chemo brain," but the changes in my father far exceeded my worst nightmare. His theretofore amazing memory seemed to disappear overnight. He lost his car in the company parking lot during out next trip to Oak Hill; he began repeating the exact same questions to me (and others) multiple times each day. His ability to understand our business also declined dramatically. I recall forwarding him a memo from our Chief Financial Officer summarizing an interest rate swap (something we had done routinely for years) we had just executed; my dad returned the memo to me with the notation, "Alas, I cannot understand this at all." It was heartbreaking.

He began interrupting formal business meetings, wearing shorts and a dirty T-shirt, to ask inappropriate questions. For months, I wrestled with the question of what I should do before finally admitting to myself that my father, with his typical prescience, had anticipated this precise scenario a decade earlier. He had extracted a promise from me, and he had trusted me to keep that promise for the benefit of the company he loved. It was the saddest and most difficult business decision of my career, but I knew what I had to do.

When I told Werner Stiefel I did not think he was mentally able to continue as CEO of the company that bore his name, I had no idea how he would respond. To his credit, he calmly smiled, thanked me, and said that he would retire at the next meeting of the Board of Directors. In May 2001, at the age of 80, my father stepped down as Chairman and CEO of Stiefel Laboratories; and the Board elected me to succeed him.

My primary goals as CEO were threefold. Sales in the International Division still vastly exceeded US sales, representing 70 percent of the total; I believed that a healthier ratio would be closer to 50:50. Consequently, my first goal was to increase sales in the United States so dramatically they would equal or exceed our ex-US sales. My second goal was to achieve my father's dream of making Stiefel a billion-dollar company. The challenge was, after years of double-digit growth, the company had stopped growing—annual sales had been stuck at approximately $250 million for four consecutive years. And finally, my third goal was for Stiefel Laboratories to become the largest and most respected dermatology company in the world. At that time, we already were the largest privately-held dermatology company, but my goal was to eliminate that "privately-held" modifier.

However, it is important to note not everything was completely under my control at this time. Although I was nominally the corporate CEO, the 1966 agreement between Werner and Herb remained in effect until 2006; my Uncle Herb still had full autonomy in running all of our overseas operations. Happily, Herb and I got along extremely well, and together, we began planning for the day when the "US Division" and the "International Division" would no longer exist, and Stiefel would become one united global company.

It is the responsibility of every CEO to maximize shareholder value. But philosophically speaking, what is the value of a share of stock one cannot sell? In the history of Stiefel Laboratories, only a negligible number of shares were purchased by buyers other than the company itself, so unless the company itself was willing to step up to the plate, there was essentially no market for Stiefel shares. Consequently, I felt part of my duty to maximize shareholder value included the duty to maximize the potential for our stockholders to monetize their investments.

Back in Chapter 11, I mentioned Dick Sandler's advice for Stiefel to accept offers from stockholders seeking to sell shares to the company, as long as their proposed selling price was lower than our most recent stock appraisal. We dutifully followed this practice throughout the 1990s, accepting redemption requests to the extent we could do so without impairing our business. Our shareholders universally appreciated the opportunity to sell, and not one person ever groused about having to sell at a discount. A company can become the victim of its own success, however, and as our stock price rose higher and higher, our shareholders grew increasingly anxious to liquidate their investments. We received so many requests each year that Matt Pattullo, our Corporate Secretary, began maintaining a waiting list of holders desiring to sell as soon as the company was in a position to buy.

We tried to accommodate everyone as best we could, but there were always a number of people on Matt's waiting list. Due to cash constraints, we sometimes needed to limit how many shares we could redeem at a particular time from any one stockholder; fortunately, nearly everyone understood and accepted these limitations. A few large stockholders, however, insisted the company buy all their shares immediately, and they retained attorneys who tried to apply pressure by threatening lawsuits. I was not worried about these threats, recalling Sandler's advice from years earlier that the company had absolutely no legal duty to redeem anyone's shares (except for Participants in our Employee Stock Bonus Plan). I nevertheless felt very conflicted. On one hand, my philosophy had always been to afford our shareholders the opportunity to sell if they so desired; but on the other hand, we could not afford to pay anywhere near the appraised price if a large block of shares was being offered.

The solution to this dilemma was provided by Columbia University, which one day sent me an unsolicited offer to sell all its shares. Columbia's offer was based upon a formula whereby the price per share decreased as the number of shares we were willing to purchase increased. By redeeming all Columbia's shares (which the Board voted to do), the average discount off our appraised stock price became quite significant. The result of this transaction was Columbia benefitting by being able to monetize its entire investment and all other Stiefel shareholders benefitting because the value of their stock increased.

It was a true win-win transaction; and given our guiding principle to treat all shareholders equally, we thenceforth communicated to others seeking to sell large blocks of stock we would only entertain offers conforming to the discount schedule introduced by Columbia. Not surprisingly, given we were a family business, the largest blocks of stock ever offered back to the company were by members of the Stiefel family. After my dad retired, he and his wife Marie (who by then held his power of attorney) approached me, wanting to monetize all their holdings; happily, we succeeded in negotiating a deal to accommodate them. Then my brothers Jay and Ned, both approaching retirement age, asked to cash in. Their request was much more complicated, however, because virtually all their stock was owned indirectly through D'Anconia (the holding company set up by my father), and legally, it was not deemed a prudent investment for Stiefel to purchase a minority interest in D'Anconia.

By then, Dick Sandler had retired, but another excellent attorney, Michael Kavoukjian of White & Case, devised a complex plan whereby D'Anconia would be merged into Stiefel, with no tax consequences to either company, and D'Anconia's stockholders would become Stiefel stockholders. As part of this plan, my two brothers were able to sell all of their shares as they had requested; thereafter, D'Anconia ceased to exist. No sooner was the D'Anconia merger completed than Herb asked me if his holding company, Bacamachli, could be merged into Stiefel on similar terms. Naturally, I wanted to accommodate Herb and his five daughters, so less than a year later, Bacamachli likewise ceased to exist, with many of its Stiefel shares being redeemed as part of the merger process.

Unbelievably, in the five-year period from mid-2003 to mid-2008, the Stiefel family sold more than 31,000 shares back to the company for total consideration exceeding $140 million! Fortunately, the company's sales began to increase dramatically in 2003, so we were able to oblige these family members without endangering our cash position. This family stock represented more than 40 percent of the company's total equity, and since these shares were purchased at average discounts exceeding 50 percent, the value of the stock owned by everyone else (including the Participants in our Employee Stock Bonus Plan) increased very significantly as a result.

I was mindful, however, of Dick Sandler's advice that the company treat all stockholders similarly. So, when my friend (and Vice Chairman of the Board) Dick MacKay approached Stiefel in mid-2008 wanting to sell 750 shares owned by his Canadian holding company for estate planning purposes, I felt we needed to give Dick the opportunity to redeem these shares using the same Columbia University formula we had used for members of Werner and Herb's families. (Of course, since Dick was selling fewer shares, his discounts did not grow nearly as large; so the average price per share he received was more than twice what was paid to the D'Anconia and Bacamachli holders.) Dick seemed quite happy at the time, pocketing approximately $9 million in cash, while retaining the vast majority of his Stiefel stock. Unfortunately, the old adage "no good deed goes unpunished" sometimes proves to be true. If you are interested in the sad ending to this story, or if you simply like to read about lawsuits, make sure to check out this book's epilogue.

Many people throughout the years have asked me about my management style; I would characterize it as egalitarian rather than dictatorial. I considered all our employees around the globe to be important members of the Stiefel team, not just boxes on an organizational chart. Everyone was deemed a peer—no one a subordinate—and my door was always open. I always fetched my own coffee, and I never issued a direct order without first trying to build a consensus. I strived to foster a corporate culture whereby all employees, regardless of rank, would be treated with equal respect and dignity. I gave every employee in the company my direct office phone number and e-mail address, and I encouraged them to contact me day or night with any comments, questions or concerns they might have.

My egalitarian style did not prevent me from occasionally challenging my colleagues. One strategem I sometimes employed was to utilize an extreme example in order to make a point. For example, Stiefel once marketed an acne product, Clindets®, which comprised a box of small pledgets soaked in 1 percent clindamycin phosphate solution. Each pledget was individually wrapped in foil—similar to the towelettes you might receive in a rib restaurant. Stiefel did not own a machine capable of packaging Clindets, so we outsourced this function to a company called Sharp Packaging. The initial demand for this product was much stronger than we expected; within a few weeks after launch, our warehouse was nearly out of stock. Backordering a new product just as it is gaining momentum is a marketing person's worst nightmare; we desperately needed Sharp to package more Clindets for us immediately!

Sharp's schedule was extremely busy, however, and Stiefel was not slated to receive more Clindets for two months. Our people begged and pleaded, to no avail. At a meeting of our New Products Committee, they delivered the disastrous news—nothing could be done to induce Sharp to package Clindets sooner. "Suppose," I asked with a straight face, "we offered them one billion dollars?" Someone responded that we could probably buy the entire company for that amount, so naturally a sum that large would entice Sharp to move Clindets forward in their schedule. "We don't have a billion dollars anyway," I replied, "but suppose we offer to pay them a significantly higher price per unit than we are paying them now?" Some people were skeptical about this idea, but our liaison with Sharp was eager to try. Sure enough, we were able to negotiate a deal whereby Sharp scheduled an emergency packaging run of Clindets in exchange for a 25 percent premium over their normal price.

My philosophy was to delegate authority and accountability to our executive team and then try to refrain from micro-managing them. I would not hesitate to intervene, however, if I believed that an important business principle was at stake. I felt strongly, for example, Stiefel should never waste money. In speeches to our global executive team, I would frequently emphasize it was okay to spend millions of dollars on a project, but wasting even one cent was not acceptable. Some managers felt any expenditure should be permissible as long as they stayed within budget, but I insisted they spend their budget dollars prudently, as if it were their own money.

One of my pet peeves involved our corporate logo, which you can see on several of the photographs included within this book. Nearly every time we hired a new marketing executive, that person would almost immediately propose we change our corporate logo to make it appear more modern. I would always respond the same way, pointing out the enormous cost associated with changing our logo on every building sign, every piece of product packaging, every custom metal die used to press bars of our soap, every sales aid, every business card, and every other miscellaneous place where our logo appeared.

"What," I would ask, "will be the ROI (return on investment) for this expenditure? What incremental sales and profits will the company earn due to this modernized logo?" No one could ever answer these rhetorical questions, so the proposal would eventually be withdrawn—with the marketing person no doubt thinking that I was stubborn and old-fashioned. Interestingly, one of the first things the Stiefel team did after I left the company in 2009 (after GSK acquired us) was to change our corporate logo! I sincerely hope Stiefel earned a return on that investment.

In 2009, a business magazine asked me what advice I might offer to aspiring executives, and I want to end the chapter on myself by reiterating my answer to that question:

1. Ask questions rather than dictate answers.
2. Seek input from all stakeholders.
3. Continually search for best practices.

4. Facilitate open and honest communication throughout the organization.
5. Build consensus.
6. Drive the decision-making process.
7. Understand the nature of business is risk, but the amount of risk a company undertakes should always be commensurate with the potential reward.

Oak Hill, NY manufacturing facility

Campus of Stiefel Brazil

Global Research Headquarters
Research Triangle Park, North Carolina

Manufacturing facility in Sligo, Ireland

Stiefel Research Institute, Oak Hill, NY

Stiefel UK

Singapore manufacturing plant

Research facility in Maidenhead, UK

Stiefel Mexico

Stiefel Canada

CHAPTER EIGHTEEN

INVESTING IN PEOPLE

"Leaders don't create followers, they create more leaders."
— TOM PETERS

T hroughout the years, Stiefel Laboratories has employed more than its share of interesting characters. One of our early corporate treasurers, for example, decided the company's finances were becoming too complicated for his skill set, so he quit to take a job driving a truck (in the summer) and a snowplow (in the winter) for the local township. As a youth, I considered his decision to be bizarre; as I matured, however, I grew to admire his sense of self-awareness. Taking a cut in pay in order to reduce one's stress level is probably a pretty reasonable trade-off.

Jay Pittman, a Princeton graduate with a photographic memory, worked several years as our plant manager in Oak Hill. One of the smartest people I've ever known, Jay once asked me my date of birth; without writing down my answer, he thereafter called me every year on that day to wish me happy birthday. What made this feat particularly impressive was he did the same thing with dozens of other people. Jay's father was likewise very interesting. A man of modest means, he nevertheless assembled (through skillful purchasing and trading) a multi-million-dollar coin collection that was unrivaled in scope and quality outside of the Smithsonian or the British Museum. When Jay's father passed away, Jay left the manufacturing sector to help manage his dad's world-famous collection.

I worked with one person (let's call him Tom) for a few years before my dad confided in me; Tom (whom my dad had hired) had been convicted of murder while serving in the military. I assumed there must have been extenuating circumstances, but I was wrong. Apparently, a fellow soldier had infuriated Tom, so Tom stealthily crept in the night to this fellow's bunk and stabbed him to death with a knife. Tom was dishonorably discharged and subsequently served time in a military prison before eventually landing a job at good old Stiefel Laboratories. I am a believer in second chances, but I was deeply troubled that neither I nor any of my fellow employees had ever been warned about Tom's background. Fortunately, Tom never murdered anyone else (to my knowledge).

I mentioned earlier in this book my father's favorite author was Ayn Rand; henceforth, he hired quite a few Ayn Rand disciples throughout the years. One of these disciples called himself Gary Cooper. I never learned this gentleman's real name, but I always assumed his pseudonym was chosen because the actor Gary Cooper had played the role of protagonist Howard Roark in the movie version of Ayn Rand's *The Fountainhead*. Our employee Gary was a recluse with a deep distrust of the United States government, so my dad hired him to work at our tiny facility in Grand Cayman. Most of the time, Werner would fly to Cayman to meet with Gary, but on the rare occasions Gary would travel to Coral Gables, he requested to meet my father very early in the morning, so he could leave the office without having to encounter anyone else. Over time, Gary began to distrust the Cayman government too, so he decided to quit his job and simply disappear. His final instructions were to burn without opening any mail that came for him, and "If anyone asks where I've gone, tell them to go to hell!" Gary Cooper was never seen or heard from again.

The human brain is the most complex organ in the body, which perhaps explains why the behavior of some people is so difficult to comprehend. Stiefel once employed two sales executives who, it was reported, told racist and sexist jokes at a sales meeting. I confronted both of them in our Coral Gables conference room, and they both readily admitted telling these jokes. They insisted they harbored no bias against anyone and were just trying to be funny. Everyone knew they were joking, they insisted, and our society is becoming too politically correct.

I told them anything they said while representing Stiefel Laboratories reflected on the company, and if they ever again told inappropriate jokes at a company meeting, I would have no choice but to terminate them. They nodded, assured me they understood, and thanked me for giving them a second chance. Incomprehensibly, at the very next sales meeting, both men not only told racist and sexist jokes once again, they handed out photocopied sheets with the jokes written on them! Needless to say, they were both fired immediately; to this day, I cannot think of any logical explanation as to why they intentionally committed career suicide in this manner.

Sadly, careers are also sometimes cut short by tragedy. Dennis Sherman was a marketing manager who developed very rapidly-progressing Parkinson's Disease at a very young age. Shortly after he was diagnosed, he was no longer able to work, but our long-term disability insurance did not begin to pay benefits for the first six months. I always thought of my fellow employees as part of the extended Stiefel family, so (with my father's consent) I asked our finance people to continue to pay Dennis his full salary until he qualified for long-term disability payments. Tragically, Dennis had to move into a nursing home almost immediately, and within a couple of years, he passed away. He was a great guy, and I will never forget him.

Another tragic case involved a sales manager I will call Rick. A true gentleman, Rick lived in a nice Miami home located across the street from a park. Late one night, a large group of teenagers was partying loudly in this park, so Rick stepped outside onto his front porch and yelled for the revelers to quiet down so that people could sleep. An unknown assailant threw a rock that struck Rick squarely in the head; horribly, he suffered a severe injury to his brain. I visited him in the hospital, where he was in a coma, and again in his home, where he sat silently and did not seem to know me. No longer able to work, Rick was faced with the same six-month waiting period Dennis Sherman had faced. Once again, we decided to continue paying him his full salary until his disability payments commenced. I saw Rick a few years later working out in the same gym I frequented, and I was surprised and happy that he recognized me.

One of my father's greatest disappointments involved a young man (let's call him Pete) who joined Stiefel as a blue-collar worker right out of high school. Impressed with Pete's intelligence and work ethic, Werner arranged for the company to pay for Pete's college education and promoted him to a job in the front office. Pete performed well, so the company paid for him to earn an advanced degree, promoted him to a senior management position, and gave him a company car. Over time, Pete became one of the highest paid and most respected executives in the entire company, wielding a considerable amount of power and influence. One of my father's most trusted advisors, Pete was almost like a son to Werner.

No one at Stiefel had a company credit card at that time, so we adopted a practice whereby employees traveling on company business could request a "travel advance" (typically a few hundred dollars), so employees did not have to spend their own money and then wait for Stiefel to reimburse them. When these employees filed their expense reports, the amounts they spent were set off against the travel advance, and then either the company or the employee would write a check for the balance. A handful of senior executives (including Pete), however, were given a large "permanent travel advance," so they would never need to advance even a penny of their own money. These permanent advances would never need to be repaid, as long as the executive stayed with Stiefel. One day, as I walked past Pete's office, I noticed on his secretary's desk a request for a $500 travel advance, which had been both requested and approved by Pete.

I was instantly suspicious. Firstly, it is highly inappropriate for an executive to approve a check payable to himself. Secondly, one of the primary purposes for the "permanent travel advance" was to obviate the need to request an ordinary travel advance every time one traveled on company business; Pete's check request was tantamount to double dipping. I could think of no valid reason for what struck me as serious impropriety, so I decided to undertake a secret investigation. I started returning to the office late at night, when the office was closed, and reviewing boxes and boxes of old accounting records. Much to my dismay, these records showed that Pete had been embezzling from the company for years, and the total amount stolen was quite significant.

I initially showed the telltale records to my father, who was visibly stunned. After everything the company had done for Pete, he could not possibly be guilty of such treachery, my father reasoned, and perhaps there was some mistake. We both agreed to involve our corporate auditors, Coopers & Lybrand; after reviewing all the documents I had copied, they confirmed Pete's longstanding embezzlement. The next morning, Werner and I met with Pete in the conference room, confronted him with the stack of evidence, and fired him. He agreed to pay back most of what he had taken by transferring all his retirement benefits, as well as some Stiefel stock he had acquired, back to the company. We had no desire to hurt his family by having him arrested, so we never involved the police. But my father remained devastated someone he had trusted so implicitly could betray him like that.

Sadly, Pete was not the only senior executive whose greed led him astray. Stiefel's House Accounts Division, which manufactured well-known brands for other companies, had always been quite profitable—at least partially due to the extensive industry contacts of its president, whom I will call Ralph. As time passed, however, Ralph began selling more and more of his division's production to a company in New Jersey; and this middle-man (let's call it ABC Company) would then fill and/or package the product, add an additional mark-up, and book the final sale to the owner of the brand. As Stiefel owned its own filling and packaging equipment, several of us within Stiefel questioned the need for a middle-man. Why involve a third party to perform a service that Stiefel could easily perform itself? Why not earn a higher profit by selling directly to the ultimate customer—our standard practice in the past?

Once again, I was suspicious enough to investigate. My theory was Ralph owned part of ABC Company and that he was intentionally diverting Stiefel profits and customers to ABC, with a view toward eventually quitting his job at Stiefel and working there full-time. Initially, I met with buyers at several customers of the House Accounts Division, and they confirmed my suspicion Ralph had suggested involving the middle-man, claiming ABC Company could perform filling and packaging better than Stiefel. I also interviewed several of Ralph's colleagues at Stiefel; Ralph had, unwisely, told one of them of his plan to leave Stiefel and work at ABC. Finally, I called ABC's bank, told them (truthfully) I worked with Ralph, and asked them to fax me a copy of the signature card for ABC's bank account.

Surprisingly, this actually worked! But not surprisingly, Ralph's signature appeared prominently on the card as an authorized signatory on ABC Company's bank account! Late that Friday afternoon, I shared everything I had learned with my father; he immediately decided he would fire Ralph first thing Monday morning. Fate, however, had its own plan for Ralph. The very next day, Ralph flew his Cessna (yes, he owned his own plane) to New Jersey to meet with his partner at ABC Company; shortly after taking off to return home, he was killed in a mid-air collision over Livingston, New Jersey. The National Transportation Safety Board report noted that the Cessna had entered controlled airspace without radioing the tower and also cited "the failure of the pilots to exercise adequate vigilance to detect and avoid each other." To this day, I wonder whether Ralph was distracted that day, because he knew that his scheme was unraveling around him. There is, however, a macabre postscript to this story. Two years before Ralph's death, one of his adoptive sons was jailed for raping and bludgeoning to death a retired editor of the *Reader's Digest*. And two years after the mid-air plane crash, another adopted son killed Ralph's father and critically wounded Ralph's mother before being shot and killed himself by the police.

Unlike Pete and Ralph, the overwhelming majority of my Stiefel colleagues were honest, intelligent and diligent. Many of them were so talented they became CEOs of other pharmaceutical companies after leaving Stiefel. Why did they leave, you might wonder? In most instances, they were recruited away by larger companies offering superior compensation packages. If you are a sports fan, as I am, you have undoubtedly observed some college and professional teams consistently excel year after year. The primary reason for their success, in my opinion, is that these teams have accumulated the most talented collection of players and coaches. But professional teams are restricted in their personnel choices by salary caps and the draft; and college teams are restricted by the number of scholarships available. Businesses, on the other hand, have no such restrictions and are limited only by what they are willing to pay.

Consequently, when I became the CEO of Stiefel Laboratories, I was determined to recruit the most talented and hard-working player for every single position on the Stiefel team. If we could assemble the "dream team" of the pharmaceutical industry, I was confident Stiefel would be successful. My philosophy was to hire people smarter than I was, motivate them, empower them, and then get out of their way. I knew that the company would need to pay higher salaries to recruit the best people, and I was more than willing to do this. I viewed this increased compensation not as an incremental cost decreasing our profits, but rather as an investment that would lead to increased profitability in future years.

Instead of losing our best talent to larger companies, we began recruiting people away from such pharmaceutical industry giants as Allergan, Amgen, Sanofi-Aventis, Bristol-Myers Squibb, Merck, Johnson & Johnson, Schering, Pfizer and GlaxoSmithKline. Adding these new recruits to the wealth of talent already at Stiefel created what I considered to be the best executive team in dermatology. Some of these key individuals are mentioned in other chapters of this book; the backgrounds of the rest of Stiefel's most senior leaders at the time we sold the company are outlined below.

Bill Humphries is one of the most talented pharmaceutical executives I have ever met. He and I have been friends for many years; while he was running the skincare business at Allergan, we always made it a point to get together at dermatology meetings and share our thoughts about news and trends in the industry. Extremely organized and analytical, Bill never failed to impress me with his knowledge and insights. I had wanted for years to recruit him, but every time I prepared to do so, Allergan would promote him again— and I assumed he would not want to leave right after accepting a promotion. Finally, the time was right, and in March 2004, Bill joined Stiefel as our Senior Vice President, Commercial Operations.

He performed so well I eventually promoted him to become our corporate President—the first time anyone outside the family had held that position—and invited him to join our Board of Directors. Bill ran Stiefel for nearly three years after GSK acquired us before accepting a position as President and CEO of Merz Pharmaceuticals. Ultimately, he was recruited by Valeant to run their extensive dermatology business.

I recruited Devin Buckley away from the Pratt & Whitney

division of United Technologies in 1997, the year I stopped serving as General Counsel. A graduate of Yale University and Georgetown Law, Devin is a highly-skilled attorney who believes corporate lawyers should help facilitate sound business deals, rather than kill them by raising an endless list of objections. Devin's philosophy was to point out the legal issues associated with a proposed transaction or course of action, but then work together with the business people to conceive solutions. Stiefel's legal department included several attorneys around the world, and Devin managed all of them as our Senior VP and General Counsel.

How Matt Pattullo came to work for Stiefel is an unusual story. Matt and his wife, Angie, met as undergraduates at the University of Michigan and were working in Connecticut. Angie's parents were close friends of mine in Miami, and they asked if I would give Matt a job so he and their daughter would move there. Through the years, I received dozens of similar requests from dermatologists and other friends, and my practice was always the same—I promised to interview the job candidate, but I cautioned there would be no offer unless we had an opening matching the candidate's skill set. In Matt's case, I conducted a lengthy interview over the phone, and I was highly impressed with Matt's intelligence, personality and willingness to undertake new challenges.

It was 1990, and Stiefel had an opening for a human resources position in Coral Gables, which is part of the greater Miami area. Matt had no HR experience at all, but I had a strong hunch he would learn rapidly, so I offered him the job and he accepted.

While working full-time, Matt earned his MBA from the University of Miami; during his two-decade career at Stiefel, he repeatedly demonstrated his organizational and leadership skills. At various times, Matt ran our global HR group, our risk management group, and our corporate facilities group, saving us millions of dollars in the process. He also served as our Corporate Secretary, arranging and attending all Board meetings and stockholder meetings.

As an aside, the move to Miami also worked out pretty well for Angie. After earning her law degree at the University of Miami, she rose through the ranks at Ernst & Young. As of this writing, Angie is in charge of the tax group for the entire southeast, managing hundreds and hundreds of tax professionals!

We recruited our Chief Scientific Officer away from pharma giant Amgen; he had also previously worked at Schering Plough and Bayer. An infectious diseases physician originally from South Africa, Gavin Corcoran, M.D. is the perfect blend of scientific expertise and business acumen. With his enthusiastic and cooperative personality, Gavin was the perfect choice to coordinate the efforts of all of our researchers around the world. During his tenure at Stiefel, several important new drug applications were approved by the FDA, allowing us to expand dramatically our portfolio of products. Gavin stayed at Stiefel for a year after we were acquired, but other companies recognized his talent. As of this writing, he is the Chief Medical Officer at Allergan.

When I took over as CEO, the company was very fortunate to employ two first-rate finance chiefs—one in the US Division and the other in International. Only one of them could become our new global Chief Financial Officer, and I was conflicted about which one to choose. I had worked more closely with the US individual, so I was initially somewhat biased in her favor. On the other hand, the International person had naturally forged closer relationships with the executives and accountants in our numerous foreign subsidiaries, and the International Division at that time generated nearly 90 percent of our total profits.

Wanting to choose as objectively as possible, I solicited the opinions of every single senior executive who had worked with both of them; I also spoke to our outside auditors and bankers. Overwhelmingly, they recommended the International person, and soon thereafter, Mike Cornelius became Stiefel's CFO. During Mike's tenure, Stiefel closed a number of complicated financial transactions, but Mike handled all this complexity with ease. Intelligent, focused, honest and diligent, his performance was consistently excellent. He left the company a few months after GSK acquired us, but not surprisingly, he almost immediately landed another CFO position.

Having the most talented and best-coached team obviously does not guarantee you will win the championship. Egos, insecurities and personality conflicts all need to be managed; and I often lamented that, like a kindergarten teacher, the most difficult part of my job was "getting the children to play nicely together." Furthermore, injuries, bad luck and outstanding play by your competition are important factors that are essentially beyond your control. But if you have the best talent, the probability of outstanding performance is certainly enhanced. So how well did Stiefel's new "dream team" perform? During my eight years as CEO, the company's worldwide sales quadrupled from $250 million to nearly $1 billion—all due to the efforts of the talented colleagues with whom I had the honor and pleasure of working.

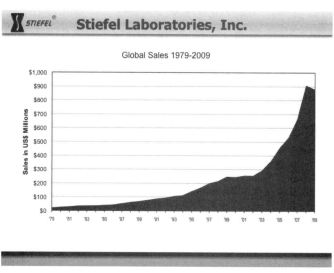

Three decades of Stiefel sales

CHAPTER NINETEEN

TODD AND BRENT — THE SIXTH GENERATION

"There are no secrets to success. It is the result of preparation, hard work, and learning from failure."

— COLIN POWELL

T here is an old adage about family businesses: "The first generation builds the business, the second makes it a success, and the third wrecks it." Or as Andrew Carnegie phrased it, "Shirtsleeves to shirtsleeves in three generations." While this is obviously a gross generalization, it is nevertheless frequently true. According to a 2016 article in *The Economist*, only 30 percent of family businesses survive into the second generation, only 12 percent into the third, and only 3 percent into the fourth. These statistics partially elucidate why the Stiefel saga is so unique. My sons, Todd and Brent, represented the sixth generation of Stiefels to serve in senior management roles at Stiefel Laboratories!

There are numerous theories as to why children of successful business owners often ruin what their ancestors worked so hard to create. One leading theory is that some of these children grow up lacking the ambition and hunger that drove their parents—cursed with an overblown sense of entitlement, they are arrogant and lazy. Or as legendary football coach Barry Switzer put it, "Some people are born on third base and go through life thinking they hit a triple." I am extremely proud of the fact my two sons are exactly the opposite. Firstly, they did not grow up wealthy; secondly, they are both decidedly modest; thirdly, they have always exemplified an exceptionally strong work ethic. In both of my sons, this work ethic manifested itself at an early age.

Throughout their years in school, Brent and Todd were always at the top of their classes academically, despite engaging in numerous extracurricular activities. During the summers, they continued to work hard at outside jobs. In high school, Brent worked at K-Mart and a bowling alley, in addition to umpiring little league baseball games. Brent was a very talented baseball pitcher, scouted by the major leagues, and his college choice was Notre Dame—at least partially because Notre Dame's pitching coach called him every single week during his senior year in high school. In college, Brent worked at Glades Pharmaceuticals for two summers and spent one summer with Network KKO, a concert and event production company in New York City. In addition, he worked as a graphic designer at *The Observer*, Notre Dame's student newspaper. He also played varsity baseball at Notre Dame, and one day he happened to meet a lovely classmate, Courtney Banks, who played varsity soccer on the powerhouse women's soccer team. Brent graduated from Notre Dame in 2000, having majored in Management Information Systems, and married Courtney in 2002. They are the proud parents of daughters Sienna and Tyler.

Todd's high school jobs were cashiering at Winn Dixie, selling Cutco knives, umpiring little league games, and selling magazine subscriptions for the Sierra Club. Todd only applied to one college— Duke University—so my wife and I were very relieved when he was admitted! During his Duke years, he worked every summer at Glades, where he created and implemented a telemarketing system, set up Stiefel's first e-mail server, optimized the pharmacy database, and made sales calls to the small and mid-sized pharmacy chains and drug wholesalers. Todd graduated from Duke in 1997 with a major in psychology and a minor in economics.

Both sons were drawn to the family business, and I told them the company would be lucky to have them, but I recommended they both go through the process of creating a resume and applying for jobs elsewhere. I wanted them to learn how much the marketplace valued their talents and to recognize they had attractive career options beyond Stiefel Laboratories. They both followed my suggestion, and both received job offers at salaries considerably higher than the family business was offering—Todd from IBM, and Brent from Capgemini, a global IT consulting firm. Happily for me, both sons opted to forego the extra money to join the company their great-great-great-grandfather had founded in 1847.

The offer Todd chose to accept was from Brendan Murphy, the president of Glades and Todd's boss for the previous three summers. Glades was headquartered in Atlanta, and Todd worked there as Marketing Manager until late-2001, when I recruited him to join me in Coral Gables as Stiefel's first Director of Strategic Planning. (He brought with him his beautiful bride, Diana Gentry, a scientist and University of Georgia graduate whom he had met in Atlanta. They are happily married with a son, Cole, and a daughter, Amber.)

I had become corporate CEO only a few months earlier, and the challenge I asked Todd to undertake was monumental. The company was 154 years old, yet we had no Mission Statement and had never had a global Strategic Plan. Werner and Herb had provided excellent leadership for the US Division and International Division respectively, but the two divisions had often moved in totally different directions. Clearly, we needed a unified strategy, but with no one within Stiefel knowing how to approach this problem, Todd engaged an outside consultant to help. He also took several executive education classes at Wharton to expand his expertise, earning a Certificate of Professional Development. As he assumed more and more responsibility within the company, he recruited new talent into the department to advance its important function.

One such recruit, Martin Floreani, came to Stiefel from Merck, and he eventually became our Vice President of Global Strategy. Martin is extremely bright, and after leaving the company shortly after GSK acquired us, he went on to become a CEO elsewhere. (Todd too was promoted—first to VP, then Executive VP, before ultimately becoming Chief Strategy Officer, with our Finance, Strategy, Risk Management and Facilities departments all reporting to him.) Striving to develop a plan that would motivate and inspire every employee, Todd and his team solicited input from executives all over the world. Working together, each business unit and corporate function utilized a common format to develop its own strategic plan; these individual plans, once approved, rolled up into the overall corporate plan.

Significantly, the annual strategic plans were integrated with the budgeting process; for the first time ever, the objectives and tactics of all areas and functions were tied not only to their individual budgets, but to the overall corporate budget. Chairing our Enterprise Leadership Team, Todd created an Enterprise Program Management Office to identify, prioritize and approve all significant capital expenditures all over the world. After so many years of being managed as if we were two different companies, it was extraordinarily beneficial to finally have a consistent, disciplined approach to the capital and operating budgeting processes!

With the strategy group driving consensus, we crafted the Stiefel Mission: "The mission of Stiefel Laboratories is to be the world's most valued and respected dermatology-focused specialty pharmaceutical company, improving the quality of human life by providing high-quality, innovative, safe, and effective products for the prevention and treatment of skin diseases." Todd's group also agreed upon and disseminated our corporate values: "To embody and promote honesty, fairness, integrity, enthusiasm, entrepreneurship, excellence and courage."

This positive development was particularly important to me. When making speeches to colleagues within Stiefel, I had frequently showed a slide entitled "Corporate Values" which listed four words in large print—"Communication, Respect, Integrity, Excellence," and I then asked the group if they could guess where I had found this slide. No one ever guessed that those words came directly from the 2000 Annual Report of Enron Corporation, which had declared bankruptcy the following year due to massive internal fraud!

What I emphasized to my colleagues was anyone can write down words on a sheet of paper and claim those words to be their values, but the words are meaningless unless everyone actually lives these values. Within Stiefel Laboratories, Todd's group established a system whereby our mission, vision and values were communicated personally to every single employee in the company by that employee's manager. The goal was for everyone to understand accomplishing our goals was not enough—we also wanted to do it the right way.

When Brent graduated from Notre Dame, he turned down offers from Capgemini and Network KKO (where he had worked one summer) to accept an offer from Stiefel's National Sales Manager to become a sales representative stationed in Denver, Colorado. We still had a relatively small sales force at that time, so Brent's territory was huge, covering Colorado, Utah and Wyoming. He learned a great deal about our products, the competition, and dermatology in general, so after two years, I asked him to join me in Coral Gables as our Business Development Manager.

I was confident Stiefel could grow nicely organically (increasing the sales of our own products) through the efforts of the dream team I was in the process of assembling. But to achieve my goal of becoming a billion-dollar company, we needed to make some significant acquisitions—and for that we needed a very strong business development group. Historically, Stiefel had mostly steered away from acquisitions, primarily because of Werner's zero debt philosophy. We almost deviated from our conservative nature in 1983, when we made a valiant effort to acquire Elder Pharmaceuticals, a small dermatology company focused on selling psoralen products.

Many dermatologists were using PUVA therapy to treat various skin diseases, and PUVA entailed exposing the patient to psoralens (drugs that react with ultraviolet light), followed by ultraviolet A, or UVA. Adding Elder's psoralen products to our existing product line would have been a perfect fit, so my father and I flew to Bryan, Ohio to meet with Tom Elder, the owner and CEO of the company. Tom Elder was very nice, but he struck me as quite eccentric. For example, as he drove us to dinner on a country back road, he suddenly slammed on the brakes, reached into his glove compartment to pull out a loaded handgun, rolled down his window, fired several shots out the car window into a small pond in the middle of an empty field, rolled up the window and placed the gun back in the glove box. Then he just drove on—without ever saying one word!

Perhaps this was his way of warning us he would be a tough negotiator, but we were nevertheless able to reach an agreement that very night, and we shook hands on our deal. The next morning, however, he added one proviso—a significant percentage of the purchase price needed to be paid to an entity in the Cayman Islands. There may have been a very legitimate reason for this request, but neither Werner nor I could think of any reason other than tax evasion; we certainly did not want to be accomplices to that. Consequently, our deal fell apart, as acquisitions so frequently do. Back in Coral Gables, it occurred to me that maybe Tom Elder had experienced seller's remorse and had raised the Caymans issue knowing that it would kill the deal. Whatever his thinking, we were a bit frustrated when he sold his company to a third party less than a year later.

Stiefel's only significant acquisition before Brent's involvement came in 1996, when we purchased Trans Canaderm, our largest competitor in Canada, for approximately $16 million. Dick MacKay and I negotiated that deal, which was huge for us at the time; it solidified our position as the number one dermatology company in Canada for the remainder of our existence as a family business.

We financed this acquisition with a term loan from our bank, which at first blush might seem like a violation of the zero-debt doctrine. Instead, it serves as yet another example of Stiefel being operated as if it were two different companies. Operation ZD (zero debt) was Werner's program, and thus not binding on Herb. Since Trans Canaderm was a Canadian company, this acquisition was handled entirely by the International Division. (I was involved because, as General Counsel, I served both divisions.) My hope when I recruited Brent from the sales force was he would identify more potential opportunities and finalize more licensing and acquisition transactions. What happened exceeded my wildest dreams!

One of Brent's first moves in his new role was to join the Licensing Executives Society (LES), an organization comprised primarily of corporate development people and attorneys interested in licensing and acquisitions. The LES hosts excellent meetings, which not only offer specialized seminars on various aspects of licensing, but also provide numerous opportunities for networking. In fact, I had met Gary Nath, who subsequently became Stiefel's outside patent counsel, at an LES meeting only a few years earlier.

Brent learned a lot from LES, but the complexity of a typical licensing contract convinced him he needed some additional formal education. Consequently, he enrolled in business school at the University of Washington, where he earned an MBA with a focus on finance and global business. Returning to Coral Gables, he began building his department; his first addition was someone strongly recommended by Bill Humphries.

Jim Loerop was (and remains) the consummate corporate development professional, and when Stiefel recruited him in May 2006, he already had nearly 15 years of experience in pharmaceutical licensing. Jim and Brent worked extremely well together, and they talked about potential deals so frequently, at all hours of the day and night, they joked it was almost like having a second spouse. Between them, they knew virtually every business development person in dermatology; Jim, through his years of closing deals, was on a first-name basis with the players at all the major investment banks.

Jim also knew from experience exactly what steps a company should take anytime it even considers a potential acquisition; we immediately adopted Jim's recommendations (which follow) as our standard practice. Firstly, since confidentiality is always so vitally important, we should give each project a code name, involve only those individuals with a need to know, and maintain a list of everyone who knows about the project. Secondly, we should engage an outside expert (usually, but not always, an investment bank) to advise and assist us when considering a potential business transaction. Thirdly, if discussions advance far enough to involve attorneys, choose a law firm with lots of experience doing M&A (mergers and acquisitions) work. And finally, everyone with knowledge of the project should be cautioned to maintain absolute secrecy about the project until such time, if ever, as an acquisition agreement is signed—at which time a formal public announcement is made.

Maintaining this strict confidentiality is even more critically important if the stock of one of the companies involved is publicly traded, because in that event, news of a possible acquisition could impact the stock price and trigger potential violations of federal securities laws. We were reminded of this danger shortly after we completed our first major acquisition later that year.

Connetics Corporation was a publicly-traded dermatology company based in California; with sales (just in the United States) exceeding $200 million, their US sales were almost as high as ours. Consequently, I initially was shocked when Brent and Jim suggested we try to acquire a company that large. Obviously, the price tag would be enormous, so even if we could raise enough money (which seemed questionable), the deal would entail a significant amount of risk. On the other hand, I have always maintained that "the nature of business is risk," and this acquisition made sense in several regards.

Firstly, Connetics enjoyed an excellent reputation among dermatologists. Secondly, their products were complementary to Stiefel's products, rather than competitive. Thirdly, their sales were entirely in North America, so we could potentially increase sales dramatically by leveraging their product portfolio into our global footprint. Lastly, Connetics not only marketed a strong portfolio of existing products, they also owned the rights to some excellent drug delivery technology we could employ in future products. Connetics had just licensed its elegant foam delivery system to Pfizer for use in its well-known Rogaine® Foam for hair loss, and another big pharma company was utilizing the Connetics liquid patch technology in a product for the treatment of onychomycosis (nail fungus).

Still uncertain as to whether we could afford to make this acquisition, we nevertheless engaged the investment banking group at Deutsche Bank to advise us. Working together, we created detailed financial models examining the impact of a potential deal utilizing three different scenarios—optimistic, pessimistic and realistic. We analyzed the history of their stock price and determined how much of a premium over the current stock price we could afford to pay and still achieve a positive return on our investment. We studied other recent acquisitions in the specialty pharma sector (which includes dermatology), and we considered which other companies might try to outbid us for Connetics. The Deutsche Bank investment banking group introduced us to their debt group and their private equity group; the final conclusion was acquiring Connetics should be extremely beneficial to Stiefel, if we could strike a deal at or below a specific price target.

Furthermore, Deutsche Bank agreed to help us finance this deal, either entirely with debt or via a combination of private equity and debt. It was time to retain a law firm with an excellent M&A group, and after careful consideration, we chose Willkie, Farr & Gallagher, a highly-regarded New York firm with offices in several other countries. The Willkie attorneys proved to be so talented and so diligent that we asked them to represent us in every one of our subsequent deals.

The Deutsche Bank and Willkie teams both echoed Jim Loerop's advice that we create a code name for our project to acquire Connetics, and we chose the name "Project Clear." Thereafter, everyone used the name "Clear" instead of "Connetics" in both oral and written communications. Personally, I found this cloak-and-dagger practice to be sort of fun, but more importantly, it served as a constant reminder of Deutsche Bank's and Willkie's strong advice we use maximum efforts always to preserve confidentiality when dealing with M&As.

We needed to take particular caution when dealing with Connetics—their stock was publicly-traded on the NASDAQ, so any rumors about an acquisition offer could impact their stock price. Consequently, our deal team included only those few individuals who absolutely needed to be involved, and we maintained a list of everyone who knew about Project Clear. Our first approach to Connetics was via a phone call from me to Tom Wiggans, the Chairman and CEO of Connetics, and I made him a verbal offer lower than what we would be willing to pay, but not so low it would be rejected out of hand. Tom Wiggans was (and is) the consummate pharmaceutical executive and he became a good and trusted friend.

Tom told me he would discuss our offer with his Board of Directors and revert back to me. Extensive negotiations ensued, and eventually we agreed on an all-cash deal whereby Stiefel would pay $17.50 for each share of Connetics stock—a price representing a 62 percent premium over their average stock price for the previous four weeks. Clearly this was a great deal for Tom's shareholders, and with a total acquisition price of $666.1 million, it was a game-changing deal for Stiefel Laboratories.

Public companies typically do not disclose any information about pending acquisition negotiations until a definitive contract is signed, at which time the negotiations are deemed by the SEC to be material enough to mandate disclosure. Consequently, once we signed our contract in October 2006, both Connetics and Stiefel issued press releases announcing our deal. In reality, however, the deal was nowhere near final, because we still needed the Federal Trade Commission to review this potential acquisition from an antitrust perspective. Fortunately, we overcame this hurdle relatively easily; on December 28, 2006, we successfully closed what was by far the largest transaction in the history of our company.

Parenthetically, not long after this closing, NASDAQ sent us a list of all individuals who had purchased Connetics stock shortly before our deal was announced, and they asked us to identify any names on this list we recognized. Much to our surprise, one of these purchasers was a gentleman who worked in our finance department! This person was not part of our deal team, but he had come across confidential information about our plans one night while working late. It turned out this person had not only purchased Connetics stock himself, he also shared our secret plans with a few friends who also purchased stock!

Once our deal was announced, the stock price skyrocketed, and they all made a hefty profit. Naturally, we terminated this finance person, and we all assumed that the SEC would prosecute him for what seemed like an open-and-shut case of insider trading. I subsequently learned, however, that this did not happen. Why not, you might wonder? A securities expert speculated to me the SEC likes to make headlines and prosecute cases that can jump-start the careers of staff attorneys; the dollars involved in this particular case were simply too small to satisfy those criteria.

Over the next two years, Brent Stiefel, Jim Loerop and the rest of their Corporate Development team looked at dozens (if not hundreds) of other opportunities, but typically, only a tiny percentage of business development opportunities considered actually result in a finalized deal. Frequently, Stiefel lost interest after learning the confidential details about a particular product or company; sometimes we were outbid by a competitor; other times our prospective business partner was not interested in pursuing a deal on our terms.

Although some people view corporations as ruthless and motivated solely by profits, we walked away from one potential deal for humanitarian reasons. DUSA Pharmaceuticals had pioneered the use of photodynamic therapy in dermatology, and Stiefel strongly believed that DUSA was an excellent acquisition target. We made two offers to acquire DUSA (another public company) at prices vastly exceeding their stock price, but each time our offer was summarily rejected without any negotiation.

The lawyers from Willkie explained how we could attempt a hostile takeover, and we felt that our probability of success was high. We were in the process of deciding whether or not to "go hostile" when I learned my friend Dr. Geoffrey Shulman, a Toronto dermatologist and the founder of DUSA, had recently been afflicted with a virulent form of abdominal cancer. I did not have the heart to add to Geoff's stress level, so I told the Willkie and Stiefel teams to discontinue our efforts to acquire Geoff's company. Geoff passed away four years later, in 2012, and later that year, DUSA was acquired by another company. DUSA would have been a great strategic fit for Stiefel, but I have never once regretted my decision to stand down.

Notwithstanding my interference in this particular matter and the aggressive competition for any valuable asset in dermatology, Brent and Jim successfully negotiated several other important deals for Stiefel—including two of particular strategic importance. Throughout its history, Stiefel had focused primarily on medical dermatology; but for an ever-increasing percentage of dermatologists, aesthetics represented a vitally important part of their practice. Neurotoxins like Botox® and dermal fillers such as Juvéderm® and Restylane® were enjoying immense popularity; yet Stiefel had no presence whatsoever in this lucrative aesthetic device sector.

This all changed in May 2008, when we acquired two French companies (ABR Invent and ABR Development) that had developed a dermal filler called Atlèan®. Atlèan was already on the market in Europe, and we planned to move aggressively to seek approval in the United States and elsewhere. Atlèan comprised particles of tricalcium phosphate (which stimulated the production of new collagen in the treated area) suspended in a hyaluronic acid gel; and we planned to develop an entire line of fillers bearing the Atlèan trademark. The principals of ABR were experts in filler technology, having previously developed a popular filler called Sculptra®, and they believed Atlèan and its future line extensions could become the most popular line of dermal fillers in the world.

Three months after the ABR deal, Stiefel acquired another public company called Barrier Therapeutics (Project Bengal) for approximately $148 million. Barrier had some excellent products already on the market, but what attracted us most was their pipeline, which contained some potential blockbusters. The atmosphere at Stiefel was electric. The March 31, 2008 fiscal year had been the best in company history, with sales exceeding $912 million; our product portfolio was both popular and diverse; we believed our research pipeline was the best in dermatology. The future looked incredibly bright.

I mentioned earlier in this chapter the promotions my son Todd had earned during his tenure with the company. The success of the Corporate Development group led to a series of similar promotions for my son Brent—first to Vice President, then to Executive VP, and ultimately to a C-suite position. As Chief of Pharmaceutical Operations, Brent was responsible not only for Corporate Development, but also for R&D and Supply Chain (which included manufacturing, logistics and distribution). But as fate would have it, several of Todd's and Brent's most significant contributions to Stiefel Laboratories had nothing whatsoever to do with their job titles.

In August 2002, Todd and Brent were elected to Stiefel's Board of Directors, filling the vacancies created by my father and his wife Marie after my dad retired. For more than a decade, our corporate bylaws had authorized the Board to create an Executive Committee vested with the authority to manage the affairs of the company between Board meetings, but the Board had never seen the need to activate such a committee. Everything changed on December 20, 2006—eight days before we closed the Connetics acquisition— when I was diagnosed with advanced stage metastatic head and neck cancer.

It was devastating news that became even scarier when, a few days later, the newspapers reported the death of NASCAR champion Bobby Hamilton, who lived only eleven months after receiving the same diagnosis I had just received. Immediately, I started researching the best place to be treated. I visited the Sylvester Cancer Center near my home in Miami, as well as Beth Israel and Memorial Sloan Kettering in New York. Each cancer center recommended a different course of treatment—which was very disconcerting, since I had no way of knowing which option was best.

Discouraged, Daneen and I were about to fly home to Miami when my friend Steve Mandy (Miami Beach dermatologist and co-founder of DVM) called to advise he had made an appointment for me the next day at MD Anderson Cancer Center in Houston, and he strongly recommended we fly there immediately. My dad had once warned me about the danger of "spending too much time sharpening the axe and not enough time chopping wood," and I really wanted to start treatment somewhere rather than continue to investigate different cancer centers. But Steve told me of a friend who had been cured at M.D. Anderson, and after our initial visit there the next day, Daneen and I made the difficult decision to seek a cure in Houston—far away from our home, our children and grandchildren, most of our friends, and my office.

The best-case scenario would cause me to miss a lot of time from work, and I did not even want to think about the worst-case scenario. It was vital someone at Stiefel be empowered to make important decisions while I was indisposed, so the Board of Directors appointed Todd, Brent and me to the Executive Committee—with only two votes needed to make a decision. This proved to be an excellent move, because I hit every imaginable speed bump over the next several months.

My treatment regimen began with six weeks of induction chemotherapy, utilizing two different cancer drugs. Except for losing my hair, I tolerated these drugs extremely well; since my infusions were only once per week, I commuted back and forth between Houston and Coral Gables while continuing to work full-time. For the next phase of therapy, Daneen and I moved to Houston for two months, so that I could undergo six more weeks of chemo plus six weeks of almost daily radiation. I have always prided myself on being a very stoic patient, with a high tolerance for pain and discomfort; but these radiation treatments were no fun at all! I was fitted for a plastic mask that was molded precisely in the shape of my face; and to receive the radiation, I had to lie face up on a metal table, with my face mask screwed down so that I could not move. Before donning the mask, I had to insert into my mouth a heavy custom-fitted radiation stent comprised of lead and other materials and designed to protect my tongue and other non-cancerous tissue from the radiation. This stent did not bother me during my initial treatments, but it caused me to gag frequently during the last few weeks. I lost my sense of taste after my very first treatment and did not regain it until about nine months after I completed therapy. During my time in Houston, I spent a few days in the cardiac intensive care unit after developing a pulmonary embolism (both cancer and chemotherapy are risk factors for PE), and three weeks later I was hospitalized again with a dangerously high fever and a mouth filled with radiation sores.

Eventually, I could not eat at all, so for four months, my sole nourishment was via a feeding tube. I developed third degree burns on my neck, but (like so many other times in my life) dermatologists came to the rescue—particularly MD Anderson's Sharon Hymes. My heart was always racing erratically (I developed atrial fibrillation immediately after the feeding tube was connected), so sleep was nearly impossible; and I could barely talk above a whisper. MD Anderson's Head and Neck Center has a tradition whereby patients "ring the bell" after their final radiation treatment. Daneen brought a bottle of champagne so that we could toast the occasion when I rang the bell—and celebrating with us was my close friend, Houston dermatologist Margaret Waisman. My mouth was burned raw from the radiation, so the champagne felt like I was drinking sulfuric acid; but I relished every drop!

As fate would have it, however, my ordeal was not yet over. Daneen and I moved back to Miami in May 2007, but when we returned for my very first checkup the following month, it was discovered (completely unrelated to the cancer for which I had just been treated) I also had thyroid cancer. My surgeon (Randal Weber), my medical oncologist (Merrill Kies), and my radiation oncologist (David Rosenthal) had been weighing the pros and cons of surgically removing some lymph nodes in my neck; but now that a thyroidectomy was necessary anyway, Dr. Weber performed a neck dissection at the same time, removing 27 lymph nodes in the process. The surgery went perfectly, and thankfully, there was no evidence of cancer in any of these lymph nodes. Back in Miami, however, a cardiologist who was justifiably concerned about my pulmonary embolism prescribed two different blood thinners simultaneously. Nearly four weeks had passed since my surgery in Houston, so one would expect that this would be a safe move; but unfortunately, I developed a massive hematoma in my neck that required emergency surgery. The operation was successful; but due to the two neck surgeries, I could not lift my right arm normally and I also developed significant lymphedema. These issues were not serious, but they required months of physical therapy to remedy. My final cancer treatment was in February 2009, when radioactive iodine was administered to kill any lingering thyroid cancer cells. I hit a few other speed bumps after that, but I was finally out of the woods. Many years have now elapsed since my last cancer treatment, and I have officially been deemed a "survivor." Eternally grateful, Daneen and I endowed a Professor Chair at MD Anderson in honor of the three wonderful physicians (named above) who cured my cancers and literally saved my life. And subsequently, we decided to endow the entire head and neck center, in an effort to increase cure rates and improve patient outcomes for future generations.

In a book about Stiefel Laboratories, why do I share the gory details of my bout with cancer? The point is that not only did I miss a great deal of time from the office, but there were numerous instances when I was not even able to participate in phone calls.

I did manage to keep up reasonably well via e-mail, but Todd and Brent (wearing their Executive Committee hats) stepped up to do most of the heavy lifting. They represented Stiefel Laboratories at numerous face-to-face meetings I otherwise would have attended, and they kept the company moving in a positive direction. Their most important accomplishment, however, was the negotiation of the Blackstone deal.

When we acquired Connetics in December 2006, our original plan had been to finance the deal with a combination of private equity and debt. With Deutsche Bank advising us, we ran a process whereby we interviewed nine private equity firms, solicited preliminary, non-binding bids from five of them, and then made detailed management presentations to three finalists— Blackstone, Apax and TA Associates.

Then we made a critical mistake. We chose Blackstone as the winner of our process—the firm with which we would attempt to negotiate a final contract—and we duly notified all three firms of our decision. We thought this was the most honorable way to proceed, because we did not want to waste the time of the two firms not selected; nor did we want to waste our own time. The problem was once Blackstone knew they were no longer part of a competitive process, they could negotiate much more stringently on every contractual point.

Fortunately, we had kept open the option to finance the Connetics transaction entirely with debt. Deutsche Bank had assembled a consortium of banks willing to lend us all of the money we needed. We continued to negotiate with Blackstone until five days before the Connetics closing, at which point I notified them we were terminating discussions. Instead, we borrowed $773 million from the Deutsche Bank consortium. This term loan was divided into two tiers—a first tier of $623 million with an interest rate of LIBOR + 2.25 percent, and a second tier of $150 million bearing interest at LIBOR + 5 percent. At that time,

Todd Stiefel (left) and Brent Stiefel

LIBOR (the London Interbank Offered Rate) exceeded 5 percent, which meant that the interest rate on the second tier of our loan was more than 10 percent. Although we were very happy with Deutsche Bank, we wanted to pay off that second tier as quickly as possible; and we also wanted enough cash to fund additional acquisitions. Consequently, while I was away being treated for cancer, Brent and Todd reopened discussions with Blackstone and TA Associates and held several meetings with each firm. This time, they informed the two firms they intended to negotiate contractual terms with both of them simultaneously, and Stiefel would sign the first contract containing terms we deemed favorable to us.

This tactic placed pressure on Blackstone and TA to make concessions, and to do so before we signed with the competition. It worked. Both private equity firms made bids superior to what they had offered only a few months earlier, and in August 2007, we finalized a deal with Blackstone whereby they invested $500 million in exchange for shares of a newly-created convertible preferred stock.

This infusion of cash was precisely what Stiefel needed! We immediately paid off the second tier of our term loan and added the remaining $350 million to the cash line on our balance sheet. Having this cash enabled us to pay for the Barrier and ABR acquisitions and still have a healthy amount of cash left over. Thanks to the hard work and business acumen of Todd and Brent, Stiefel Laboratories was able to continue moving aggressively toward its goal of becoming a one-billion-dollar company.

CHAPTER TWENTY

GROWING ORGANICALLY

*"There is only one boss. The customer. And he can fire everybody
in the company from the chairman on down,
simply by spending his money somewhere else."*
— SAM WALTON

The acquisitions we made during my tenure as CEO obviously contributed significantly to the company's overall growth. But the majority of our sales increases emanated from organic growth—increased sales from Stiefel's own product lines. A healthy percentage of these sales increases came from our acne gel, Duac®—the best-selling product in the history of our company.

When I became CEO in May 2001 (two months into our 2002 fiscal year), I was immediately confronted with a major business challenge. Our worldwide sales had been stuck at approximately $250 million for four consecutive years, and most of our hopes for emerging from this rut were tied to Duac. As you may recall from Chapter 15, however, our New Drug Application for Duac had been stuck in the morass of FDA bureaucracy for five years; we had no idea when or if our NDA would ever be approved.

Making matters much worse, Dermik's product Benzaclin®, with a nearly identical formulation, had been approved fifteen months earlier and was already on the market, growing rapidly. Dermik was owned by Aventis (which became Sanofi-Aventis two years later), a French pharmaceutical giant approximately 75 times our size. At that time, Stiefel employed 34 medical sales representatives in the United States—a number that had remained unchanged for over two decades—while Dermik employed about six times that number. If Duac did get approved and we went head to head with Dermik, how could we compete against their nearly identical product with a significantly smaller sales force?

We were faced with a very difficult decision. It takes a long time to recruit and train a new sales representative, and it typically takes several months (at a minimum) for sales reps to meet all the doctors in their territories and become truly effective. If we did not dramatically increase the size of our sales force immediately, we would not be prepared to compete with Dermik if Duac received approval. On the other hand, if we did expand our sales force and the FDA did not approve Duac, we would be forced to eat the enormous incremental cost of the larger sales force—which would have severely impacted our bottom line.

I decided to take the risk. Over the next several months, we hired and trained 115 additional sales representatives, as well as some new sales and marketing executives. Fortunately, the gamble paid off. In August 2002, Duac was approved in the United States, and, thanks to our expanded sales and marketing team, we took market share from Benzaclin every year thereafter. To improve our sales reps' productivity, we purchased a state-of-the-art sales force automation system, whereby the details of every single sales call were tracked and transmitted to sales management.

We also purchased the best available data on physician prescribing practices, thereby enabling our reps to concentrate their efforts on the doctors with the most potential to prescribe Stiefel products. These prescribing data were also utilized to develop a new bonus system which provided both greater accountability and greater bonus potential for our sales force. Our enhanced sales muscle helped our entire product line, not just

Duac, and after Bill Humphries joined our team in March 2004, we became even more of a force in dermatology. During my first four years as CEO, Stiefel's US sales nearly tripled and total worldwide sales more than doubled—and this was before any of our major acquisitions. Doctors began to take notice.

Early in my tenure as CEO, we assembled a focus group of dermatologists to ascertain how Stiefel Laboratories was perceived. The results were both disappointing and disconcerting. Dermatologists felt Stiefel was "sort of like a boring next-door neighbor, who's a nice, honest guy you can count on to bring in your newspaper, but who's not very interesting or exciting." We were considered to be a "very conservative company" with an effective, but somewhat mundane, product line—a company that one would expect to be a follower rather than a leader or innovator. I was really surprised because over the years, Stiefel had pioneered a number of "firsts" in dermatology. But for some reason, we were not receiving the recognition I thought we deserved.

You may recall one of my goals when I became CEO was for Stiefel to become the largest and most respected company in dermatology. Clearly our corporate image was sorely in need of repair! To enhance our visibility and elevate our reputation within both the dermatology community and the pharmaceutical industry in general, the company implemented a number of programs, a few of which are the following:

1. Recognizing many job applicants, customers, and potential business partners derive their first impression about a company from its website, we retained a team of professional designers to modernize our corporate website and enhance its content, appearance and user-friendliness. In addition, several product-specific websites were developed, including www.duacgel.com, which won a highly-coveted award within the pharmaceutical industry.

2. We established a Corporate Advisory Board comprised of several of the most influential dermatologists in the United States. Separate advisory boards were established for each of our three most important products.

3. We started donating important dermatology textbooks to every single dermatology resident in the country each year.

4. We initiated several other special programs for residents, including "The Miami Review," an on-line tutorial to assist them in preparing for their boards.

5. Stiefel became the sole sponsor of all supplements to the Blue Journal.

6. In conjunction with the American Society of Dermatologic Surgery, we sponsored a writing competition for residents with a particular interest in cutaneous surgery.

7. Stiefel became the sole sponsor of a new American Academy of Dermatology televised program entitled, "Your Skin, A Health Guide for Hispanic Americans."

8. Stiefel became a major presence at virtually every dermatology meeting in the world. A much larger, more modern, and more efficient exhibit booth was designed and constructed for use at the annual meeting of the American Academy of Dermatology. No longer were there separate, smaller booths for the International Division and the US Division.

9. We dramatically increased our product sampling in physician offices and the quantity and quality of advertisements we placed in medical journals.

10. All across the country, we hosted dinners at which I would make a presentation to several dozen dermatologists about the history of Stiefel Laboratories and our aspirations for the future.

The above changes definitely made a positive impression on the dermatology community. In March 2005, we assembled another focus group, and once again we inquired about Stiefel's corporate image. This time, the group overwhelmingly rated us as the dermatology company that was "the most dynamic and rapidly-changing" and concluded that Stiefel was "the company to watch."

I loved growing up in the rural hamlet of Oak Hill, New York, and the company never encountered a problem finding skilled, hard-working people to work in our manufacturing plant there. Unfortunately, however, recruiting scientists to work across the parking lot at Stiefel Research Institute was an ongoing challenge. At every meeting of the SRI Board of Directors, President Dan Nicolai would report the number of scientists he had succeeded in hiring versus the number who had left; and oftentimes we lost more people than we added. Compounding this problem was the issue of the talented people we did have spending much of their time doing work for outside customers, rather than concentrating their efforts on advancing our own research projects.

To me, the lifeblood of a pharmaceutical company is its pipeline of new products; so in February 2004, the Stiefel board voted (at my recommendation) that thenceforth, SRI would cease performing research and development work for anyone other than Stiefel Laboratories. Recruiting scientific personnel to Oak Hill remained an issue, however, so our head of R&D recommended we find a new location in the United States to become our global research and development headquarters. We engaged a consultant to help us identify the optimum location, and after considering a myriad of factors, we narrowed our choices to a handful of geographic areas—one of which was Research Triangle Park, North Carolina.

By fortuitous circumstance, pharmaceutical giant Eli Lilly had recently built a new, state-of-the-art research facility in Research Triangle Park to pursue a project they subsequently decided to discontinue. The campus was ideal for our needs, with ample room for future expansion; since Eli Lilly was highly motivated to sell, we were able to conclude the purchase at a price representing a fraction of what it would have cost us to build such a facility. And, as a bonus, we convinced Lilly to throw in all the expensive laboratory equipment in the building!

We continued to utilize the SRI complex in Oak Hill for other purposes, but we transferred a number of scientists to North Carolina, where we were able to recruit a wealth of new talent. Our future Chief Scientific Officer, Dr. Gavin Corcoran, moved there too; over the next few years, Gavin's team successfully achieved FDA approval of a number of new dermatological drugs.

As our sales grew, so did our global headcount—from 2200 employees in 2002 to nearly 4000 in 2008. Consequently, in 2006, we recruited Steve Karasick to manage both Human Resources and the newly-created function of Organizational Development on a worldwide basis. I first met Steve when he was consulting for us on a special project, and he immediately impressed me with his intelligence (he had been a Morehead Scholar at the University of North Carolina at Chapel Hill), his insight, and his enthusiasm. Steve is extremely honest and sincere, and since he genuinely loves people, he hit the ground running in his new role.

Steve and I wanted to make Stiefel a place where employees would want to spend their entire careers, and we wanted people to be treated equitably and consistently in all of our subsidiaries across the globe. Since becoming CEO, I had already implemented numerous changes in this regard, including adding a paid holiday (Martin Luther King Day); adding more vacation and sick days; enhancing medical, dental and eye-care insurance coverage for employees and their families; increasing our 401(k) matching contributions; increasing the size of our annual Employee Stock Bonus Plan contribution; and improving employee life insurance and disability insurance benefits. I had also changed company policy so benefits that previously had been available only to spouses of married employees would thereafter be available to partners of unmarried employees—including same-sex partners.

I thought that Stiefel's new enhanced fringe benefits package compared favorably to that of our competitors, but when we acquired Connetics in December 2006, I learned I was wrong. Connetics offered several benefits Stiefel did not, whereas we offered only a couple they did not. Steve Karasick engaged a top benefits consultant, Towers Perrin (now Towers Watson), to compare the two companies' benefit packages and make recommendations as to how Stiefel could improve. Pursuant to these recommendations, we adopted a new global compensation philosophy, whereby the target compensation for every employee worldwide would be the 60th percentile (significantly above average) among all pharmaceutical companies.

Historically, only sales people and senior managers had been eligible for a bonus (I was ineligible for the first 16 years of my time with Stiefel), so we implemented a program whereby hundreds of additional employees became eligible. We took care to ensure the bonus criteria lined up with corporate and individual objectives. One of Towers Perrin's strongest recommendations was to merge our 401(k) and our Employee Stock Bonus Plan into one plan, with Stiefel stock being just one of many investment options the employee could choose. The ultimate goal was to offer our people greater flexibility and control over how their retirement money was being invested.

To effect this goal, Towers Perrin emphasized that we needed to amend our ESBP to allow employees to sell some of the Stiefel shares in their accounts annually—not just when they left the company. We learned this diversification option would be legally mandated if we were a public company, but in the post-Enron era, it was strongly recommended for every company with an ESBP. Towers Perrin made a number of other recommendations, including creating a new Long-Term Incentive plan, and we adopted essentially all of them.

Other changes were happening simultaneously. Bill Humphries, who was managing our entire worldwide sales and marketing effort, further increased the size of our US sales force. With 255 medical sales reps and 30 managers divided among 4 different sales forces, we gained the ability to promote all our key products to the doctors simultaneously. Bill also took steps to ensure our promotional message was consistent from country to country, and he recommended increased marketing spend in subsidiaries where he felt we would realize a return on this investment.

With the global regulatory environment becoming increasingly complex, we hired a seasoned compliance expert, Jeff Klimaski, who became our first ever Chief Compliance Officer. Integrating our US Division and International Division into one unified company necessitated investing millions of dollars in infrastructure; but we were growing rapidly and generating the cash flow needed to cover these expenditures. Our fiscal year ending on March 31, 2008 was by far the best in company history. Our sales had nearly quadrupled in six years, and with US revenues finally exceeding foreign revenues, one of my primary goals had been achieved. And perhaps even more exciting was our forecast for the coming year projecting Stiefel would reach a milestone that had seemed out of the realm of possibility only a few years earlier—exceeding one billion dollars in annual sales!

CHAPTER TWENTY-ONE

BAD LUCK AND THE GLOBAL ECONOMIC COLLAPSE

"September and October of 2008 was the worst financial crisis in global history, including the Great Depression."
— BEN BERNANKE

A las, it was not to be! As we observed earlier in this book, a company's fortunes can often be influenced by circumstances totally outside its control—sometimes by world events, other times by simple bad luck. When we acquired Connetics in December 2006, most of their present and future products were based on their proprietary foam technology, and this important technology was protected by a series of patents. Naturally, given the high price Stiefel was paying, we conducted extensive due diligence to ensure this patent portfolio was valid and enforceable. We retained two different highly-regarded patent law firms to review the history of these patents and render an opinion on them; both firms opined the Connetics patents were very strong.

These opinions were critically important to us, given Perrigo, a leading generic company, had already challenged the validity of these patents (generic companies routinely challenge patents as part of their business model), and litigation was pending between Connetics and Perrigo. I distinctly recall being on a conference call in early-2007 with the attorney representing us in this lawsuit (which we took over from Connetics), and he expressed great confidence we would prevail. Then, on April 30, 2007, everything changed. The United States Supreme Court, in the case of *KSR International Co. v. Teleflex, Inc.*, changed the decades-old standards used in determining whether a patent claim is "obvious."

Without getting into the legal nuances, suffice it to say that this game-changing case suddenly made it much more likely Perrigo would succeed in invalidating the Connetics patents. Another phone call with our patent counsel ensued, and this time, he strongly urged us to settle. I inquired about our chances of success if we did not settle, and his answer was painfully straightforward—we would almost certainly lose the case. Perrigo had already developed a generic equivalent of our third leading product, Olux® (a so-called "superpotent" topical corticosteroid foam), and this generic was approved by the FDA in March 2008. As you might, correctly, assume, we could not settle the lawsuit without allowing Perrigo to launch this product. We attempted to minimize the damage by having our Glades subsidiary launch an authorized generic of Olux, but we still took a huge hit.

From March 2008 to March 2009, sales of Olux dropped from $67 million to $15 million! And this was just one of our foam products. The Supreme Court's ruling threatened all of them—some more than others because of the different patents involved—and our competitive intelligence sources advised us Perrigo was already working to genericize our other foam products. Overnight, the value of what we had purchased in our Connetics acquisition had decreased dramatically.

Meanwhile, the economy was encountering problems of its own. The collapse of prestigious investment bank Bear Stearns in March 2008 heralded the beginning of what Ben Bernanke, former

Chairman of the Federal Reserve, called "the worst financial crisis in global history, including the Great Depression." In September of that same year, financial giant Lehman Brothers declared bankruptcy—the largest bankruptcy filing in the history of the world. Less than two weeks later, Washington Mutual went under, marking the largest traditional bank failure in American history. Numerous other banks followed, as did automotive giants General Motors and Chrysler. In total, more than 2.5 million individuals and approximately 133,300 companies filed for bankruptcy in 2008 and 2009. The banks that managed to survive significantly tightened their lending criteria, and the credit markets essentially dried up.

How, you might wonder, did this global financial crisis impact Stiefel Laboratories? Firstly, in any recession, consumers tend to reduce their discretionary spending, and (unfortunately for us) many individuals consider dermatology products to be non-essential. Consequently, although Stiefel sales remained surprisingly strong in the fiscal year ending March 31, 2009, we fell short of our budgeted sales number in every one of our top ten subsidiaries. Not only did we fail to hit our billion-dollar sales forecast, global sales actually declined by $25 million from the previous year!

Secondly, the company had planned to continue making strategic acquisitions, but the severe credit crunch rendered it extremely difficult for us to secure the necessary financing for any major deal. Finally, and most importantly, the global financial crisis totally changed the dynamic of our banking relationships. To clarify, every time Stiefel ever borrowed money from a commercial bank, the loan agreement contained various covenants requiring us to maintain specific financial ratios. This is a standard banking practice, and it had never before been a concern for us. Throughout the years, there were many times when we expected to breach one of these loan covenants, but since our banks were always eager to keep our business, they would immediately fax us a waiver.

Our loan agreement with the Deutsche Bank consortium

contained two significant loan covenants—a minimum interest coverage ratio (EBITDA divided by total interest expense) of 2.75, and a maximum net leverage ratio (net debt divided by EBITDA) of 3.75. (EBITDA, short for Earnings Before Interest, Taxes, Depreciation and Amortization, is a measure of a company's performance that many financial experts consider more significant than net income.) In November of 2008, Stiefel's finance people projected we were going to breach both of these covenants in the near future. As noted above, this would not have been a concern for us in the past, but in the midst of a global credit crisis, it presented a problem of enormous magnitude. We still enjoyed a close association with Deutsche Bank, but we had no relationship whatsoever with the other banks in the consortium.

We knew if we could obtain a waiver at all, it would come at an extremely high price; with so many companies failing, the more likely scenario would be the banks refusing to issue a waiver. In that event, Stiefel breaching a loan covenant would entitle the bank consortium to declare our entire loan due and payable immediately. And since our total debt exceeded our total cash by more than $400 million, there was no way we could have paid off this loan. We would have been forced into bankruptcy!

Clearly, we needed to act urgently and do everything within our power to avoid breaching a loan covenant. Both our key financial ratios were based on EBITDA, so increasing EBITDA became our top priority. To increase EBITDA, we needed either to increase sales or decrease expenses. As we were already trying our best to increase sales, it became imperative to focus on reducing our expenses. Immediately, I announced a corporate austerity program whereby we froze virtually all corporate travel (except for sales personnel); halted any new hiring; directed all functional managers to eliminate all spending that was not mission-critical; cancelled plans for a new global headquarters in Coral Gables; and even eliminated our traditional holiday parties around the world.

I appointed Dick MacKay and Martin Floreani to head a task force (comprised of numerous senior managers) in charge of making further recommendations, and with speed befitting the urgency of our situation, they submitted a comprehensive report code-named Project CREO (Corporate Restructuring for EBITDA Optimization) six days later. The report contained both short-term and long-term measures, the most painful of which was that Stiefel engage in its first ever global layoff—eliminating 114 positions the first week in December, with plans for a further reduction in force the following year.

My personal policy was to avoid layoffs if at all possible, so this was a very depressing time for me—particularly since a few of the positions eliminated were held by individuals with years of service to the company. Only eight months earlier, we had recorded the best year in company history; now we were seriously worried about going out of business. I asked our finance people for daily reports on where we stood with respect to breaching our loan covenants.

Simultaneously, we were pursuing several other courses of action. Our debt was trading at 25 percent below its face value, so we tried to buy back some of our own debt from the Deutsche Bank consortium. Unfortunately, such an action required the unanimous consent of every bank in the consortium, and one bank refused to consent. We approached Blackstone to ascertain if they would be willing to invest more money, but due to the probability we would breach a loan covenant, Blackstone had written down the value of their $500 million investment in Stiefel by 30 percent. They now deemed us to be an "impaired asset," meaning they considered it unlikely they would recoup their investment. Given Blackstone's considerable financial expertise, their gloomy view of Stiefel's future was obviously enormously concerning.

Another interesting idea we explored was given the code name Project Yoda. At that time, there were numerous Stiefel facilities in the United States, and the concept was to consolidate these multiple locations into a new Global Headquarters at our existing site in Research Triangle Park, North Carolina. Moving all personnel to one place would reduce expenses significantly while simultaneously enhancing communication and efficiency. Project Yoda would have saved a lot of money in the long run; the problem was, in the short run, the moving expenses associated with relocating so many people would have caused us to breach a loan covenant.

We decided to start small by moving only three senior executives initially (Bill Humphries, Todd Stiefel and myself), with a view toward moving everyone else if and when we could afford to do so. North Carolina was aggressively trying to attract business to the state, so Steve Karasick and I met with Governor Bev Perdue and several other state officials to learn about the type of incentive package that could be ours once we implemented the full Project Yoda. First, however, we needed to get the loan covenant problems behind us.

Although it might seem counterintuitive, we also explored the possibility of making a major acquisition. Medicis Pharmaceutical Corporation, a New York Stock Exchange company, was a star player in the US dermatology market, and they were highly profitable. We knew Medicis would cost a minimum of $1 billion (less than four years later, Valeant acquired Medicis for $2.6 billion), but if we could somehow make it happen, our combined EBITDA would be so high that we would no longer have to worry about loan covenants. Furthermore, Stiefel Laboratories would become the most powerful dermatology company in the world by far. I arranged a meeting with Jonah Shacknai, the founder and CEO of Medicis, in the fall of 2008, and he expressed willingness to consider a merger if our price was high enough.

Following our normal practice, we code-named this potential deal Project Arnold, and we engaged a financial expert (the healthcare investment banking group at J.P. Morgan) to advise us. Our bankers prepared detailed financial models which confirmed this deal would be a home run for Stiefel. But alas, it was not to be. In principle, Blackstone loved the idea of Stiefel acquiring Medicis. But since Blackstone was already concerned about their existing investment, they understandably did not wish to invest even more money in Stiefel—not even to finance such a great deal—and we could not move forward without their consent. Project Arnold ended only two months after coming into existence, and we at Stiefel remained seriously worried about breaching one or both of our loan covenants.

CHAPTER TWENTY-TWO

PROJECT JUMP

"Any business today that embraces the status quo as an operating principle is going to be on a death march."
— HOWARD SCHULTZ

njan Mukherjee was a Senior Managing Director at Blackstone and my primary liaison with that firm. With a Harvard undergraduate degree and a Harvard M.B.A., Anjan is one of the smartest individuals I have ever known. The more I interacted with Anjan, the more I was impressed with his keen business insights and superb analytical skills. We became friends; and given that Blackstone was entitled to one seat on the Stiefel Board of Directors, I asked for Anjan to be designated to fill that seat. Regardless of one's political views, I think most people like the idea of having honest, highly-intelligent people involved in government; so I was proud and impressed when, in late-2008, President Obama tapped Anjan to join his transition team—focusing on economics and international trade matters.

In mid-November 2008, Anjan is the one who told me Blackstone viewed Stiefel as an "impaired asset." I told him how terribly I felt we were missing our forecasts, and I pledged we would do everything within our power to avoid breaching a loan covenant.

He agreed such a breach would be a disaster that could force Stiefel Laboratories into bankruptcy, and he volunteered to help us in any way he could. Three days before Thanksgiving, Anjan called to advise me Chris Viehbacher, CEO of pharmaceutical giant Sanofi-Aventis (and owner of our competitor, Dermik Laboratories) was interested in acquiring Stiefel and wanted to meet with me. "I already told Chris that Stiefel is not for sale," Anjan added, "but he wants to meet with you anyway."

I had always believed that becoming acquainted with senior executives of big pharma companies was beneficial for Stiefel, and I also felt I had a fiduciary duty to Stiefel stockholders to at least listen to what Chris Viehbacher had to say. Consequently, I informed Anjan I would be happy to meet with Chris, but given Stiefel's austerity program, I was not willing to fly to Sanofi's headquarters in France. Anjan assured me Chris visited the United States frequently, and he would attempt to arrange a meeting.

For the past several years, Todd, Brent and I had met every year on the day before Thanksgiving to discuss a variety of topics—both personal and corporate—that we seldom had time to discuss during regular business hours. At one of these meetings, for example, I told my sons that (unlike my dad) I did not plan to work until I was an octogenarian. I loved my job and had no desire to retire in the immediate future, but I was designating them as my successors, and I planned to step down as CEO when I turned 65. After that, I wanted to remain involved on the Board for a few years, but I would no longer be involved in the day-to-day management of the company.

At our 2008 pre-Thanksgiving meeting, I told my sons about Sanofi-Aventis wanting to acquire us. We had never before discussed, or even remotely considered, the notion of someday selling the company. Working together to build our family business was both intellectually stimulating and immensely satisfying; I loved interacting with dermatologists and working with my two sons and my other Stiefel colleagues. However, I did feel a strong moral obligation to enable our shareholders to liquidate their stock whenever they wanted, so I thought we would probably want to file for an IPO (initial public offering) eventually, thereby making Stiefel Laboratories a publicly-traded company.

I had no particular date in mind, but I was mindful of the fact our Deutsche Bank loan came due the end of 2013, and Blackstone could demand repayment of their $500 million investment (plus 4.5 percent compounded in-kind dividends) in 2015; so it seemed likely Stiefel would need an outside source of funds at some point in that general time frame. (As an aside, Blackstone was guaranteed at least the aforesaid amount, even if Stiefel's value were to decrease. But if Stiefel were to sell the company or go public at a high enough valuation, Blackstone had the right to convert its preferred shares to common shares and potentially receive a much higher amount. Unlike the common shareholders, they were essentially in a no-lose situation.) Todd, Brent and I had already asked Mike Cornelius (our CFO) and several other senior executives to take appropriate steps so that we would be ready for an IPO whenever the time was optimal. But selling the entire company was, as my Uncle Herb used to quip, "a horse of a different wavelength."

After telling Todd and Brent about Sanofi's interest in acquiring Stiefel, I inquired as to their thoughts. It is often said that timing is everything in life, and on that particular day, all of us were pretty depressed about our family business. Our first ever global reduction in force was about to take place; we were operating in austerity mode; our sales and profits were down from the previous year (and far below budget); and even though the company was still financially strong, we were paradoxically facing the possibility of being forced into bankruptcy due to a technical breach of a loan covenant.

Such a disastrous outcome would have seemed absurd in normal times, but in the midst of "the worst financial crisis in global history," it was a distinct possibility. After we had worked so hard to increase shareholder value, was all Stiefel stock (with the possible exception of Blackstone's preferred stock, which had a liquidation preference) about to become worthless? All of these negative thoughts were in our minds as we wrestled with the Sanofi issue. On one hand, selling the company might solve all our problems and eliminate all our stress simultaneously. On the other hand, we were the fifth and sixth generations of Stiefels running our family business, and we were sad even thinking about the possibility of selling the company to outsiders.

Complicating matters further, I did not have the power to sell, even if I wanted to do so. Selling Stiefel Laboratories required the affirmative vote not only of the Class B shares (which I controlled), but also the Class A shares and Blackstone's preferred shares. Emotionally conflicted, we ultimately decided to explore the possibility of a sale, but we resolved not to proceed unless we received what we considered a highly compelling offer—or, as the Godfather might say, "an offer we couldn't refuse." No one voiced aloud our tacit awareness that receiving a home-run offer in such a dreadful economic climate was extraordinarily unlikely.

Throughout the years, quite a few giant pharmaceutical companies had expressed an interest in acquiring Stiefel, but Werner had always responded by stating we were honored by their interest, but we were firmly committed to remaining private and independent. End of discussion! Consequently, we had never gleaned even the vaguest notion as to what price ranges these companies may have contemplated. Since we now wanted to ascertain how much Sanofi-Aventis might be willing to offer, we first needed to give them access to an enormous amount of confidential information ... and uploading thousands of documents into a virtual data room takes a great deal of time. Why invest all that time just to allow one company, Sanofi-Aventis, to access our confidential information? Why not allow some of the companies that had expressed interest in the past to view the same documents and possibly submit bids of their own?

Even if Sanofi were to submit a compelling offer to purchase us, sound business practice would require us to conduct a "market check" anyway, just to make sure some other company wasn't willing to submit a higher bid. We had learned the importance of competitive tension from our private equity negotiations. Why not, we reasoned, avoid the time and expense of doing a market check later by running a competitive process from the outset? So, we set out to explore how much, if anything, Sanofi-Aventis and a few select other companies might be willing to pay to acquire Stiefel Laboratories. This endeavor was eventually given the code name Project Jump. (Chris Viehbacher had also expressed a potential willingness to sell Sanofi's dermatology business, Dermik Laboratories, to us, so Project Jump included this exciting concept as well.) Following our standard practice, we kept Project Jump highly confidential, involved only those individuals with a need to know, and engaged an expert advisor to help us. The advisor we chose was an arm of Blackstone called Blackstone Advisory Services. But I am getting ahead of myself.

Thanksgiving weekend of 2008 was a busy one for me. I wanted to calculate for myself how much an interested pharma company might be willing to pay for Stiefel Laboratories, as well as figure out what a possible sale at that price would portend for our shareholders. Firstly, as you would assume, our loan from the Deutsche Bank consortium needed to be paid in full before any sale proceeds could be distributed to Stiefel stockholders. Secondly, the preferred stock owned by Blackstone had a long list of special features making it much more valuable than our three classes of common stock; and one of those features was a liquidation preference. This meant if we were to sell the company, Blackstone was entitled to be paid its entire investment, plus accrued dividends, from the sale proceeds, before the other stockholders received a penny. Finally, selling a company is a costly proposition in terms of legal fees, financial advisor fees and other expenses.

Adding up all of the foregoing, I calculated we would need a sales price exceeding $1.2 billion in order for our common stockholders to receive anything at all. A price below $1.2 billion would render everyone's shares (except Blackstone's) worthless. Our most recent independent appraisal, done for purposes of our Employee Stock Bonus Plan (ESBP) as of March 31, 2008, valued our common stock at $16,469 per share; we would need an offer of $1.8 billion in order for our non-Blackstone shareholders to receive this price per share.

Next, I used three different methods to calculate how much an interested and motivated buyer might offer. Our EBITDA for the current fiscal year was projected at that time to be $130 million (it turned out to be considerably less), and before the economy had tanked, the average acquisition price in our specialty pharma sector had been slightly below a multiple of 12 x EBITDA. Multiplying $130 million times 12 suggested to me a company that considered Stiefel to be a good strategic fit might reasonably pay a price of $1.56 billion—which equaled approximately $11,000 per share for our Class A, B and C common stockholders. I tried two other methodologies to predict what a willing buyer might offer us, and these two estimates, while slightly lower, reinforced my belief that, if we were to receive an offer at all, it would probably be in the neighborhood of $1.56 billion. Independently, our Chief Financial Officer, Mike Cornelius, ran his own calculations, and his valuation was nearly identical to mine.

On one hand, this seemed like an enormous sum to a guy who had grown up drinking powdered milk. On the other hand, a price per share 33 percent lower than our most recent ESBP appraisal was hardly a home run for our stockholders. I nevertheless felt strongly we should move forward with Project Jump, for three reasons. Firstly, I had the strong impression this would appease Blackstone, which was pressuring us to improve our precarious financial situation; I felt really badly Stiefel had become what they deemed an impaired asset. Secondly, accepting a non-compelling price, while undesirable, was vastly superior to going bankrupt. And finally, one can never know what factors might influence a potential buyer; even in a terrible economy, the remote possibility existed that some company out there would make us an offer we couldn't refuse.

Business decisions, however, should be based on reality, not remote possibilities. If there existed a realistic probability we might sell the company, it made no sense for Stiefel to incur the expense of moving Todd Stiefel, Bill Humphries and me to North Carolina, given that an acquiring company (if it opted to retain us) would probably want us to live in its headquarters city. And Sanofi-Aventis, the only company in the picture at that time, had no corporate presence in North Carolina. But my calculations on Thanksgiving weekend of 2008 convinced me selling the company was not a likely scenario.

Consequently, that same weekend, pursuant to Project Yoda, I contacted a real estate broker in Raleigh and started looking at houses that were within commuting distance from the Stiefel facility in Research Triangle Park. Daneen and I signed a contract to purchase what is now our home in Raleigh on March 11, 2009— before Stiefel had received even a non-binding offer from anyone. Bill Humphries and Todd signed contracts on Raleigh homes within the same time frame.

Disturbingly, I kept receiving news suggesting that the value of Stiefel Laboratories was spiraling downward. Shortly before Thanksgiving, I had received some competitive intelligence our oral product for psoriasis, Soriatane®, was expected to go generic in a few months. This report was extremely worrisome, because Soriatane was our second largest seller with an excellent profit margin. Making matters worse, I learned in mid-December a generic company had just completed a successful clinical trial comparing their product to Duac®—our largest and most important product. If both of these products were genericized, our profitability would take a huge hit, thereby vastly increasing the probability of our breaching a loan covenant. Around the same time, I learned from Blackstone Advisory that the EBITDA multiple I mentioned in the last paragraph had decreased to 7.8, which implied a more reasonable estimate of what price Stiefel might command was $1 billion. As noted previously, selling the company at that price would leave nothing for the common shareholders.

Even more pessimistic was the report that hit my desk on December 18, when J.P. Morgan, our advisors in Project Arnold (the potential acquisition of Medicis) submitted their detailed financial analysis for our consideration. As part of this analysis, they calculated the Total Enterprise Value (TEV) of Stiefel to be $837 million. Since the TEV included the amount of our net debt as well as the value of Blackstone's preferred stock, this valuation suggested all Stiefel's common shares were worthless, and the preferred shares were worth considerably less than what Blackstone had paid for them in August 2007. The terrifying possibility Stiefel might become yet another victim of the global economic crisis was looking increasingly likely.

Project Jump entailed a number of sequential steps, but before we could start, we first needed to identify which companies to involve in the process. Blackstone Advisory compiled a relatively short list of pharmaceutical companies that had demonstrated an interest in the dermatology space, and Todd, Brent and I suggested some additions to and subtractions from this list. If we had been committed to selling the company, we would have involved as many companies as possible, but given our resolve not to sell unless we received a home run offer, we did not want to share any confidential information with a direct competitor.

Galderma, owned at that time by European behemoths Nestlé and L'Oréal, was our leading competitor in virtually every country of the world; so even though Galderma had previously expressed interest in Stiefel, we opted not to include them. Blackstone executives personally knew the CEO at every company we considered; without mentioning Stiefel, they were able to develop a final list of five companies that might potentially be interested in acquiring a dermatology company: Sanofi-Aventis, Johnson & Johnson, Novartis, Allergan and GlaxoSmithKline. We initiated Project Jump by having Blackstone send each of these companies a Non-Disclosure Agreement (NDA), whereby they would promise to keep all of the information shared with them strictly confidential.

All five companies signed the NDA, but three of them first modified it to prohibit Stiefel from revealing to anyone we were even considering the possibility of selling the company. Once these five companies were bound to secrecy, the next step was to send them a "teaser" document, which provided some brief highlights about us—the intent being to enable them to decide if they wanted to learn more details by scheduling a Management Presentation. Johnson & Johnson lost interest and dropped out of the process, but the other four companies wanted to learn more.

Consequently, each of these four companies sent a team to Coral Gables, where they spent four or five hours listening to presentations from Stiefel's senior executives. The visiting companies were free to ask questions at these Management Presentations, but there were no negotiations or even general discussions about price or contractual terms.

The purpose was simply to introduce each interested company to our management team and provide more information about Stiefel Laboratories. On March 3, 2009, we took the next step in Project Jump by opening Phase I of a virtual data room—thereby enabling (for the first time) the four companies to view confidential documents about nearly every aspect of our business. A few days later, we sent out a formal Bid Process Letter, which requested each company that remained interested to submit a non-binding bid on March 24, 2009.

Per our counsel's advice, we attached a draft acquisition agreement, and we requested any bid submission be accompanied by a marked-up version of this draft contract. There were three significant advantages to sending potential bidders this draft agreement. Firstly, we would be starting with contractual terms that, while not unfair or one-sided, were reasonably favorable to Stiefel. Secondly, if multiple parties were to bid, we would be working with one basic draft rather than multiple ones—thereby saving our lawyers and us a great deal of time. And finally, we had learned through experience the terms of a deal can be just as important as the price of the deal (sometimes more so), and we would gain important insight into potential acquirers' thinking by reviewing what changes they deemed necessary.

We heard from two of our interested parties prior to March 24, when non-binding bids were due. Novartis notified Blackstone Advisory they were no longer interested and would not be submitting a bid. We were disappointed, but not surprised—it is a very common occurrence for companies to lose interest in a potential acquisition target after learning more about the target's business.

Allergan's CEO, David Pyott, called me to advise that they would not be submitting a bid either because he knew their valuation of Stiefel would not be acceptable to us. Allergan believed, he noted, that many of Stiefel's most important products would go generic in the near future; they also felt our major research projects had a relatively low probability of receiving FDA approval. Consequently, Allergan had concluded our total value was $1 billion. As you can imagine, this was very disconcerting news—particularly since this valuation was so close to what J.P. Morgan had computed three months earlier. Allergan understood our business better than any of the other companies, and their expert opinion was that Stiefel's value was so low that all of our common stock was totally worthless!

There was nothing we could do, however, other than work harder than ever and wait to see if GSK or Sanofi might have a different opinion. I believed these two companies would submit non-binding offers because Chris Viehbacher (CEO of Sanofi-Aventis) and Andrew Witty (CEO of GlaxoSmithKline) had both recently asked me if they should bid one lump sum for the entire company, or if they should submit separate offers for each class of common stock. Obviously, both men felt the Class B shares (of which I owned about 90 percent) were more valuable than the other common shares, because the Class B stock could elect a majority of the Board of Directors (Class C shareholders could not vote at all).

I told them both, however, that Stiefel viewed all common shares as having equal value, so they should not bid different amounts for different classes of stock. On the morning of March 24, the two non-binding offers arrived—GSK's for $3.5 billion, and Sanofi's for $3.2 billion. The Stiefel team had agreed we would terminate Project Jump on March 24 if we did not receive a compelling offer, but these two bids were beyond compelling—they were amazing!

Consequently, we opened Phase II of our virtual data room (which contained our most top-secret documents) two days later, and we granted access to both GSK and Sanofi. We allowed them to tour Stiefel facilities of their choosing, and we engaged in numerous conference calls to answer whatever questions their teams wanted to ask. In addition, we finally started to negotiate price and contractual terms for the possible sale of our family business.

Trying to negotiate a mutually satisfactory acquisition agreement was a monumental challenge. Sanofi-Aventis refused to mark up our draft agreement at all and instead sent us a long list of issues that needed to be resolved. GSK did mark up the draft as we had requested, but they objected to virtually every provision our attorneys, Willkie, Farr & Gallagher, deemed important. Blackstone and Willkie both stressed to us how vitally important it was to continue maintaining strict confidentiality about Project Jump—particularly since Sanofi and GSK were public companies—but this was becoming increasingly difficult as time passed. As a result, we informed GSK and Sanofi our deadline for executing a binding contract was April 24.

To maintain competitive tension, we negotiated with each party as if it were the only finalist, but as we drew closer to the deadline, it began to appear one particular issue with Sanofi-Aventis was insurmountable. We knew even if we were to sign a binding contract with either party, the deal would fall through unless it was acceptable to the Federal Trade Commission (FTC) and the relevant antitrust authorities in other countries around the world. Sanofi's dermatology subsidiary, Dermik, owned Benzaclin®, a product very similar to our product Duac®; our lawyers considered it probable the FTC would require Sanofi to divest Benzaclin as a condition of approving a merger with Stiefel.

Chris Viehbacher expressly told me, however, Sanofi was unwilling to divest Benzaclin; and this refusal essentially took Sanofi out of the running. To me, the three critical elements of any deal are price, terms and deal certainty. If you sign a contract with someone, you always want to be as certain as possible that the deal will actually close. If we entered into a contract with Sanofi that did not require them to divest Benzaclin if necessary, then Sanofi would have the right to opt out of our deal for any reason whatsoever, as long as the FTC objected to them owning both acne products.

In essence, Stiefel would be legally bound, but Sanofi-Aventis would not. Consequently, we felt GSK was the only potential acquirer remaining—if we could not make a deal with them, then Project Jump was over. As it turned out, Sanofi never submitted a binding offer, so apparently, we were reading the tea leaves correctly.

Stiefel and GSK were able to compromise on the small issues relatively easily, but there were several major issues both sides deemed deal-breakers—and as the deadline approached, none of these major issues had been resolved. There were so many of these major issues that I could fill another book if I provided the details of all of them. Suffice it to say, everyone was working day and night to try to get us across the finish line; but new challenges kept arising.

GSK informed us, for example, they wanted to announce publicly their acquisition of Stiefel just before the London Stock Exchange opened on Monday morning, April 20; if we had not signed a contract by then, they were walking. So suddenly, we faced a new, shorter time limit. Another example related to the terms of my employment post-merger. GSK had asked me in mid-April to fly to New York City to negotiate a new employment contract (which seemed like a positive development), but I politely suggested that we wait until after we had inked the acquisition agreement.

My fear was if they offered me a sweetheart deal, I might become biased in favor of selling to GSK, thereby losing the objectivity I owed to Stiefel shareholders. Apparently, GSK interpreted my suggestion to mean I intended to quit once our deal closed (the furthest thing from my mind), because just prior to our new deadline, GSK's lawyers informed Willkie, Farr & Gallagher that Todd, Brent and I were required to sign agreements preventing us from competing in the dermatology space for three years after the closing.

I objected strenuously because, at age 58, I wanted to work for several more years; and this agreement was so broad it would essentially kick me out of dermatology unless GSK opted to retain me. And I knew very well acquiring companies often endeavor to save money by laying off the acquired company's highest-paid executives as soon as possible. GSK's lawyers responded to my objections very tersely—this issue was a deal-breaker. The attorneys agreed upon an appropriate amount to pay us to sign these agreements, because in the absence of adequate monetary consideration, the IRS could allocate a significant percentage of the purchase price to the value of the non-competes and tax us accordingly. With conflicting emotions, we all signed—knowing that there was a significant chance our careers in dermatology would soon be over.

By working around-the-clock the last few days before the deadline, we managed to overcome all remaining contractual obstacles, and we even convinced GSK to increase their offering price somewhat. Our Board of Directors voted unanimously in favor of the deal, with our common shareholders ratifying the acquisition agreement in the wee hours of April 20—just as GSK's deadline was expiring. Blackstone likewise endorsed this transaction, which would enable them at closing to convert their preferred stock to common stock and thereby earn a 37 percent profit. (This did not represent a home run by Blackstone standards, but given the terrible economy, it was not too shabby for a 23-month investment.)

That same morning, Stiefel and GSK issued a joint press release announcing the deal, which was priced at $3.6 billion. There were still significant regulatory hurdles to clear, but fortunately, the FTC and other antitrust authorities around the world approved the merger without forcing either company to divest any products. This outcome had been far from certain because GSK had been a skincare powerhouse for years, with global dermatology sales approaching $600 million. Particularly exciting for me was the fact GSK wanted to retain the Stiefel name and move its entire dermatology business under the Stiefel umbrella. The merger officially closed on July 22, 2009, and Stiefel Laboratories, Inc. became "Stiefel, a GSK company."

Overnight, Stiefel became a $1.5 billion enterprise—the largest dermatology company in the world. Our dreams of surpassing the one-billion-dollar mark and becoming #1 in dermatology had come true! The vision that had seemed so fanciful only a few years earlier had become a reality! But after six generations, Stiefel was no longer our family business. It was the most bittersweet day of my life.

CHAPTER TWENTY-THREE

STIEFEL, A GSK COMPANY

"Good business leaders create a vision, articulate the vision, passionately own the vision, and relentlessly drive it to completion."
— JACK WELCH

W hy, you might be wondering, did GlaxoSmithKline pay such a monumental price for Stiefel Laboratories— seemingly far in excess of what we were worth? Only insiders at GSK truly know the answer to this question, but I believe several factors were influential.

Firstly, when Andrew Witty was promoted to be GSK's CEO in May 2008, one of his two primary rivals for the position was Chris Viehbacher, according to several industry publications. A 20-year veteran of GSK, Chris left the company shortly thereafter to become CEO at Sanofi-Aventis. As Project Jump neared its final stages, it became crystal clear GSK and Sanofi both knew the other company was interested in acquiring Stiefel. Would it not be logical to assume the past rivalry between Witty and Viehbacher significantly magnified the competitive tension between the two companies?

Secondly, the amount someone is willing to pay for any given asset often depends on the needs and circumstances of the buyer. I lived through Hurricane Andrew in Miami, and those of us without power were willing to pay many times the normal price for a bag of ice. For GSK, Stiefel Laboratories represented a unique strategic fit, which undoubtedly made us considerably more valuable to them than to most other companies. Our existing dermatology products were complementary, not competitive, to theirs; our pipeline offered the potential for a steady stream of new products in the future.

Furthermore, by acquiring us, GSK could become the leading player in the dermatology sector. Another (arguably the most important) factor that clearly influenced how much GSK was willing to pay relates to cost synergies. Whenever one company acquires another, there is a potential opportunity to remove certain costs from the combined business. The magnitude of these synergies can vary, depending on such factors as the size of and similarities between the two companies and the strategy of the acquiring company.

Does the combined company need two legal departments, for example, or could one suffice? Typically, a number of redundant positions are eliminated, not only from support functions such as Legal, HR, IT and Finance, but also from senior management. (If your company is getting acquired and your job title starts with the word "Chief," you should probably be updating your resume!)

At a luncheon with Andrew Witty on March 20, 2009, he confided to Todd, Brent and me that, if GSK were to acquire Stiefel, he wanted to maintain Stiefel as a separate entity rather than integrate us into their huge corporate infrastructure. The reason, he continued, was he did not want to kill the entrepreneurial spirit that had caused Stiefel to be successful for so many years. I inferred from this conversation that GSK would seek minimal synergies if they were to purchase us.

Later, just before the acquisition agreement was signed, the two companies agreed upon the language of a joint press release; but prior to contract execution, the exact amount of anticipated synergies was left blank. Imagine my surprise when I subsequently read GSK expected "to deliver annual pre-tax cost savings of up to $240 million by 2012." This number was considerably higher than Stiefel's entire worldwide payroll! Obviously, some very dramatic changes were planned.

Todd, Brent and I were among the first to encounter these changes. We were all asked to remain at Stiefel, but at vastly decreased salaries and with dramatically reduced responsibilities. None of us were pleased with our offers, but I would have accepted mine anyway if not for one proviso. Changing our conditions of employment in this manner contractually entitled us to receive substantial severance payments, but agreeing to GSK's terms would have given them the discretion not to make these payments—in which case we would, in effect, be paying GSK for allowing us to continue to work at Stiefel.

Working for a negative salary was obviously unacceptable, so our only viable alternative was to leave—and with heavy hearts, we all advised GSK accordingly. On August 3, 2009, I e-mailed the following farewell letter to everyone at Stiefel:

> Dear Esteemed Stiefel Colleague,
>
> As I write this message, my heart is filled with an overwhelming sense of pride at what we, working together, have accomplished. For the past 27 years, I have dedicated myself to the dream that, one day, Stiefel would be the #1 dermatology company in the world. Today, as a GSK company, that dream has become a reality. And given our world-class pipeline and financial muscle, the future for Stiefel looks even brighter than the past.
>
> Notwithstanding the above, however, the time has come for me to move on to other endeavors. I still love Stiefel, I still love dermatology, and some of my closest

friends are dermatologists. And I still care very deeply about each of you. But as many of you know, I enjoyed a rewarding career in law prior to my tenure at Stiefel; and there are other interests that now beckon me. Quite simply, it's just the right time for me to bid you farewell.

As I depart, I am filled with confidence about Stiefel's future. With Bill Humphries as your President and Gavin Corcoran as your Chief Scientific Officer, the sky is the limit for Stiefel, a GSK company.

I would like to thank each of you from the bottom of my heart for sharing my vision and striving so diligently to achieve it. I have always felt that the Stiefel team was the best in the pharmaceutical industry, and I will forever be indebted to you, my wonderful teammates. It has been a profound honor and privilege for me to have had the incredible opportunity to work side by side with you to build Stiefel into the #1 dermatology company in the world. I wish you and your loved ones a lifetime filled with excellent health and much happiness.

Thanks again and warmest personal regards,
Charlie

I never dreamed anyone at GSK would be upset by this farewell letter, but I was severely mistaken! The very next day, Human Resources called me and ordered me to turn in my company car, credit cards, computer, office key, and any other company property in my possession immediately! I subsequently was told by a friend in HR that GSK had been preparing its own announcement to employees about my departure, and their spin would have given the impression I wanted to retire so I could spend more time with my grandchildren.

My decision to draft my own farewell message had clearly

infuriated somebody, because suddenly, GSK began to play hardball with Todd, Brent and me. In order to receive some benefits to which we were legally entitled, we were asked to sign away our rights to other such benefits. We were forced to retain attorneys to argue on our behalf; fortunately, after a few stress-filled weeks, everything was peacefully resolved. To this day, I remain flabbergasted anyone could have been so furious about my heartfelt farewell to my colleagues!

I would like to be clear I have the utmost respect for GlaxoSmithKline, and I harbor no bitterness towards them whatsoever. They are a great company, they paid our stockholders a great price, and once they acquired us, they were legally entitled to make whatever cuts they wanted. I was well aware of this, so the fact that many of these cuts surprised me is irrelevant. I mention synergies only because they help explain why GSK was willing to pay so much money to acquire us. Almost immediately after the acquisition was completed, GSK began to close Stiefel facilities around the world; and to the best of my knowledge, by 2016 there were none left.

Originally, GSK planned to close our manufacturing plant in Oak Hill, New York, but trying desperately to save those workers' jobs, we happily convinced them to keep it open. (They converted it into a GSK facility that manufactures toothpaste, and they even expanded it.) Sadly, outside of Oak Hill, vast numbers of Stiefel employees were laid off, and many others left voluntarily to take jobs elsewhere. Almost all our senior managers were gone within the first year. Our Glades subsidiary, which had been successfully marketing authorized generics for Stiefel products within the United States, was closed, and GSK chose to pay an outside company to do this for them instead. Our Travel, Meetings and Conventions Department, which had saved us huge sums of money over the years, was likewise closed, and all their work was outsourced.

All the research and development being conducted on our

Atlèan line of dermal fillers was abruptly halted because a GSK policy prohibited the development of any product requiring animal testing if that product was purely aesthetic in nature. I immediately contacted GSK and offered to purchase worldwide Atlèan rights, but they said no. (Five years later, they sold European rights to Sinclair Pharma and subsequently surrendered US rights back to the original inventors.) GSK also negotiated early terminations of all Stiefel's distributorship relationships around the world, reportedly at a cost exceeding $60 million.

This move particularly surprised me, because I believe all these agreements would have expired under their own terms within a couple of years anyway. Over time, most of our products were divested or discontinued, and I am unaware of any ongoing promotional activity. At the 2018 annual meeting of the American Academy of Dermatology, for the first time in more than six decades, Stiefel did not have an exhibit booth. There are still a handful of products bearing a Stiefel trademark being sold in some countries, but less than nine years after GSK acquired us, the Stiefel company essentially ceased to exist.

Dermatologist friends often ask me why GSK bothered to acquire us, if their intent was to destroy the company. I truly believe; however, this was never their intent at all. I pride myself on being a fairly good judge of character, and Andrew Witty impressed me as a very honorable person. When he shared his vision for Stiefel with Todd, Brent and me, I believe that he meant every word. Giant companies have so many layers of management, however, it is virtually impossible for the CEO to know everything going on within the company. For GSK, buying Stiefel was a relatively small deal, and my guess is some of the people tasked with integrating Stiefel into GSK did not fully comprehend their CEO's vision. For them, it was just business as usual, which, in the case of an acquisition, means maximizing synergies.

A couple of years after leaving Stiefel, I briefly encountered

Andrew in Research Triangle Park. We smiled and shook hands, but there was no opportunity to converse. I was told, however, that shortly after our encounter, Andrew commented wistfully "I thought Charlie was going to stay on with us." Clearly, he had no idea I had been forced out by individuals a few steps down the chain of command. I felt badly for him, and worse for myself, because I respect Sir Andrew Witty (he was knighted by Queen Elizabeth II in 2012) very much and would have enjoyed working with him.

A great number of former Stiefel employees have contacted me since 2009, expressing gratitude to the Stiefel family for giving them an opportunity and lamenting how much they miss our corporate culture. Many state their time at Stiefel was the happiest time in their careers, and several have suggested I buy the company back from GSK and revive the "old Stiefel." In 2011, I actually discussed this concept at length with Blackstone, but we jointly concluded GSK could not sell the company for anywhere near what it was then worth, because that would entail taking a huge loss on their books—which would infuriate their stockholders. Regrettably, it is now too late—our corporate infrastructure has vanished; and except for a few miscellaneous products, there is essentially nothing left to acquire.

Sometimes I reflect on whether, if I could go back in time, I would still vote in favor of selling to GSK. I loved my job and was not ready to retire, so from a career perspective, I definitely did not want to sell. Nor were we forced to sell to avoid breaching loan covenants. The austerity program implemented in November 2008, worked well enough to keep us fully in compliance with the terms of our loan agreement. In the end, I voted in favor of the GSK deal because I felt it was my moral duty to help our shareholders maximize the value of their stock. GSK's offer was so staggeringly high, it was, quite simply, an offer we could not refuse.

Friends ask me if it makes me sad to think about what happened to our family business after the acquisition, and the answer is yes.

I think of Johann David Stiefel and his sons, toiling in Offenbach to build their fledgling soap company. I think of Werner, Herb and August struggling for decades to resurrect Johann's dream and build upon it. I think of six generations of Stiefels who dedicated their lives in pursuit of their singular vision. I think of the thousands of incredible men and women who shared this vision and helped make it a reality. It took 162 years of blood, sweat and tears to build that tiny soap business into the largest dermatology company in the world. Then suddenly, like the last fleeting echo of a magnificent fireworks display, it was gone forever. *Requiescat in pace.*

A DECADE OF LAWSUITS

"Of course, people are getting smarter nowadays; they are letting lawyers instead of their conscience be their guides."
– WILL ROGERS

According to a January 30, 2015, editorial in the *Wall Street Journal*, 94 percent of corporate acquisitions at a price exceeding $100 million result in at least one shareholder lawsuit. Unfortunately, Stiefel was not among the fortunate 6 percent that escaped this fate. The first lawsuit against us was filed in July 2009—even before our deal with GSK had closed. This suit was brought by Norm Segall, the Miami attorney who represented my Uncle Herb's third wife in their divorce proceedings (small world, eh?), and four additional suits were subsequently filed by this same gentleman and his co-counsel.

A total of eight lawsuits were filed, and when I started writing this book, my intent was to discuss each of them with some level of detail. All eight named Stiefel Laboratories and me as Defendants, and most of them named some other Stiefel executives as well. GSK retained an excellent law firm, Greenberg Traurig, to represent us in all these cases: with Dave Coulson, Hilary Bass and Todd Wozniak leading our defense team. It is 2018 as I write this, and unfortunately two of these lawsuits are still awaiting trial. Consequently, to avoid revealing our trial strategy, this epilogue will be somewhat shorter than I originally planned.

Seven of the eight lawsuits made claims on behalf of former Stiefel employees who exercised their put options to sell shares of Stiefel stock (about 800 shares total) from their Employee Stock Bonus Plan accounts back to the company prior to February 2, 2009. Pursuant to the terms of the Plan, these individuals received $16,469 per share—the price established in the most recent appraisal. At the time, this was the highest price ever paid for Stiefel common stock in the history of the company. In contrast, the Stiefel family in the previous five years had sold more than 31,000 shares at prices averaging less than $5000 per share.

When we were acquired on July 22, 2009, however, the home run price per share GSK paid was approximately four times what these employees had received six months earlier. Understandably, the people who had sold shares regretted their decision and wished they could receive the GSK price; and quite frankly, I deeply sympathize with these former colleagues. Unfortunately, however, stockholders sell shares all the time just before positive news causing shares to skyrocket is announced; while this may be unfortunate, it is the reality of the market. The only viable chance for these Stiefel sellers to receive more money was to file a lawsuit alleging fraud.

Sure enough, a few ex-employees concluded they indeed had been defrauded. It was painful for me to be sued by individuals I considered my friends, but I was gratified the vast majority of the people who sold ESBP shares opted not to sue. Some of the people who did sue had their cases dismissed, others settled, and two (so far) went to trial. The first case that went to trial was brought by Tim Finnerty, a long-time sales rep who had been laid off after Stiefel acquired Barrier Therapeutics. Tim and a Barrier sales rep were working essentially the same territory, and our sales management group decided to retain the Barrier person and let Tim go. Tim was a good guy and a friend, so I felt badly when he called me to advise that he was no longer with Stiefel. He was applying for a job at another dermatology company, and since I knew their CEO, I called on Tim's behalf to put in a good word. (He got the job.)

Tim's lawsuit was very complicated; Dave Coulson wanted jurors either with a college degree or some business experience, so they could understand such issues as the difference between convertible preferred and common stock, and why businesses typically maintain strict confidentiality when running a sales exploration process. Tim's lawyers, on the other hand, wanted exactly the opposite. Unfortunately for us, the presiding judge—a very kindly and distinguished jurist—advised the assembled jury pool that anyone who would be inconvenienced by serving on the jury (due to work or family issues) could get up and leave. Out the door went most of the potential jurors who (in our opinion) were capable of understanding the complexities of this case!

Next came jury selection, and the lawyers on each side had the right to issue a few peremptory challenges—thereby dismissing potential jurors without stating a reason. I was very impressed when Peter Prieto, one of Finnerty's attorneys, approached Dave Coulson and advised him the father of one prospective juror—a college graduate who was about to enter law school—was close friends with one of Peter's partners. I whispered to Dave what a nice gesture this was, which caused Dave to smile and opine Peter was merely hoping this information would cause us to challenge this young woman. Dave did not challenge her, but sure enough, Peter did! Clearly, he did not want any college-educated individuals on the jury.

Ultimately, we ended up with a jury containing no one with a college education or business experience. Nevertheless, the trial seemed to go well for us—so well, in fact, our legal team felt so confident we would win that they opted not to call several of our witnesses. The jury took a very long time deliberating, but eventually they returned a verdict in Tim's favor. The story was not over, however.

By strange coincidence, a close friend of my son Todd lived next door to the jury foreperson, who (after the trial had ended) volunteered to Todd's friend that the jury really liked me and did not believe the company or I had done anything wrong. In addition, she confided the jury had ruled for the plaintiff solely because they felt Tim was a nice guy who needed the money, whereas Stiefel Laboratories was a giant company with money to spare! I excitedly shared this revelation with Dave Coulson and asked if we could get a mistrial, but he said no—this particular judge was very protective of his jurors and would not want to see this juror questioned in court. It was frustrating to know the jury verdict had not been based on the evidence, but there was nothing I could do about it. For better or for worse, jurors frequently make decisions based on sympathy or emotion.

The other lawsuit that went to trial was commenced by Richard Fried, who had served as our Chief Financial Officer for about ten years. Richard was also a friend of mine, but unlike Tim, Richard had quit his job at Stiefel to take a new job he expected to be much more lucrative. I could be wrong, but I think this fact made Richard a less sympathetic figure in the eyes of the jury. In addition, in the Fried trial, our jury included someone with both a college degree and business experience; and the other jurors elected her as their foreperson. Lo and behold, when the jury returned its verdict, they ruled completely in our favor! I am a huge fan of our nation's system of jurisprudence, but I do think our system could be improved. It is no longer permissible, for example, to issue peremptory challenges based on race; I think that it should likewise be impermissible to issue challenges based on level of education. During the Finnerty trial, I saw one juror blatantly sleeping. How can one be expected to render a fair verdict in a complex case when one does not even bother to listen to the evidence?

The lawsuit that shocked and hurt me the most was filed in July 2011 by Dick MacKay (technically by his personal holding company, to which he had transferred his Stiefel shares), my long-term friend whom I had honored by naming him Vice Chairman of the Board of Directors. Naturally, this suit raised a lot of eyebrows, given Dick's former stature within the company, and I believe the serious allegations he made may have influenced the SEC to file its own civil suit six months later. (After a lengthy investigation, the SEC had previously informed us they were not going to file a lawsuit.)

A few times throughout the years, Dick had asked the company to purchase some of his shares, and Stiefel had always tried to oblige him. One such stock redemption, for example, had enabled Dick to construct a beautiful ski chateau in Mont Tremblant. (I had dinner with him there once, and it is spectacular.) His lawsuit, however, related to his sale of 750 shares of stock back to Stiefel in June 2008.

Initially, Dick had contacted Steve Karasick and asked if, for estate planning purposes, he could sell 100 shares back to the company every year. You may recall my Uncle Herb had asked me this exact question a few years earlier, and Dick Sandler had advised me not to do something for one shareholder we would not do for all shareholders. Since Stiefel's willingness to redeem stock at all was based on its cash position and other factors, the company could never guarantee its ability to make stock purchases in future years at prices not yet known. I had related this to Herb, and he fully understood. Consequently, when MacKay posed this question to Steve, I advised him to answer Dick the same way we had answered Herb—we were willing to repurchase some of his shares at that time, but we could not promise in advance to do the same thing in future years.

Dick then asked if Stiefel could purchase 750 shares instead of 100, and Steve said yes, but to be consistent, Stiefel would only accept an offer to sell such a large block of stock if Dick were willing to accept the same discount schedule utilized when we had purchased large blocks from Columbia University, D'Anconia and Bacamachli. At the time, Steve advised me Dick seemed very happy to be getting the same deal as Werner, Herb, and their children. Dick subsequently wrote to me on May 16, 2008 as follows:

> "Good morning Charlie,
> This will confirm that I wish to sell 750 shares held by 100079 Canada Inc. to SLI pursuant to the discount schedule outlined in the attached spreadsheet.
>
> Kindest regards, Dick."

The spreadsheet calculated a total price of just under $9 million, and on behalf of the company, I accepted his offer.

This seemed like a total win-win for everyone—Dick was getting to monetize as many shares as he wanted, and the rest of the Stiefel shareholders' stock would increase in value. More than a year elapsed, and when we closed the sale to GSK, Dick was ecstatic. He and his wife, Francine, invited Daneen and me to dinner, at which time Dick presented me with two extraordinary bottles of wine—a 1981 and a 1982 Lafite Rothschild. According to his sworn deposition, he told our mutual friend, dermatologist Steve Mandy, I had been a phenomenal CEO and the moves I had made as CEO had increased his wealth by a multiple of three or four. Imagine my shock, then, when two years later he sued the company, Todd, Brent and me for more than $40 million!

Dick's Complaint alleged my sons and I had "conspired to repurchase a substantial portion of Plaintiff's shares at prices they knew were grossly undervalued," and we had "knowingly cheated Plaintiff out of over $40 million and lined their already deep pockets." To me, this allegation is so absurd no comment is necessary, so I will only note in passing that Todd and Brent had no involvement whatsoever in the purchase of Dick's shares—to the best of my recollection they did not even know about it until after the fact.

As for poor Steve Karasick, MacKay alleged he and I "pressured Mr. MacKay to sell Plaintiff's shares at an artificially low price in June 2008." Steve is the nicest guy in the world, and if you were to read through all the correspondence between Steve and Dick, I am confident you would not find even the remotest evidence of pressure. Quite the contrary, by his own admission, Dick approached us and asked us to purchase a small portion of his holdings at a discount. The sole reason I said yes was to do him a favor.

You will recall Blackstone and TA Associates were competing in mid-2007 to purchase convertible preferred stock from Stiefel, and Blackstone ultimately made an aggressive bid reflecting a total enterprise value of $2.9 billion and an equity value of $2.1 billion. Incidentally, these were not appraisals of the value of the company, but merely bids to determine how many preferred shares Blackstone would receive for its $500 million investment. (Both firms, for example, submitted initial bids on July 31; but 3 days later, Blackstone increased its "valuation" by $25 million to win our business. Obviously Stiefel had not suddenly increased in value by that amount.) MacKay alleged in his lawsuit, "Although Defendants were aware that Blackstone had given the Company these valuations, Plaintiff and Mr. MacKay were not aware of this information. Only the Stiefel Family Defendants—not the other directors—had access to this information." Continuing, MacKay alleged "the Board, including Plaintiff, was not told, for example, that Blackstone was paying $60,000 per share when it acquired its interest in the Company."

During MacKay's sworn deposition, however, our attorney showed him an e-mail I had sent to all Board members with the entire Blackstone bid attached and then asked, "This shows Mr. Stiefel, in fact, did inform you of the valuation that was presented by Blackstone as part of its bid to make a private equity preferred shares investment. Is that correct?" MacKay answered, "I still don't understand it all," so our attorney persisted and asked the following: "But nevertheless, isn't it true Mr. Stiefel informed you of the valuations that Blackstone used with its bid in 2007?" MacKay responded, "This would say that, yes." Our attorney then showed MacKay another e-mail from me to the entire Board, wherein I advise, "Pursuant to my last e-mail, attached below are the latest versions of the documents being negotiated with Blackstone. We are working hard to finalize all open terms by Friday at the latest, and I will send you updated red-line versions as soon as available." MacKay was then asked if he received this e-mail, and he admitted, "I am on the list. Yes, I must have."

Next, our attorney showed MacKay the paragraph within these documents which specified that the stated value of a preferred share was $60,407 and asked MacKay if he had read that portion of the documents back in August of 2007. MacKay's answer was, "I don't recall reading it." Dave Coulson, continuing his masterful job in this deposition, then asked, "When you as a shareholder and a director voted in favor of accepting a Blackstone investment, you had all of the contract documents between Stiefel and Blackstone, is that correct?" MacKay's answer was "I must have, yes." Mr. Coulson did not let up. He asked, "So you yourself decided not to read the contract terms and other information in writing that Mr. Stiefel gave you?" Dick MacKay answered, "I didn't have the background to really be able to understand a lot of this stuff." He subsequently admitted he did not think I had made any misrepresentations whatsoever with respect to the Blackstone investment.

I apologize for going into some detail about the MacKay lawsuit, but since it was dismissed by a judge without ever going to trial, I feel this is my only opportunity to set the record straight. In my opinion, the false accusations made in his Complaint were extremely libelous in nature; but (believe it or not) the law allows plaintiffs to state whatever they want—even total fabrications—in a Complaint, without being liable for defamation. With your indulgence, I would like to correct just a few more erroneous accusations.

MacKay alleged in his lawsuit the valuations by our ESBP appraiser "completely ignored Blackstone's valuations of the Company, or its purchase of Company stock in August 2007 for $500 million." If you were to read the March 31, 2008 appraisal, however, you would see the appraiser specifically refers to the $500 million preferred stock investment; he opts to treat 75 percent of this investment as debt—exactly the position adopted by Moody's. (Standard & Poors, the other top rating service, had treated 100 percent of Blackstone's investment as debt.) So not only did the appraiser not ignore the Blackstone investment, as MacKay claimed, but he specified in writing how he factored it into his evaluation.

Yet another fabrication in MacKay's Complaint asserted, "By virtue of their long relationship with Bogush (the appraiser), the Stiefel Family Defendants knew that Bogush was legally unqualified and not competent to perform the annual appraisals." In reality, neither Todd nor Brent had ever even met Terry Bogush, and I had talked to him only once or twice in the previous quarter century! Not only did I not know then he was unqualified and incompetent, but I still believe to this day that he was both qualified and competent.

Finally, this Complaint claims: "The Bogush valuations were chronically, severely undervalued for over a decade, and this fact was well known by Defendants. Defendants purposely used this inside knowledge to the detriment of any shareholder who sold stock to the Company, including Plaintiff." This allegation is absurd when one considers the fact my father, my uncle, my siblings, my cousins, and I personally (on two separate occasions) all sold stock back to the company at discounts to these valuations.

In reality, and contrary to the implications in most of these lawsuits, the Participants in the Employee Stock Bonus Plan

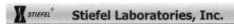

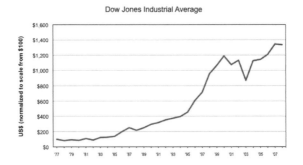

Performance of the DJIA over three decades

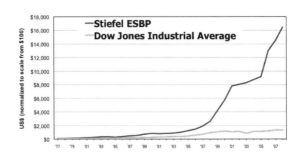

Performance of Stiefel stock versus the DJIA

earned excellent returns on the Stiefel stock given to them. Many investment professionals view the Dow Jones Industrial Average as a yardstick by which to measure how well equities perform over time. Above are two charts—one looking at the performance of the Dow over three decades, and the other comparing that performance to the price of Stiefel stock, as calculated by our ESBP appraiser. As you can readily see, Stiefel stock outperformed the Dow by a very significant margin.

In fact, the appraised value of our stock increased so much throughout the years that I knew blue collar workers who retired as millionaires, and many managerial employees became multi-millionaires. Until the first lawsuit was filed, not one employee had ever complained about our appraiser or his work product. During the decade before Stiefel was sold, I had occasion to review several other in-depth appraisals of our stock—one calculated a price comparable to what Mr. Bogush had determined, and all of the others valued our stock considerably lower.

Mr. Bogush was a CPA who passed the certifying examination administered by the Institute of Business Appraisers, and he served as our independent appraiser for over two decades. The Department of Labor requested his appraisals for three separate years as part of a comprehensive review of our Plan, and they had no negative comments to make. Likewise, the appraisals were examined in detail every single year by an external auditor retained specifically to audit our Employee Stock Bonus Plan, and this auditor likewise never voiced an objection. The IRS audited the Plan and raised no issues. And finally, Dick Sandler reviewed the Bogush appraisals personally on several occasions, and he deemed them to be in full compliance with all applicable laws and regulations. The methodology employed by Mr. Bogush was consistent through the years, and I firmly believe the work he did greatly benefited Stiefel employees.

So why would Dick MacKay betray me by making defamatory

allegations he later admitted in his deposition were untrue? Why would he sue a loyal friend whom he had previously credited for tripling or quadrupling his personal wealth? Was the $190 million he made selling his Stiefel stock not enough? Personally, I will never understand why he chose to act as he did, but being somewhat cynical, I have 40,000,000 suspicions!

Attorneys in private practice are paid to be zealous advocates on behalf of their clients. A government lawyer, however, according to the US Supreme Court, "is the representative not of an ordinary party to a controversy, but of a sovereignty whose obligation…is not that it shall win a case, but that justice be done." The Honorable Patricia M. Wald, former Chief Judge for the United States Court of Appeals for the District of Columbia Circuit (after the Supreme Court, arguably the most important court in our nation), wrote a 1998 article opining government lawyers should be held to a higher ethical standard than ordinary lawyers. Referring to the American Bar Association's Model Rules of Professional Conduct, she notes, "A government lawyer in a civil action…has the responsibility to seek justice and to develop a full and fair record." She states further that "unlike a private practitioner, the loyalties of a government lawyer…cannot and must not lie solely with his or her client agency."

The SEC filed a civil suit against Stiefel Laboratories and me (as its CEO) in December 2011; in the intervening years, I have developed the overwhelming impression they do not subscribe to the ethical tenets above. In their Complaint, for example, they state, "The Defendants (note use of the plural) purchased substantial amounts of the Company's stock at artificially low prices by purchasing shares from current and former employees." Stiefel maintained meticulous stock records, however, and it is incontrovertible I did not purchase any of these shares. A Miami newspaper, after reading the SEC Complaint, inferred I had personally purchased all of the shares in question and so stated in a highly defamatory article (no,

I did not bother to sue the paper), so it was (and remains) very important to me to set the record straight.

Our attorneys tried their best to get the SEC to admit only the company had purchased shares, but amazingly, to this day, they have refused to do so! We perhaps could have used this falsehood against them at trial, so when the attorneys for both sides were asked to list for the judge the factual issues to be tried, the SEC simply omitted any reference to me personally purchasing shares. In other words, for purposes of the trial, they have indirectly admitted their lie, but as far as the general public is concerned, this untrue allegation is still on the record. Furthermore, instead of accepting their responsibility "to develop a full and fair record," the SEC is aggressively attempting to keep out of evidence any facts that might damage their case.

For example, the SEC's position is the company should have disclosed the details of Project Jump to all ESBP Participants, and our failure to do so constituted securities fraud. For this to have been fraud, however, it is necessary that the company acted with "scienter", a legal term meaning "a mental state embracing intent to deceive, manipulate or defraud." There are numerous facts demonstrating Stiefel lacked scienter, just one of which is the fact three of the five companies involved in Project Jump required us to sign confidentiality agreements which prohibited us from disclosing what the SEC maintains we should have disclosed.

Personally, I have never breached a contract in my entire life, and I would have shut down Project Jump rather than allow Stiefel to break its written commitment to these three companies. The SEC, however, made a motion asking the judge to prevent us from even introducing these confidentiality agreements into evidence! There are many other similar examples, but in the interest of brevity, I will cite just two more.

In its Complaint, the SEC alleges I fraudulently concealed the detailed methodology of the annual stock appraisal from Stiefel stockholders. I will note in passing my attorneys and I are unaware of any requirement to announce this methodology in the first place. Nevertheless, in order to disprove this false allegation, Dave Coulson would like to introduce into evidence the fact that my philosophy was to give a copy of this appraisal to anyone who requested it, and I did so on several occasions. Twice, in fact, we mailed this appraisal to every shareholder in the company. Once again, the SEC is trying to prevent the jury from hearing these facts!

Finally, the SEC alleges I concocted a massive scheme to defraud our shareholders, starting in late 2006 and continuing well into 2009. You may recall I was diagnosed with advanced-stage cancer in December 2006, causing me to be out of the office (literally fighting for my life) during a significant portion of the time when I was supposedly advancing this fraudulent scheme. Naturally, therefore, the SEC is trying to keep out of evidence the fact I ever had cancer at all!

In reality, anyone who has ever been diagnosed with a life-threatening condition can attest to the fact it forever alters your perspective. The love and support of friends and family become much more important, and you become uniquely focused on trying to stay alive. To me, it is patently absurd to suggest I would select precisely that moment in time to mastermind a lengthy and highly complex multi-year scheme to cheat some of my fellow stockholders (including family members!) out of some money.

This is particularly true given both Chris Viehbacher and Andrew Witty asked me if I would like to receive separate bids for each class of stock. It would have been perfectly legal for me to answer "yes, please," and had I done so, I probably would have been offered as much as 40 percent more for my shares (this was Blackstone's opinion). Who in their right mind would reject a simple, legal way to make a lot more money and opt instead to embark upon a lengthy, complex illegal scheme that may or may not make any money at all?

In my opinion, the most egregious behavior exhibited by the SEC took place before their litigation was even commenced. I noted above that, after investigating for nearly two years, the SEC advised us they were closing their file and would not bring a lawsuit. They subsequently changed their mind, however, because (they informed our counsel) their original decision not to sue did not sit well with the Stiefel people who had been complaining to them. The SEC then advised us that they intended to sue on behalf of all the ESBP Participants who had sold shares during and after December 2008, seeking to recover about $40 million—the difference between what these people actually received and what they would have received from GSK had they not opted to sell.

A routine conference was held to determine if there was any basis for a settlement. When I walked into that settlement conference, I was shocked. One of the SEC officials from the Miami office stared at me with a look of sheer hatred—as if I had just murdered his entire family. Even though this individual had never before met me or even spoken with me, his look silently screamed, "Don't bother me with the facts! I've already made up my mind!" My shock continued when the SEC then informed us they do not settle cases.

Firstly, as a faithful reader of the *Wall Street Journal*, I have read about numerous cases the SEC has settled. And secondly, what was the point of this settlement conference if the SEC never settles? Subsequent to that conference, the SEC followed up with one of my attorneys, who informed me the SEC had just issued a threat. If we would not pay the full $40 million they were seeking, then they would broaden their lawsuit and sue on behalf of everyone who had sold stock to Stiefel since late-2006! I could not believe what I was hearing! If the SEC believed in good faith Stiefel had cheated the individuals who had redeemed shares during this earlier time period, then they should be suing on behalf of these people, regardless of whether or not GSK was willing to pay the SEC the $40 million they were demanding.

But, if the SEC did not believe in good faith that these people had been defrauded, then they were blackmailing us! Either way, their position struck me as extraordinarily unethical. I have no idea what they truly believed, but suffice it to say GSK did not give them their $40 million, and the suit the SEC subsequently filed did indeed go all the way back to late-2006. As an aside, I am not the only one who harbors strong feelings about the SEC. Mark Cuban, owner of the Dallas Mavericks and star of the television series *Shark Tank*, was once sued by the SEC. After the jury ruled in his favor, CNBC asked him, "You refused to settle and went to trial. You had to spend more money on lawyers than on the potential fines you would have had to pay. Why was this so important to take this to the mat?"

Mr. Cuban's answer was enlightening: "Because I hate to be bullied. I love this country. The idea that the people who...ran the SEC could ignore facts and care only about winning and losing and have no interest in justice, turned my stomach. I have the resources to fight. I felt compelled to take up that fight."

It has been nearly nine years since this legal nightmare began, and there is still no end in sight. During that time period, there have been two trials, numerous legal Complaints, scores of motions, dozens of depositions, and thousands of pages of documents produced. A long-term friend and colleague, Mike Martinolich, who had steadfastly refused to sue me, changed his mind after reading the vicious allegations in the SEC lawsuit and accompanying press release. I believe that many people assume if the government sues you, you must have actually done something wrong (I used to make the same assumption); so I harbor no ill will towards Mike. Since July of 2009, there have been numerous untrue accusations or implications of wrongdoing, and before ending this saga, I would like to set the record straight on just a few more of these falsehoods.

In the very first lawsuit filed, for example, it was asserted the global reduction in force Stiefel effectuated as part of our austerity program was done in order to "harvest" the shares of the employees who lost their jobs. In other words, this layoff was supposedly part of my scheme to get more retiring employees to put their ESBP shares back to the company. This particular allegation was not only 100 percent false, but unbelievably insulting as well.

Firstly, a high percentage of the individuals who lost their jobs either worked overseas (and thus did not participate in the ESBP) or had ESBP accounts that were not yet vested and thus contained no shares to put. Secondly, these layoffs were suggested by Dick MacKay and Martin Floreani to help us avoid breaching loan covenants; the individuals to be let go were chosen by their departmental managers—not by me; I did not even learn any names until after the fact. Finally, the written guidance I gave these managers requested them, if everything else was equal, to retain the employees with the most tenure—typically the people with the most stock in their ESBP accounts.

Thus, my guidance ran directly contrary to the "scheme" I supposedly was advancing. Ironically, at virtually the same time (July 2009) this lawsuit was commenced, the law firm (Ruden McClosky) that filed this suit engaged in some layoffs of their own; two years later, it filed for Chapter 11 bankruptcy protection. I guess they learned not every layoff is a subterfuge, and there actually was a global financial crisis!

Several of the lawsuits suggest I made concerted efforts to convince people to sell their shares back to Stiefel Laboratories. This is a total fabrication. I never once asked or encouraged anyone to sell, and the facts demonstrate the exact opposite was true. Whenever non-ESBP stockholders approached the company and asked to sell, Matt Pattullo (our Corporate Secretary, who handled these transactions) would read a script to them. A handful of people asked to sell shares in June 2008 (the same time as Dick MacKay), for example, and Matt's script notified these shareholders "there are several important factors you should consider before deciding to offer shares for sale," including that as of April 1, 2008, a new fiscal year had begun, and a new appraisal "is expected in a few months" and "may be higher." Matt then cautioned, "Please be advised that sales for FY2008 came in (unaudited) around $908MM, an increase of 37 percent over last year." If anything, Matt's scripts encouraged people to wait rather than sell, but seeking liquidity, most opted to sell anyway.

On rare occasions, people would ask me for my opinion, and I consistently suggested they consult their financial advisors. It is undisputed that (except for the two tender offers in 1985 and 1990) every single one of the non-Plan shareholders who redeemed shares approached the company (never the other way around) and offered to sell at a discount. The company derived no benefit whatsoever by accepting these offers—in fact, we always had better uses for the cash we paid these sellers. The only reason I tried to accept these offers when we could afford it was because I knew from personal experience the disadvantages of owning stock enjoying virtually no liquidity.

As you learned earlier in this book, merging the ESBP into our 401(k), adding a diversification option to the combined plan, and implementing a new Long-Term Incentive Plan were all recommended by Towers Perrin as part of an early-2007 HR initiative to improve employee benefits; these recommendations were strongly endorsed by Steve Karasick and our HR group. All of these recommendations were made in writing about 18 months before we even dreamed of selling the company; it goes undisputed my only role in adopting these programs was to vote to accept Towers Perrin's suggestions. Yet the Complaints in the various lawsuits would cause one to believe I personally dreamed up and then implemented all of these changes for the sole purpose of enriching myself.

Speaking of enriching myself, all of the lawsuits strongly imply I derived some immense and unique benefit because of the ESBP shares put back to the company shortly before GSK acquired us. In reality, as Dick Sandler counseled, since these shares were sold at the appraised price, the value of all the remaining shares did not change at all at that time. About six months later, solely because of the home run price paid by GSK, I received about 1.8 percent more for my shares than I would have if these ESBP shares had not been sold. Stiefel Laboratories had approximately 100 shareholders at that time, plus more than 700 Participants in the ESBP; all of these people (except, of course, the few who chose to sell) benefited by the exact same 1.8 percent I did.

Ask yourself this question: if you had the opportunity to sell something you own for $100, would you intentionally cheat your friends and colleagues in order to receive an additional $1.80? Personally, I do not know anyone capable of such amoral behavior, yet this is precisely what these lawsuits claim I did. Also, please remember when these ESBP people were selling between January 12 and February 2 of 2009, no one could possibly have predicted what, if anything, someone might offer us. We had not yet finished writing the "Teaser", let alone the Management Presentation; we had not met with any of the potential acquiring companies; there had been no negotiations whatsoever; and it was seven weeks prior to us receiving even a non-binding bid.

If GSK had acquired us at a price anywhere near the values calculated by J.P. Morgan, Allergan, our CFO Mike Cornelius and myself, then all of our shareholders (including me) would have received less money (rather than 1.8 percent more money) because of the ESBP shares that were sold, as well as a price well below the $16,469 per share received by the ESBP Participants. If this scenario had occurred, there undoubtedly would have been no lawsuits filed. I wonder, however, if the handful of individuals who sued to get the higher price received by their co-workers would have volunteered to return some of their proceeds if their co-workers received less than they did?

Several of the Complaints purport to contain quotes attributable to Todd, Brent or myself. Taking a partial quote totally out of context, however, can grossly distort its true meaning. Since much of this book relates to dermatology, let us examine an imaginary quote from a female dermatologist: "I have a cynical friend who thinks I got into medical school by sleeping with the Dean of Admissions; but I never even met the guy." If we were to abbreviate this quote and take it out of context, we have the following: "I got into medical school by sleeping with the Dean of Admissions." Note the shorter version captures verbatim part of what was actually said, but would anyone consider this to be fair and accurate?

In the lawsuits against Stiefel, one partial quote from Brent supposedly supports the theory that he, Todd and I were conspiring to cheat the ESBP Participants who were selling stock in early-2009. When one looks at the timing and context of his words, however, they actually prove Brent did not even know these people had sold until after the fact! He would have no reason to know, since he had nothing whatsoever to do with this routine process. Many other quotations in the Complaints are similarly misleading, either because they are taken out of context or intentionally twisted during the process of paraphrasing.

Most of the lawsuits relate primarily to the ESBP Participants who sold shares between January 12 and February 2 of 2009, and Stiefel's repurchase of these shares is alleged to be part of our corrupt scheme to cheat our employees. It is vitally important to understand, however, Stiefel did not voluntarily purchase these shares—all of these individuals exercised put rights, which meant the company did not have the power to refuse them. The lawsuits claim we should have refused to redeem these shares anyway, but if you were to read our lengthy Employee Stock Bonus Plan document, you would not find any provision allowing us to do this. Quite the contrary—the Plan document specifically grants to the Participants the absolute right "to require the Company to purchase the Bonus Stock."

Our purchases from stockholders who were not part of the ESBP were indeed voluntary, but the last of these discretionary stock purchases took place in June 2008. Accordingly, the SEC's lawsuit is unlike any I have ever seen before. They claim Stiefel Laboratories (not me personally, because they realize that I did not purchase any shares) committed insider trading, despite the fact the company's "trading" was not even voluntary!

Everyone involved in these lawsuits agrees no one at Stiefel told the ESBP Participants about Project Jump. The plaintiffs contend this omission was the final element in my malicious scheme to trick my colleagues into selling their shares. Nothing could be further from the truth. You may recall from Chapter 11 that Dick Sandler, an expert in securities law, specifically advised me in 1985 that not only was Stiefel not required to furnish detailed company information to ESBP Participants, but we should never provide any confidential information at all to these individuals.

Throughout the following years, we diligently followed Sandler's advice, and it never even occurred to us to deviate from this practice. But this was far from the only reason why we did not disclose the existence of Project Jump. I already alluded to the fact our confidentiality agreements with GSK, Sanofi and J & J specifically forbade us from making such disclosure, but there were several other important reasons as well. When we first started learning about the acquisition process in 2006, our attorneys (Willkie, Farr & Gallagher), our outside advisors (Deutsche Bank) and our in-house expert (Jim Loerop) all emphasized the importance of maintaining strict confidentiality when even considering an acquisition deal—particularly in situations (like Project Jump) when public companies are involved.

As noted earlier in this book, this became our standard operating procedure, and we followed it meticulously thereafter. An important point the plaintiffs' lawyers try to ignore is the Project Jump team continued to maintain strict confidentiality long after the ESBP Participants had sold. Why do this if our sole motivation was to cheat these people out of their stock? To be completely candid, we never even considered the notion of disclosing Project Jump to anyone outside of the small group of people who were working on the project. Not one of our lawyers, our Blackstone advisors, our executive team (several of whom had significant public company experience), or anyone else ever suggested that perhaps we should consider making such disclosure.

If anyone (our General Counsel, for example) had advised me Stiefel needed to disclose the existence of Project Jump, I would have cancelled the project immediately rather than disclose it. Why, you might wonder? Why do so many experts stress the importance of confidentiality when undergoing a sales exploration process?

Firstly, employees become nervous about job stability, and they may seek employment elsewhere. During my career at Stiefel, every time there was even a rumor a competitor was for sale, we were flooded with résumés from that company's employees. And it is a business reality that your key executives—the ones you most need to retain—are the ones who find it easiest to get a new job. The fact Stiefel was operating in austerity mode would undoubtedly have enhanced employee nervousness. In addition, morale suffers and employee productivity declines.

Secondly, vendor relationships can be damaged. Not knowing with whom they might be dealing in the future, vendors may impose more onerous credit terms or perhaps demand price increases. Thirdly, licensing relationships can be disrupted, with your business partners examining their options in the event of a change in control. And potential new licensing partners can be scared away. Fourthly, customers can become nervous, wondering if a new owner will honor existing pricing, warranty and returns policies. Would you buy a product from a company that you hear might be disappearing?

Finally, your competitors will instantly circle like vultures, trying to recruit away your top talent and steal your customers. In the words of the Florida Business Exchange, "The combined effects of all these factors can be devastating for a business. The knowledge that your business is for sale will often affect the viability of the enterprise. It can cause the value of your business to decline or may even put you out of business." Given Stiefel's precarious financial situation in early-2009, I sincerely believe disclosing we might be sold would have seriously damaged the company, and it might indeed have put us out of business. If someone—anyone— had remotely suggested to me back then we might need to disclose Project Jump, I would positively have killed that project rather than risk the viability of the company.

Except for the MacKay case, all the lawsuits are based on the overriding assumption that if I had told our employees Stiefel might possibly be sold, then no one would have sold any shares, and everyone would have received the GSK price. But remember Dick Sandler's warning about Stiefel not disclosing one confidential development to ESBP Participants without disclosing all confidential developments? Disclosing only one fact out of many would be grossly misleading.

Consequently, if I had opted to inform these individuals the company might be sold, I would also have been required to inform them about all the bad news, including but not limited to the following: we were projecting to breach a loan covenant, which might force us into bankruptcy; Blackstone considered us an impaired asset; our sales and profits were far below budget; our two lead products might soon be going generic; the value of the foam technology we had acquired from Connetics had greatly diminished in value due to a recent Supreme Court decision; and the valuations calculated by J.P. Morgan, Mike Cornelius and myself all suggested a lower, rather than higher, price per share. If you received all of this news, and you had the option either to hold your shares or sell them at the highest price in the history of the company, what would you have done?

The lawsuits against Stiefel Laboratories are a classic example of what psychologists call "outcome bias," a natural tendency to judge a decision based upon the ultimate outcome. Coaches in sports routinely deal with outcome bias when they call plays in critical game situations—if the play works, the coach is brilliant; if it fails, the coach is an idiot. If Stiefel had gone bankrupt in 2009, no one would now claim fraud had been committed. But knowing the company was sold for $3.6 billion makes it easy to second-guess earlier business decisions and assume ulterior motives.

In reality, every single decision I made that was supposedly part of a fraudulent scheme was based upon the advice of either outside experts or trusted members of Stiefel's senior management team. I never once told a lie to anyone. I controlled the Board of Directors, so if I had wanted more money at the expense of the stockholders, I could simply have asked the Board to award me a huge bonus. If, on the other hand, I had not owned any Stiefel stock at all, then there would have been no basis for a lawsuit against me, because I would have received no financial gain.

The actions I took and the decisions I made as CEO were extremely beneficial to the overwhelming majority of Stiefel stockholders; the sole basis for the lawsuits against me is that I was one of these stockholders. Ironically, although a CEO's job is to maximize shareholder value, I was sued because this is precisely what I did. Consequently, the litigation against Stiefel Laboratories could have important ramifications throughout the business world. Virtually every CEO I have ever met owned stock in their company. It is scary to think any corporate decision benefitting a company can potentially be viewed as fraudulent, simply because the CEO was one of the individuals who benefited.

I will not attempt to predict the outcome of the two cases still awaiting trial. These cases are extremely complex, and the ultimate jury verdicts may well depend on the ability of the jury to understand these complexities. Win or lose, however, I am happy I had the opportunity to work for such a great company—and with such a wonderful group of colleagues. Perhaps more importantly, I am proud I can look at myself in the mirror and know I always acted with integrity and did my absolute best on behalf of Stiefel's employees and stockholders. At the end of the day, who can ask for more?